QUEER FOOTPRINTS

'An incredibly powerful exploration of a London that has been deliberately hidden, by one of the most courageous and insightful activists we have.'
—Owen Jones, author of *Chavs*

'An electrifying adventure through London's untold queer past. Every page is packed with inspiring, moving and downright hilarious secrets just itching to be uncovered, and with the riotously entertaining Dan Glass as your mincing tour guide, you'll have an absolute blast as you do. A word of warning: after reading this, London will never seem the same again.'
—Sam Arbor, Director's Assistant of Netflix's *Heartstopper*

'Dan Glass is a charming raconteur, grass-roots historian, people lover and pleasure seeker who delights in guiding us from pick-ups to pinkwashing through the queer London that he loves. He lets both the neophyte and the experienced City dweller discover the magic anew.'
—Sarah Schulman, writer

'The strength and the beauty of this book is its resolute and joyful nod to queer history, the multiplicity of our stories and the ongoing, transformative process of our queer footprints which continue to add layers onto the city I was lucky enough to grow up in. London, through the eyes of Glass, is ever-changing but always radical.'
—Juno Roche, author of *Queer Sex*

'Dan Glass, London's unofficial queer mayor, takes you bar and history hopping through former gay ghettos and new queer spaces. The oral histories Glass obtained from those who were there, much like hidden gems on less travelled side streets, bring his guide to vibrant life.'
—Peter Staley, HIV activist and author of *Never Silent:*
ACT UP and My Life in Activism

'Offers a fascinating, lively and revealing look into the capital's queer past. Like the winding streets themselves, there is something surprising at every turn. This is a queer look at London with a Capital Q and is by turns intimate, gossipy, personal and political.'
—Joseph Galliano, Director of Queer Britain,
the national LGBTQ+ museum

'A fascinating and passionate ode to queer London in all its glory. Dan Glass has inspired hundreds if not thousands of people towards social justice and the transformative power of community activism. He has created London's new essential anthology of heroic queer histories and the untold stories of queers who built the world's greatest city.

—Jeremy Goldstein, founder of London Artists Projects

'Dan Glass is a living gift from our queer ancestry with an ability to write our present with an alternative view of our past. His experience has shaped the way we appreciate the world we live in and how we choose to question the past.'

—Kieron Jina, artist

'Whether you are reading in the comfort of your own home, or following one of the tours live on the street, *Queer Footprints* brings the LGBTQIA+ history of London to life in a beautiful and visceral manner. This is no self-important history lesson that starts somewhere in the past and leads you date by date to the present. It's all rather punk and, well, queer. A love letter to queer London reminds us that although we're not always in the mainstream telling of history, we have always been here. And whilst the spaces and places we've occupied throughout the recent past may no longer be ours, or no longer even exist, this powerful book reminds us that real history, and indeed our future, doesn't lie in dates, buildings, pomp and ceremony, but within the hearts, minds, loves, lives, losses and desires of all the LGBTQIA+ people who occupied our cities before us.'

—Nathaniel Hall, playwright and HIV activist

'In his usual glorious fashion, Dan brings us truly out from the sheets and into the streets. This is more than a history book. It's a living walking guide. It's a closeted cartographer's wet dream come true. It's a brick to throw through the windows of London's most transphobic establishments … I'll be utterly shocked if there aren't queer walking guides like this across all continents in five years.'

—Phil Wilmot, member of Beautiful Trouble

'Dan Glass has uncovered the queer history of one of the world's great cities in a way that is not only eye-opening, but just as entertaining as the writer himself. Whether you've visited London, lived in London, or never been that lucky, you will see it with fresh eyes … his call to action, for activists to create similar histories of their communities today, is one I believe will be the legacy of this fabulous book.'

—Victoria Noe, author of *Fag Hags, Divas and Moms*

Queer Footprints

A Guide to Uncovering London's Fierce History

Dan Glass

First published 2023 by Pluto Press
New Wing, Somerset House, Strand, London WC2R 1LA
and Pluto Press Inc.
1930 Village Center Circle, 3-834, Las Vegas, NV 89134

www.plutobooks.com

Maps by Mark Glasgow
www.markglasgow.co.uk

British Library Cataloguing in Publication Data
A catalogue record for this book is available from the British Library

ISBN 978 0 7453 4621 2 Paperback
ISBN 978 0 7453 4626 7 PDF
ISBN 978 0 7453 4624 3 EPUB

This book is printed on paper suitable for recycling and made from fully
managed and sustained forest sources. Logging, pulping and manufacturing
processes are expected to conform to the environmental standards of the
country of origin.

Typeset by Stanford DTP Services, Northampton, England

Simultaneously printed in the United Kingdom and United States of America

CONTENTS

Dedicated to anyone struggling to come out.

And for London, my love.

Introduction

Hello, dear readers! I'm Dan Glass. I'm so excited to take you on a tour through the fumes, the regrets, the constant Costa coffees, the hangovers, the walks of shame, the moments of fame and the 'was I here last night, I can't remember?' moments that make up the experience we are part of in this phenomenal, mysterious and naughty city – London Town.

It's an enormous honour and privilege to trot these routes with you and shake our booties together. We are going to have a lot of fun marching in the steps of so many iconic souls; celebrating legendary people, moments and movements, all continuing to build the road to freedom – a legacy you are now part of too.

The idea for *Queer Footprints* rooted itself back in 2014 when I was in my favourite club, the legendary Joiners Arms on Hackney Road. This is where the importance of cherishing, and the gravity of losing, queer spaces dawned on me. Catching up with friends while smoking a cigarette, I was told that alongside the recent mass closure of other queer spaces, the Joiners doors would soon be shutting too. Rising rents and a lack of protection were dooming yet another queer place to the scrapheap of cultural life. I dropped my cigarette and sparked up an idea. 'No ^%&$%* way. Not our Joiners. Let's stop the Joiners from being shut down. Let's speak to the landlord and organise a meeting.' This is how Friends of the Joiners Arms began: with an incredible, diverse, creative collective determined to win a new space back in its place.

Through this organising experience, I learnt that fire-fighting the closure of queer spaces is not enough. We have to dig deeper.

Two years later in 2016, I co-founded Queer Tours of London
– A Mince through Time, walks that tell the stories of London's
queer herstory, shedding light on the lives, spaces, identities,
repression and resistance that form the backdrop of lesbian, gay,
bisexual, trans, queer, intersex, asexual and other (LGBTQIA+)
lives today. Ever since, the forces of queer-nature at Friends of
the Joiners Arms have been working night and day to cultivate
home through reclaiming queer space, and I've been writing this
toolkit for you.

Fast forward to 2022, and thanks to so many of you out
there – the queer community and our allies, all buying shares
and supporting our performance club nights, we recently raised
enough cash to create a new queer space opening in the Joiners
Arms' honour!

When the new space opens, I assure you, I am going to put this
pen down, and whatever protest placard I'm holding, and dance
and sweat like there's no tomorrow. I hope you'll join me there.

HOW TO USE THIS BOOK

Queer Footprints is your invitation to take up space! Get your
towel out, take to your garden, your favourite park or somewhere
comfortable to read the book. Better still, take it into the streets,
on your own or with friends, with strangers, whatever works for
you. Taking up space feels good, eh? We can change the way we
all experience our city, whether you're LGBTQIA+, an ally or
someone hungry for freedom. We are the queerdos we have been
waiting for and we don't have to hide anymore.

There is more than one way to use this book. You might find it easier to read the book first and then do the walks – or you might decide to just go for it. The Soho, Brixton, Trafalgar Square and Whitechapel routes should each take approximately 1–2 hours; for the Piccadilly, King's Cross and Ladbroke Grove routes, I would give it half a day. The 'mini minces' queer power short stops can be on the spot in various parts of town. When planning your trip make the most of London's fabulous array of queer spaces, places and events which can be seen in the resources section at the end of *Queer Footprints*. London has a huge range of yummy places to eat too, so tuck in.

The gorgeous maps illustrated by Mark Glasgow will help you navigate the route. My previous book, *United Queerdom: From the Legends of the Gay Liberation Front to the Queers of Tomorrow*, focused primarily on the period in the run up to 50 years of radical Pride in 2022. *Queer Footprints* zooms out with and from the GLF and focuses primarily on 'living herstory'. *Herstory* is history viewed from a feminist perspective. I have chosen to platform incredible queer places, spaces and people predominantly since the Sexual Offences Act, 1967, which led to the partial decriminalisation of homosexuality. The areas covered have been chosen based on curating walks that make most sense chronologically, politically and practically, as well as highlighting stories previously less known.

I didn't want to write Queer Footprints in a detached way. I chose not to write, 'in this building this happened ...', or 'In this street someone said ...' because the reality is we create community together, continually, all the time. These stories are real and they happened to real people. So I chose to give space to those who were there to speak and narrate their own experiences, and who make my heart booooom! It's been a delicious joy to sit with these icons, and their beloveds, hearing these stories from their mouths. All those who are alive, I am chuffed to call my friends. We have organised many protests and programmes for transformation together and continually fine-tune our movements so that we can scamper on effectively ahead.

Some of the iconic locations you'll visit on our walks are now luxury flat complexes, a KFC or a NatWest bank. It baffles me that these places aren't covered in blue heritage plaques and don't have flags flying outside them proudly declaring their queerstory to every unsuspecting passer-by. But however hard the corporate privatised tarmac falls on us, we still come rising up like a defiant spring. Today, I'm so excited at how queer spaces, clubs, movements and support networks are bubbling to the surface, reclaiming spaces for the masses in our ever-evolving queer city. Long may it continue!

What you will see in the pages ahead reflects only about 0.000000001 per cent of the research undertaken for this book, because queers have changed the world since the dawn of time. I have 40 giant maps of London regions printed on my wall with over 2000 case studies of people power – maybe more books like this will follow.

When you've finished with *Queer Footprints* don't leave it on your shelf gathering dust. Pass it to a friend – or, even better, think of the biggest homophobe in your life and buy it for them for their birthday. You never know, you might see them dancing to Lil Nas X or Donna Summer the following year.

INTRODUCTION

INTO THE FUTURE

London is changing so fast. The world is changing so fast. It is incumbent on us as curious people to keep telling our stories, to keep creating change and to keep expanding our horizons. There are lonely people out there who needn't be, trust me. Glorious and glittering collective action can create beauty against all odds. These stories are a recognition of our interconnection – how the person opposite you on the tube is somehow intimately intertwined in the salvation of our city for all people, against profit and greed. Reach out to them.

I feel so lucky and grateful to have written this. Every day has been a massive dose of ancestral shaking. I have cried, laughed and fallen harder in love everyday with our incredible community, so much so that now it's done I'm going to be a little bit heartbroken.

There's one last thing as you tie up your boots: *Queer Footprints* is only an appetiser, a gateway book for you to continue our lineage, by documenting queerstory. You are that story. Whatever the choppy future seas have in store for us, knowing we can drop anchor, reconnect with those who've come before us and all the wisdom and inspiration they hold, will mean we can venture more boldly into the eye of the storm and help others find their way.

So get yourself a shiny new notebook and print out a map on which you can plot the treasure of your community's story. The moment we begin to shape our own identities, everything becomes bigger out there. Do it. The world will be so much better for it.

'Queer not as being about who you're having sex with (that can be a dimension of it); but queer as being about the self that is at odds with everything around it and has to invent and create and find a place to speak and to thrive and to live' – bell hooks

I

Homosexuals Come Out!
Soho

Have you ever wondered how to break free from cultural stereo-types? Have you ever dreamt of creating a neighbourhood where everyone can be themselves in all their delicious and defiant identities? Have you ever wanted to know how to create the most exhilarating club nights, fabulous effective movements for change and how to connect with people across cultures? Great! Welcome to Soho, the pulsing Queen Bee of Queer London and meet the fierce force behind some of the legends who have paved the way.

START: TOTTENHAM COURT ROAD STATION

1. The Make-Up is Cracking – *Old Compton Street*
2. Like a Trifle! – *Madame Jojo's, 8–10 Brewer Street*
3. Life Was a Funny Thing – *Au Chat Noir, 72 Old Compton Street*
4. Queer Valentines Carnival – *Comptons of Soho Pub, 51–53 Old Compton Street*
5. Somewhere Over the Rainbow – *Admiral Duncan, 54 Old Compton Street*
6. I Don't Like the Look of You Cunty – *The Colony Club Room, 41 Dean Street*

1. *THE MAKE-UP IS CRACKING* – OLD COMPTON STREET

Stand slap bang in the centre of the street. It's a cool summer's night in 1972. All around Soho, black London cabs and red double-decker buses whizz by and a song, 'Ain't No Mountain High Enough' by Diana Ross, can be heard faintly from a cafe nearby, but here it's quiet. Knock, knock ... you can hear tapping on doors close by. Members of the Gay Liberation Front (GLF) are trotting up and down the street in multicoloured linen shirts and corduroy flares, wrapping their knuckles on doors with handfuls of the GLF magazine *Come Out!* under their arms. Some shop-workers peered out and took the magazine, others screaming that they should leave immediately for fear of police reprisal and losing their jobs.

Ted Brown, a GLF activist, remembers that time:

At the time there were no public gay bars or clubs. In London a few known gay venues existed and there were a handful of venues where secrecy was still the norm. There was only one pub that I knew of – the Salisbury pub near the Globe Theatre and two cafes – the Lyons Corner House on the Strand and one on Regent Street – with straights on one side and gays on the other. Lesbians went to Gateways Club in Chelsea or private women's parties. That's why the GLF were marching. Straight people had no idea gay pubs were there, even the GLF activists

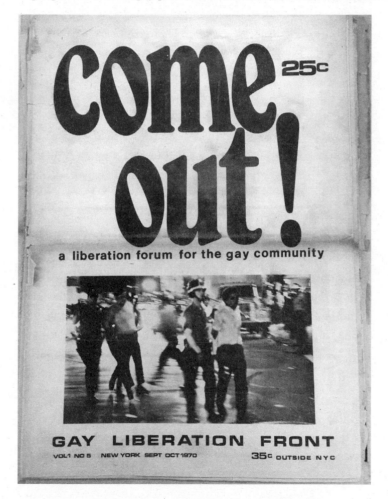

had to ask each other where they were. Windows blacked out, hidden away, you wouldn't know it was a pub.

Ghettos, the physical boundaries humans create, can be used to segregate and oppress, but also to protect. Ghettos constantly require us to reflect on whom they truly serve, and Martha Shelley's got something to say about that: 'The roles are beginning to wear thin', as she wrote in the pages of *Come Out!*

> The make-up is cracking ... The roles – breadwinner, little wife, screaming fag, bulldyke, James Bond – are the cardboard characters we are trying to fit into, as if being human and spontaneous were so horrible that we each have to pick on a character out of a third-rate novel and try to cut ourselves down to size.

Right on Martha. It's about time to flip the script and discover who we really are. 'Time to Come Out!' the GLF members called in response to the shop owners as they peeped out from the slots in their doors.

Ted continues:

> At the time, Old Compton Street was gay, but only a few people knew it and it was quite elitist. You had to be in the know, pretty or wealthy to get into any of the clubs. In order to reclaim the self-determination of our bodies, it was necessary to secure certain rights, but this was only the first step. We joined a fight against a whole system of domination, with its divide-and-rule logic that extended into the individual self. Examples were

the adoption of male and female roles among gay people and challenging being asked whether you are 'butch or bitch' when entering a bar or 'lipstick lesbians' or 'bulldykes'. There's still not enough spaces for the whole LGBTQIA+ community. But London is so much better for gay people at large now – Old Compton Street is so out now! GLF made that happen.

The GLF were on a not-so-secret mission to not only break out of the gay ghetto and into the outside world, but also to break down the elitism and stereotypes within the ghetto itself. Ted was also involved with a small group called 'Gays against Fascism'.

Coming out of the closet can result in rejection, with potentially catastrophic consequences. Coming out can also be a positive, enchanting and liberating experience and often a wild mixture of both. It is a profoundly brave and courageous act, one that happens not just once but continues throughout our lives, as Dustin Bradley Goltz explores as 'a daily and moment-by-moment negotiation, contingent upon context, social assumptions, and shared social cues'. Choosing what to wear, imagining a dream job to apply for, owning the natural pitch of our voice or pondering how to walk out the door, jeez, sometimes we've come out five times before we've even had our cornflakes.

Coming out happens constantly here on Old Compton Street, in many daring ways. Here is a small street that provides a magnitude of homes, a patchwork of places and people that are defiantly creating pathways for freedom. One of those people is Josh Hepple. He can often be found sitting here having a coffee responding to many blushing faces and online invitations.

Josh's outstanding and attention-grabbing writing explores his unique account of his experiences using Grindr, the gay dating and sex app. He has cerebral palsy, his impairment affecting his speech and mobility, relying on personal assistants 24/7. Growing up in Edinburgh, he sensed the need for wider support and so helped to establish the charity TalkTime Edinburgh providing free counselling for disabled teenagers, regardless of sexual orientation. His equality training sessions are based on the social model of disability and as a campaigner and activist Josh has worked in many different sectors such as the Edinburgh Festival Fringe. He is the spirit of the civil rights mantra 'Nothing about us, without us, is for us', written from the view of disabled people who are disabled by barriers in society and not by their impairment or difference. Enjoy the tour ahead – I have no doubt you will, with Josh by your side.

2. *LIKE A TRIFLE!* – MADAME JOJO'S, 8–10 BREWER STREET

With its go-go dancers in windows and the red lights over the alleyway doors, you know that Soho has always been naughty. Very, very naughty. Colin Vaines, a film producer and long-time Soho resident, recalls:

During the 1970s, red lights were everywhere and every other entrance seemed to be a strip club, massage parlour, sex cinema or sex shop selling magazines and 8mm home movies. Displays inside and outside the shops, sometimes plastered on entire walls of buildings, were as graphic as the law – or rather, the notoriously corrupt 'porn squad' of the time – would allow.

'A community of fringe culture' from 1960 to 2004, Madame Jojo's nightclub began with the original Madame Jojo as the host. It soon became a hotbed for everyone – gays, straights, drag, transgender, punks, hipsters and pop stars – hellbent on providing a space to be free. The crowds were a mixture of the out and fashionable with the underground and sleazy, celebrities such as Eartha Kitt, Danny La Rue, Liza Minnelli, Michael Ball and Chaka Khan mixing with prostitutes, punks and pimps. Soho showed musty old Blighty how life really could be lived, regardless of gender, sexuality or creed; and many of the shop signs are remnants of that era. 'Everybody was thrown into the melee: it wasn't corporate, it wasn't mundane. Like a trifle, colourful and glittery', recalls 'The very Miss Dusty O' who ran 'Trannyshack' here on Wednesday nights. A dazzling array of shows where young stars like actress and cabaret performer Mzz Kimberley cut their teeth here working with the original Jojo and as a show girl in a Ruby Venezuela show, six nights a week. Mzz Kim recalls with a twinkle in her eye:

> Madame Jojo's was of huge importance to me. Alongside Lily Savage, Ebony, the only Black drag queen on the scene at the time, also performed in the club. All sorts of things used to happen – Grace Jones dancing on tables, Jean Paul Gaultier and Donatella Versace doing the conga in the road outside – Soho will be more magnolia for its loss.

The club's licence was revoked suddenly in 2014 after a 'serious incident of disorder', according to the police report. The *Guardian* newspaper exposed how the council's motives were questioned when it was revealed soon after that the club had already been

Credit: Mzz Kimberley / Bishopsgate Institute

ring fenced by the owners for demolition and development over the next few years. That raid marked the start of the current phase of gentrification in Soho, where now it seems like every other building is being gutted or demolished to make way for expensive flats.

Counter-culture cannot be faked, and once it's gone it's gone. Much of the gentrification is due to plain greed overriding any kind of social commitment or social policy. It remains to be seen whether replacement music venues such as the 'new' Madame JoJo's will be able to provide a similar experience at similar inexpensive prices. Triple rent increases have since forced other local shops to shut down as well. It was in this context that the 'Save Soho' campaign began, joined by GLF activists such as Alan Wakeman. The campaign's call to arms is 'Inclusive, not Exclusive'. In the short time it has existed, it has had a number of small but significant victories, such as saving Rupert Street's historic Yard Bar from poorly initiated and destructive 'development', but at the end of the day, if we need more determination, we can always learn from Quentin Crisp.

3. *LIFE WAS A FUNNY THING* – AU CHAT NOIR, 72 OLD COMPTON STREET

'If at first you don't succeed, then failure may be your style' once quipped Quentin Crisp, charmer, actor and author of *The Naked Civil Servant*.

Around the corner on Charing Cross Road in 1947, 20 years before the partial decriminalisation of homosexuality, Quentin turned on his heels in response to a voice saying 'Just a moment, you. We are taking you in for soliciting'. He was faced with two police officers.

Crisp had been 'window shopping for shoes', a euphemism for a traditional cruising technique outside selective shops known on the queer underground. Nigel Kelly explores Quentin's experiences in *Quentin Crisp: The Profession of Being*:

I had already systematically searched all the likely windows in Oxford Street and was just starting on Charing Cross Road when I was stopped by two policemen disguised as human beings. They demanded to see my exemption papers. As always, I showed them the one that said that I suffered from sexual perversion. When my inquisitors had retrieved their eyebrows from the roots of their hair, they gave me back this rather grubby document and I moved on.

Iconic.

Quentin Crisp was famous for being himself – for being flamboyantly and unabashedly out his whole life, until 1999 when he died in New York, aged 90. Quentin's daydream as a child was of growing up to be a very worldly, very beautiful woman. In later life, Quentin was often spat at, slapped without warning, or beaten to the ground in front of jeering crowds. Each time Quentin would get up, brush off and find somewhere to fix their make-up before carrying on with their day. Hair dyed, fingernails painted and wearing a respectable amount of make-up, Quentin walked the streets of London with nothing to hide. It was here at no. 72, the Au Chat Noir cafe which opened in the middle of the First World War, that Quentin and his friends would spend day after uneventful day, night after loveless night, buying each other cups of tea, combing each other's hair and trying on each other's lipsticks. This all immortalised the courage, wit and satirical nerve of Crisp and the homosexuals of Soho in those days to be themselves against almost impossible odds, as Quentin reminds us 'Life was a funny thing that happened to me on the way to the grave'.

4. *QUEER VALENTINES CARNIVAL* – COMPTONS OF
SOHO PUB, 51–53 OLD COMPTON STREET

It's a bright Spring morning in 2017. Sitting here having a coffee is Josh, but this time he's not smiling. Josh is part of 'disability queer riot' an intervention by a group of disabled LGBTQIA+ activists who are angry at being left out in the cold for so long. They are visiting venues up and down Old Compton Street to ask the managers to commit to concrete ramps to improve accessibility. Josh shares:

There's a lot of hot air about queer freedom this year, the 50th anniversary of the partial decriminalisation of homosexuality, but for who? It's OK for non-disabled able-bodied, white cisgender gay men, but what about queer disabled people with different access requirements, or queer homeless people, or queer migrants?

Holding a placard with pink and gold lettering that reads 'I'd love to shag in your toilet, if only I could get in', Josh asked the Comptons of Soho deputy manager James Bartlett, 'Are you doing everything you can? We demand equality over profit and access for all – we'll chain ourselves to the steps by September if you don't make an explicit statement of your intentions.' Soon, James had organised for Comptons to install a doorbell at wheelchair height to notify the bar team when someone required access. Signposting to accessible toilets were included in team briefings, such as the nearby Ku Bar or Rupert Street Bar, showing the immediate change that can be achieved. Ramps and toilets only hit the tip of the iceberg around different access requirements. But the ghetto still closes its doors as around half of all bars in Soho don't have wheelchair access.

Josh and the other activists alongside him that day weren't being brushed off. Many managers committed to action, including ramp provision, visible signs, and radar keys to open disabled toilets, but did not respond to Josh's follow-up emails reminding venues in writing of their promises to take concrete action within two weeks. Josh was very disappointed with the general apathy towards any significant desire to make bars more accessible. However, the responsibility doesn't rest with the venues alone.

With increasing rents, it's the local councils and Greater London Authorities' responsibility too. It's a question of political will and whether Soho is to remain accessible to the masses, or if it is to be sold off to the highest bidder. It is a staged process, and in order for it to happen, people need to be able to simply get into the bars – and that's just for starters. Can we celebrate Queer love when so many in our community are excluded? What forms of internalised oppression do we cultivate in our gay ghettos and how do we modify our behaviours to become more palatable and assimilate to the status quo? So, who's left out in the cold right now, and how might we expand the celebration of queer love to be more inclusive?

Wind back 24 years to 13 February 1993: outside this very same pub a painted sign reading 'Welcome to Queer Street' is being lowered from the second-floor window of Comptons as the landlord sprays the crowd with champagne. At the height of the AIDS pandemic in 1987, James Anderton, one of the country's top ranking police officers, shamefully stated that 'people with Aids' were 'swirling around in a human cesspit of their own making', compounding the cold-blooded Conservative government's 'Section 28' law that had banned the 'promotion of homosexuality in public institutions'. In response, Soho's gay and lesbian community came together for the 'Queer Valentine Carnival, an Orgy of Queer Desire'. This Valentine's Eve Parade was organised by OutRage! and saw nearly 2000 lesbians, gay men and their friends gather for an afternoon party and a street parade to commemorate the takeover of the area. Partygoers amassed in Soho Square, where satirically brilliant radical gender-subversive movement the Sisters of Perpetual

Indulgence, dressed as nuns to call out sexual intolerance whilst enthusiastically teaching the crowd to whirling dervish. Dressed in gold robes, filmmaker and activist Derek Jarman declared the opening of the proceedings from a carnival float carrying gods and goddesses of gay love. Their choir – a Brazilian samba band – moved through Soho, climaxing in a street party back in Old Compton Street as revellers proceeded to 'bless' each venue with showers of confetti. The atmosphere was electric and it seemed like a change was in the wind.

But it wasn't to be forever. Only five and a half years later the pub opposite was blown to pieces.

5. *SOMEWHERE OVER THE RAINBOW* – ADMIRAL DUNCAN, 54 OLD COMPTON STREET

On 30 April 1999, here in Soho, the pulsing Queen Bee of London, the Admiral Duncan pub was the scene of the worst homophobic attack to occur in Britain on a gay venue. A nail bomb blast killed three people: Andrea Dykes, 27, who was pregnant, and her friends John Light, 32, and Nick Moore, 31. The blast wounded around 70 others. The nails fired out from the bombs had been dipped in rat urine and faeces, further infecting survivors. Neo-Nazi David Copeland planted this bomb, and two others in Brixton and Brick Lane, in an attempt to stir up ethnic and homophobic tension.

Two weeks earlier, on Saturday 17 April, a black sports bag had been placed in the busy market of Electric Avenue, Brixton. A few market traders noticed the bag and saw that it contained a bomb, but they weren't sure what to do with it. Sandra Mills was walking past the Iceland supermarket:

I remember hearing a loud, deafening blast, like a huge gust of wind that blew all the windows out sending thousands of nails flying in all directions. My heart sank to my stomach in sheer panic and I just stood still. After what seemed like an eternity of silence, I saw an injured man lying in the road who was covered in glass. I ran to his aid and saw he had nails lodged in his legs.

A week after that, on Saturday 24 April, a second bomb targeted the Bengali community of Brick Lane, East London. Once again, it was placed in a sports bag, and once again, its crass nature meant a member of the public discovered it and tried to take it to the police station, which was closed at the time. The bomb exploded in the man's car, destroying nearby buildings and injuring thirteen people.

The murderer behind these attacks was branded the only serial bomber the country has seen, but the police were slow on the uptake that the bombs had been racially motivated. After the Brixton bombing, police said 'they were keeping an open mind' about who may be behind it, despite the risk posed to other multicultural communities in the country. They also initially refused to reveal a highly pixelated image of the killer taken from CCTV footage. He later claimed his motives for the attacks were 'to spread fear, resentment and hatred throughout this country', and that he wanted to incite 'a racial war'. He also added, for the record, 'I am a Nazi. I admit that, yeah.' When the police eventually turned up at Copeland's Hampshire home, he admitted to the bombings, saying, 'Yeah, they were all down to me, I did them on my own.' Hung up in his bedroom were two Nazi flags, and a collection of newspaper clippings about the bombings.

Receiving little governmental or police support, the LGBTQIA+ community came out in force. A vigil organised by queer rights movement OutRage! in Soho Square the following Sunday was attended by hundreds. 'We remember especially today Andrea Dykes, 27, four months pregnant, who was killed here in Soho's Queer Village by the bomb, while her husband was seriously injured and their best man and another friend were killed. Seventy others were injured', said the Reverend David Gilmore from St Anne's Church. On Tuesday 4 May, the London Gay Men's Chorus gathered up the bouquets of flowers and messages placed outside the pub and, in a procession watched by people lining Old Compton Street, they walked to Soho Square to lay the flowers and create a temporary garden of remembrance.

This was a snapshot of an era of rising fascist hatred, xenophobic 'othering' and homophobic and transphobic thuggery, and there was no social media at the time to elevate mass support. Many things have still not changed on this front, except for the pumping hearts of millions of people who refuse to let the victims' stories be in vain. Whole programmes have come to life since then, demanding mental health support for the entire community, to help heal us from our social trauma. Because when one of our queer family is attacked, it impacts the collective consciousness of us all.

London's queer community instantly instigated a plethora of responses. Queer punk band Sister George (whose name was inspired by the 1968 film *The Killing of Sister George*) had just released their *Drag King* album, featured a hardcore cover of the Tom Robinson song 'Glad to Be Gay', as the band chanted 'We kill in self defence'. Discontented by the political environment, they produced anthems that rocked the nation and served as a challenge to mainstream gay culture. The band's record label manager, Liz Naylor, said, 'To me, the gay lifestyle is getting to be like just another alternative lifestyle. You go down Old Compton Street in Soho and see people sitting there in nice coffee bars with their pink pounds – and these [Sister George] are 20-year-old kids who are angry and on the dole.'

Queer self-defence strategies continued to take on a more overt form when the OutRage! office received tip-offs from anti-fascists that gay pubs and clubs in Soho were about to be targeted again by the British National Party (BNP), who were holding a fascist rally in central London. One pub, the Central Station in King's Cross, had already been the target of an explosive CS canister (tear gas) attack. So Queers Bash Back was set up in response, a separate movement using physical force against queer-bashers who were attacking cruisers. Large groups of anti-fascists and OutRage! members gathered in central Soho to defend the clubs. 'Quite what a couple of dozen queens were supposed to do to stop rampaging fascists from attacking queer pubs was never explained, but small groups were stationed in pubs, while other "mobile" units kept an eye out for any trouble', said OutRage! activist Martin Maynard.

Like birds weaving twigs in a nest, life in the gay ghetto plays a crucial role in protecting our community and the work is sometimes controversial and volatile, often life affirming and always continuous.

Fast forward to 2015 and the UK saw 5597 hate crimes against LGBTQIA+ people, a rise of 22 per cent on the previous year.

This is just one symptom of a decaying system. In 2012 the home secretary Theresa May introduced the 'hostile environment' strategy with the aim 'to create here in Britain a really hostile environment for illegal migration'. This hostile environment pervaded the social atmosphere, compounding and encouraging bigotry that had become state sanctioned. It would evolve into a catch-all brand to suffocate anyone outside the narrow status quo of acceptance. This results in a 'trickle down' effect on the queer community, women, disabled people, travellers and anyone marginalised and targeted by white patriotic patriarchal culture.

The following year, in June 2016, a homophobic attack on the Pulse gay club in Orlando, USA, saw 49 people killed and many more injured. Again a vigil was organised and this time on Old Compton Street thousands turned up to fill the entire street along its length and surrounding area to show solidarity with the victims. Despite the many advances made by the LGBTQIA+ community since the start of the twenty-first century, the attack in Orlando was a reminder of the homophobia still remaining in society. The London Gay Men's Chorus sang 'Somewhere over the Rainbow' so enchantingly, the thousands packing the street fell silent.

Today, attached to the Admiral Duncan pub ceiling, you can see remnants of the bomb, twisted into a mural that commemorates the bombing outside. Look up on the exterior wall, where you can see a blue plaque. I stuck it up there with my merry band of activists, intent on amplifying and disseminating queer herstory in 2018 on the 30th anniversary of Section 28, that banned the promotion of homosexuality in public institutions. People think it's a legitimate English Heritage plaque – and it should be. Hate may have snuffed out the mortal existence of those lost in the bombings, but the impact of their lives spreads further and deeper in our souls than the accursed ideology that killed them.

6. *I DON'T LIKE THE LOOK OF YOU CUNTY* – THE COLONY ROOM CLUB, 41 DEAN STREET

Long before Old Compton Street was the place to be free, from 1948 to 1979 the Colony Room Club was the place to be.

In 1948, Muriel Belcher became the licensee and ran the place with her Jamaican girlfriend Carmel Stuart, a leading lesbian power couple of the time. To get around the tough licensing laws, Belcher claimed the place was also an eatery – so you might have found a week-old curled up sandwich sitting on the bar in case the police asked any questions.

Belcher was known for her acid wit and razor tongue. If somebody turned up that she had not seen before, she'd just look them up and down and say, 'I don't like the look of you cunty, fuck off', then wink at the crowd and burst out laughing. 'Just don't be dull and fucking boring, that's the golden rule', she growled, when interviewing prospective members. She was a very handsome woman with strong, dark eyes, black hair drawn back from her face, and because of her blasé attitude, everybody adored her.

The place was swinging. The room was tiny and packed with photographs, trinkets and lumpy places to sit, the conversations loud and the piano pounding with jazz. Artist Francis Bacon became a regular, and Belcher jokingly adopted him as 'her daughter', giving him free drinks if he brought in fancy artsy clientele. Clients like Bacon and Lucien Freud, when hard on their luck, would pay their tabs with works of art, and so the place was full of priceless art works from this country's leading artists. It was a place where the affluent mixed with the poor, where it didn't matter what's between your legs. Gay could mix with straight, women could mix with men (and be listened to), and celebrity was practically invisible. In queer bohemia, creating a new existence away from the tense street life outside, nothing mattered but your conversation and your willingness to let people simply, just be.

7. *SEXUAL FREEDOM* – DEAN STREET SERVICES, 43 DEAN STREET

With Dean Street Clinic at no. 56 and Dean Street Express at no. 43, Dean Street is home to the Hilton of sexual health centres. With its red neon lighting harking back to the sexual prowess of Soho's underworld, it does exactly what all sexual health centres should do: enable us to live a life full of pride, joy, desires and dreams together, even if the gonorrhoea injection in your bum is still sore.

In the footsteps of the world's first venereal disease clinic for men that opened in Soho in 1862, Dean Street Clinic has supported London's gay community since 2009. It has set the world record for performing the most HIV tests in one location and supported thousands of people's access to treatment. Their care is specifically focused on the LGBTQIA+ community, a world away from centuries of pathologisation, doors slammed in our faces, and sneaking around the back of clinics for fear of being attacked.

Their strategic vision led to one important recent success: contributing to the PrEP Group, which in 2015 had been campaigning for access to PrEP (pre-exposure prophylaxis), a daily pill used to prevent HIV. PrEP catalysed a striking 90 per cent decrease in HIV diagnosis in London for men who have sex with men (MSM). They didn't stop there, and ever since have been pushing for a rollout of PrEP for all, for men, women, trans people, people of colour, migrants and anyone who needs it, all across the whole of the UK. Today their programmes include running LGBTQIA+ sex education workshops, open conversations with doctors and trans health care specialists, and urgent information sessions on the monkeypox crisis.

They fight hard so history won't repeat itself, since the days of the Queer Valentines Carnival on Old Compton Street over 20 years before. The key to their success? A holistic and reparative approach to healthcare, because we cannot look at the wellbeing of our bodies in a social or historical vacuum. David Stuart, a local hero, knew this. David spent every day disseminating one-to-one advice as the wellbeing manager at Dean Street wellbeing programme, or in cafes all along Old Compton Street listening to people and providing support that reinstilled a sense of pride in our precious community. Devastated by AIDS, silenced by Section 28 and impacted by the closure of queer spaces and oversexualisation by corporate app-culture, can all lead to chemsex culture, using drugs for the purposes of gay sex, a phenomenon often leading to HIV transmission. Encouraging access to the support that we deserve, David's work helped create vital space for liberation, space that is still only beginning to emerge.

Dani Singer is an activist with 'PrEPster' who alongside Dean Street helped lead the charge for PrEP. Dani is one of the younger generation of the Gay Liberation Front, holding the torch for freedom that Ted lit in knocking doors down on these streets 50 years before. Reflecting on the painstakingly difficult battle that was fought to make PrEP generally available, Dani says, 'It was like a four year struggle, after being told by the establishment that the community doesn't deserve healthcare, to thrive in our identities, and that's really the same sort of thinking that leads to things like gross indecency laws'.

Ted, Josh, David and Dani know that the political is always personal. Passion is needed in order to push down the ghetto walls. Internalised homophobia, shame and the underlying societal structures perpetuating them are not going to be overturned overnight.

While today's HIV and AIDS statistics paint a somewhat rosy picture, they are the tip of a very imbalanced and questionable iceberg of government cuts, mainstream ignorance and an increasing lack of provision for those living with HIV. Dean Street wellbeing services are sacred places, and any moves by governments to push through austerity measures upon communities they deem unworthy, will always be challenged.

I would lie in the road to protect Dean Street services so that they continue being a template for service provision and a roadmap to end the AIDS crisis once and for all. When I'm not having a cheeky pint at Comptons of Soho, you might find me here.

8. *I'M A LESBIAN. WHAT DO YOU DO?* – GARGOYLE CLUB, 69 DEAN STREET

At the bottom of this gorgeous eighteenth-century Georgian townhouse you will see a silver rectangular plaque to the Gargoyle Club. If you were to visit back in the 1930s, you'd have entered the top floor to perhaps see Noël Coward playing the piano, Fred Astaire singing and raucous Hollywood actress Tallulah Bankhead doing naked cartwheels for all the world to see. Tallulah 'hated wearing underwear' and called herself ambisextrous, being attracted to people of various gender identities, and introduced herself at parties with 'I'm a lesbian. What do you do?' By the time she was in her forties she claimed to have bedded 5000 people and was romantically linked with female personalities of the day including actresses Greta Garbo and Marlene Dietrich, and singer Billie Holiday, giving my favourite Billie song, 'You're My Thrill', a whole new meaning.

As a result, Tallulah had been hailed as one of the wits of Manhattan. She worked hard to make sure the reputation stuck when she moved to London in 1923, her formative years. In private, she was still sometimes besieged by childish terrors and wept in her dressing room from stage fright, but in public she could launch herself into a room with a stream of slick, blunt and seemingly impromptu one-liners, 'I'm as pure as the driven slush' she would remark, tossing back her hair while taking a calculated drag on a cigarette in her famously self-described 'mezzo-basso' husky voice. 'I don't give a fuck what people say about me, so long as they say something.'

Born into a high-profile political family, she was sent to Convent School to 'straighten her out'. That didn't work (and never does), and she was soon expelled for coming on to a Nun. Her eyes were set on breaking into Broadway, and her dad sent her packing. 'Avoid men and alcohol' was Daddy's warning, but, as Tallulah pointed out, 'he said nothing about women and cocaine' she purred in return.

Deemed 'unsuitable for the public', she topped a Hollywood blacklist for her 'verbal, moral turpitude', and was classified as 'the most immoral woman that ever lived' by a Hollywood exec who said after a film shoot, 'A day away from Tallulah is like a month in the country'. Tallulah was unapologetic, a total hoot, and roared around London in her Bentley instead, making the city her own. 'Men were for sex and women were for relationships', she exclaimed. She said her husband was 'so so', and declared, 'I've tried everything. Going down on a woman gives me a stiff neck, going down on a man gives me lockjaw and conventional sex gives me claustrophobia.' Her female fans called themselves the 'gallery girls', that critics called 'Tallulahballoo,' hollering, stamping and throwing roses at her shows.

Aged 31, she ended up in hospital after a hysterectomy from gonorrhoea, but even that didn't stop her. 'Don't think this has taught me a lesson', Tallulah shouted back over her shoulder to the doctors after her release, and it was back to acting and scandals for her. On a trip back to New York City she bumped into actress Joan Crawford, who was on her honeymoon. She told Crawford, 'You're divine – I had an affair with your husband, you are next.' One of her last acting roles was as special guest villain in the *Batman* TV series, and her antics were forever immortalised in the character of Cruella de Vil in *101 Dalmations*, based on her theatrical persona. 'Darling, don't tell me about camp, I invented it', she told the press.

Her hijinks eventually caught up with her as she retired back to the States. Sauntering down an NYC street, someone asked if she was Tallulah Bankhead; she turned back, growling, 'I'm what's left of her, darling'.

9. *BREAKING OUT THE GHETTO* – KARL MARX PLAQUE, 30 DEAN STREET

Tilt your head up to the plaque honouring Karl Marx (5 May 1818–14 March 1883) who from 1851 lived in considerable poverty with his family here at number 28. Marx was a German philosopher, economist, sociologist, historian, journalist and revolutionary socialist, notable works being *The Communist Manifesto* (1848) and *Das Kapital* (1867–1894). After all we have seen you might be looking for the answer for a life beyond the ghetto, I know I am. Luckily this guy knew a thing or two about the chains that enslave us, how to reclaim our humanity and break out of captivity as he wrote in 1875 'From each according to his abilities, to each according to his needs'. Karl's daughter Eleanor Marx, born here, also would become an important socialist campaigner.

10. *BLACK AND GAY, BACK IN THE DAY* – CANDY BAR, 4 CARLISLE STREET

In recent years, Soho has become synonymous with the 'whitewashed' frontier of gay nightlife. It is often mistakenly perceived as a playground for a predominantly white LGBTQIA+ crowd, but it was here at Candy Bar that Black queer women once danced the night away. Precious Browns, 'a haven and a nightclub for queer Black women', had its home here during the 1990s, connected to a rich tapestry of queer Black London life. You can get lost for hours in the brilliant 'Black and Gay, Back in the Day', a digital community archive honouring and remembering Black queer life in Britain. Black-friendly nights featuring Black music included those at the Prince of Wales in Brixton, Traffic in King's Cross, Sombreros in Kensington and Nwangi at the Market Tavern in Vauxhall. Yvonne Taylor, a titan of the Black LGBTQIA+ community, used to DJ here while also promoting Sistermatic, a collective of Black female promoters with a lesbian-run sound system that hosted a monthly party at the South London Women's Centre on Acre Lane in Brixton.

Today, young, Black and queer activists, such as the founder of 'the Black Curriculum', Lavinya Stennett, continue their campaigns against government ministers who weaponise 'woke culture' to preserve the ghetto of British cultural life for the elite. Marc Thompson, founder of 'Black and Gay, Back in the Day' recalls:

> We tried to carve out our own spaces. As with today, there were still racist door policies. Very often the punters in the space would treat you in a racist manner, the same way that young Black gay men today might be asked if they're drug dealers in nightclubs or fetishised in mainstream queer spaces. I can't tell you how many times I went to a club and was asked if I knew it was a gay bar when I got there.

11. *QUEER BLACK JOY* – SOHO SQUARE

You'll find Josh here on a sunny day writing his latest articles on the slow improvements to accessibility in our spaces or his tantalising sex life. Wind back to the early 1990s, where Grace Jones's 'Slave to the Rhythm' and Chaka Khan's 'I feel for you' pumping out of Candy Bar and across Soho Square would connect with an emerging, timely and powerful social fabric. Beginning in Kennington Park in 1991, the 'Black Experience', unwilling to be marginalised by mainstream Pride, transformed London through 'People of Colour' tents from Brockwell to Victoria Park to Clapham Common, self-organisation that built the foundations for UK Black Pride that began in 2006.

Looking fabulous in styles that included black shades, leather jackets and manicured slit eyebrows, Marc and his co-organisers commissioned their own tents playing Black music on a ghetto blaster for 'Queer Black joy, love, friendship, celebration for celebration's sake and fun for fun's sake', Marc remembers, a smile drawing across his face. If you watched Russell T. Davies's *It's A Sin* and want to keep dancing in tribute to the Queer Londoners of that time, listen to Marc and long-time friend Calvin Dawkins 'DJ Biggy C' spotify playlist 'It 's A Sin – The Black Album'.

Soho Square continues to be the epicentre of queer joy today with gatherings from across our community. In 2019, UK Black Pride co-hosted 'QLGBTI Womxn of Colour: My Pleasure, My Power' alongside Dean Street Wellbeing programme exploring a multitude of too-long-silenced issues to catalyse pleasure in the community. The same year, under a clear blue sky and warm sunshine, 1500 people took over the Square to 'Come Out!'

continuing the footsteps of the Gay Liberation Front in these streets fifty years before. 'We're marching for the rights of Trans people,' beamed organiser Lucia Blayke at London's first ever Trans Pride. 'For healthcare, for social housing, for education, to stop the deportation of trans refugees in the UK and many other issues. Today is the one day of the year trans people can stand in an open space and think: Wow, I'm not the outcast'.

12. *FUCK THE PAIN AWAY* – GHETTO, FALCONBERG COURT

Bear with me, dear reader, for one last stop, because if there is a place that busts myths and shakes us free from traditional social and moral forces which confine our community to a 'gay scene' – it is here, the stomping ground of my teenage years.

The club Ghetto was home to legendary nights such as 'Nag Nag Nag', where you could hear blasting out 'Fuck the Pain Away' by Peaches – the soundtrack to my youth. It was the first mid-week electro club in town, with a golden-hearted bouncer attuned to the needs of the community. She understood that yes, we were going to misbehave, and that is ok, after all we have been through a lot. Based on his own experiences on the underground scene both in New York and London, Steve Swindell says he wanted to drag gay clubbing kicking and screaming into the 1980s. He had had first-hand experience of the epochal Paradise Garage, where Black gay DJ Larry Levan would conduct marathon ecstatic weekend sessions for 3000 New York dancers sweating it out on the dancefloor. So Steve launched the Lift in

1982 back at the site of Tallulah Bankhead's old hangout, the Gargoyle Club, since moved here to Falconberg Court.

This pioneering queer, trans or intersex person of colour (QTIPOC) led club was called 'Stallions' at the time, then became 'Substation' in the 1990s and 'Ghetto' in the 2000s. 'Stallions was deliciously retro', Steve says. 'It was a disco with pillars that were fish tanks!' Musicians Mick Jagger, David Bowie and the Communards, and glam rock, together with the technical and musical innovations pioneered here, helped break up the old world's cages once and for all. As gay novelist Alan Hollinghurst remembers of nights spent in this building, 'The thump of the music, like some powerful creature barely contained, came up out of the ground and gathered around us as we went in at the door.'

WHERE'S THE PUB? ADMIRAL DUNCAN,
54 OLD COMPTON STREET

We wrap up this neighbourhood tour circling back to the Admiral Duncan and raise a glass to Andrea Dykes, John Light and Nick Moore, who lost their lives here back in 1999. Why? Because oppression always inadvertently promotes homosexuality in the end, by strengthening our resolve and fuelling our struggle for freedom.

Our queer community has a beautiful spirit and a courageous soul. When we awaken our ancestors to guide us, I pray for anyone who tries to get in our way again.

BRIXTON

MARCUS GARVEY WAY

BRADWELL ROAD

CHAUCER ROAD

RAILTON ROAD

MILTON ROAD

BETTER TO SQUAT THAN LET HOMES ROT

AJAMU X

BRIXTON GAYS
WELCOME ANTI-FASCISTS

2

Even a Homosexual Can Be a Revolutionary

Brixton

Bricks make the houses, but it's what is contained within them that can change the world. Movement by movement, the community here in Brixton's 'Frontline' have created the most magnificent physical, psychological and spiritual structures on the streets and in the human imagination. They have built a queer landscape where at times it seemed impossible. So join us to explore one of London's most shape-shifting neighbourhoods, where every building has a story to tell of unity, mischief, resilience, compassion, love and hope.

START: BRIXTON STATION

1. Bumping 'n' Grinding – *Corner of Marcus Garvey Way and Railton Road*
2. No Justice, No Peace – *Leeson Road Corner*
3. Erotic and Unapologetically Fun – *South London Gay Community Centre, 78 Railton Road*
4. Sister Love, Sister Love, Sister Love – *Brixton Black Women's Centre, 65 Railton Road*
5. My Name Is Mrs Mold – *The George, 82 Railton Road*
6. I'm Bisexual, Ya Know! – *Pearls Shebeen, 103 Railton Road*

1. *BUMPING 'N' GRINDING* – MARCUS GARVEY WAY

A people without knowledge of their past history, origin, and culture is like a tree without roots.

—Marcus Garvey, Pan-Africanist activist, journalist and entrepreneur, *Message to the People*, 1937

It's a calm September evening in 1981, with a light drizzle. The street you are standing on is part of an area known locally as 'the Frontline'.

Suburban Fiat Pandas and classic Austin Metro cars line the roadside. Mothers and their kids are clutching shopping bags from the market. A group of teenagers in Sergio Tacchini tracksuits, Fred Perry shirts, bracelets and rings are smoking and giggling on top of a pavement wall, some of them unfurling ideas for their nights ahead. On a quiet night in Brixton, you wouldn't know that blossoming hives of community organising in Black power, gay liberation and women's movements, and seductive underground parties, were to be found here.

Welcome to the home of counter-cultural swinging, magnetic and defiant London here in Brixton. 'Frontlines' are areas deprived by the government of basic resources necessary for life, and were the only tangible public spaces where Black people felt relatively safe enough to convene, especially as they were ostracised by mainstream venues. 'In the Jamaicans, you have a people who are constitutionally disorderly ... it's simply in their make-up, they're constitutionally disposed to be anti-authority', declared Kenneth Newman, commissioner of the Metropolitan police in 1982, illustrating the blatant racism the community has always faced. And so the police would invade these locations – but they were often outnumbered – as outlined in the brilliant 2021 exhibition 'War Inna Babylon: The Community's Struggle for Truths and Rights'. Throughout the 1970s and 1980s other Frontlines came into being in London's Dalston, Tottenham, Notting Hill and beyond in St Paul's in Bristol and Chapeltown in Leeds, Moss Side in Manchester, Toxteth in Liverpool and Handsworth in Birmingham.

Unlicensed house or 'blues' parties were run here by young Black people in response to racist door policies that excluded them from West End clubs at the time. 'My memories are of lots of beautiful men, much bumping 'n' grinding, clouds of weed smoke, really good vibes and no trouble at all', reminisces club promoter Steve Swindells. You paid a pound to get into a packed flat, and once you were inside, a bottle of beer cost £1, a shot of spirits £2, and the music was a mix of imports from the Black American scene and Jamaica.

1970s and 1980s Britain was saturated with political activity. Just look around you and imagine the 'Workers' power', 'Love over hate' and 'Brixton women care for kids' graffiti along the walls.

Brixton was, and still is, a community in constant transition. Attacks by fascist groups, such as the National Front, as well as discrimination in housing and employment incited buzzing chatter in cafes, school drop-off-points and market stalls. Conversations about the latest outrages of police violence were commonplace. Whispers in shop fronts and outcries on the streets shared the daily news. Increased tensions between the police and Black communities were epitomised by the 'sus' laws: the laws allowing police officers to stop and search people on mere suspicion that they intended to commit a crime.

Smell the concoctions of cannabis, sweet orange, coconut, incense and hazelnut wafting through the streets and listen to the wisdom imparted by older bohemians with beatnik influences in the 1950s handed across generations. Radical murmurings of peace, love, and brown rice from sandal-wearing hippies emanated from the communes of the 1960s influencing the community in the 1970s. This generation were then equipped and ready to stop mass evictions of squatters and launch world-changing experiments in modern dance and theatre. At the time, Brixton was a melting pot of revolutionary creativity as labour rights, trade union and anti-war struggles joined Black, women's and gay liberation movements to challenge the oppressive status quo.

Chants of 'Gay is good!', 'Free Nelson Mandela', 'Can't pay won't pay', 'Never going underground' and 'Maggie Maggie Maggie, Out! Out! Out!' could be heard at protests around these street corners on a regular basis. In Britain, gay liberation was not only closely entangled with national strikes for equity in the labour force but also against an empire crumbling under the advance of anticolonial movements. Queer people, seen as walking evidence of moral debauchery and the loss of manly character, became scapegoats for this imperial decline, just as immigrants had been before them. Queer liberation was emerging into a wider alliance of anticolonial movements in the Global South based on common solidarity. 'There was always this commitment to struggles around the world', says Jeffrey Weeks, a prominent historian and activist of the Gay Liberation Front (GLF). Throughout this period the anti-Apartheid movement, the Anti-Nazi League, Troops Out of Ireland, Red Wedge and many more programmes for civil freedom together challenged the racist regime in South Africa, the growing perils of racism and fascism and the continuing military occupation of Northern Ireland. Much of this melting pot of radical activity provided the ingredients for how politics were practised locally in Brixton.

2. *NO JUSTICE, NO PEACE* – LEESON ROAD CORNER

It's Saturday 28 September 1985 in the heart of Brixton. Screeching police sirens fill the air and barricades of bricks are piling up, ready to defend the community.

Why? Because three days earlier, 31-year-old mother of seven Cherry Groce was shot in her own home, in front of her 11-year-old son, by the Metropolitan Police. The police had raided her home to find her son Michael Groce, wanted in relation to a suspected firearms offence. Instead, the police attacked Cherry, causing her to be paralysed for the rest of her life. This sparked ongoing community movements to resist brutality, escalating in two days of uprisings which saw the death of photo-journalist David Hodge, and 43 civilians and 10 police officers being injured. During a number of fires, one building was destroyed and 55 cars were burnt out.

As queers, our history reminds us that the price to pay for police violence and indifference towards it is high, and resistance can be ground-breaking. The Stonewall Uprisings in New York in 1969 catalysed an upsurge of solidarity against all those affected by police violence, fought most fiercely by street Trans Queens of Colour. In Brixton, throughout the 1985 uprisings, similar resistance also took place, with punks, squatters, sex worker and lesbian activists nursing the wounded. Siobhan Fahey recounts: 'All night people came to our squats with injuries from the police, and we bandaged them up and sent them back out. We listened to the police radio over our shortwave Citizens Band (CB) radio, so we could give up to date info to the sheroic rioters.'

This was the second major uprising that Brixton had witnessed in the space of four years. The preceding one, dubbed 'Bloody Saturday' by *Time* magazine, was in 1981 and a result of the racist and discriminatory 'stop and search' practice used mainly by white police. This compounded existing tensions that followed the deaths of thirteen Black teenagers and young adults in the 'New Cross house fire'. In an era of white nationalist racism, this catalysed a mobilisation of political activity in Black and other oppressed communities. The South London Gay Liberation Front (GLF) showed their solidarity and took part in the uprisings too. You would think that by today the Black community would have some closure, perhaps even justice and accountability. Well, think again. Still today, nobody has ever been charged in relation to the New Cross fire and the police now claim that it was not an arson attack.

In 2014, the police eventually apologised for the wrongful shooting of Mrs Groce, only 43 years later. Cherry died in 2011 aged 63 from kidney failure, which a pathologist directly linked to the gunshot injury. An inquest jury concluded that eight separate police failures had contributed to her death and so, unsurprisingly, the community of Brixton has lost trust in the Metropolitan police, spiking an awareness of institutional racism that continues today. In 2021, a memorial to Cherry was unveiled in the heart of Brixton, at Windrush Square. Her son Lee Lawrence said in tribute to the memorial's powers:

> The injustice done to my mother on 28 September 1985 and its aftermath, catalysed our community to act together relentlessly and persistently in the pursuit of justice for more than three decades. Our achievements together in that effort can inspire us to continue to work together to make justice a reality across our society'.

3. *EROTIC AND UNAPOLOGETICALLY FUN* – SOUTH LONDON GAY COMMUNITY CENTRE, 78 RAILTON ROAD

As a gay Black teenager in 1980s Huddersfield, Ajamu fashioned himself in a sexy punk aesthetic to become the empowered sex bomb that he needed to be. Wearing studded leather cuffs and hats, a tight black vest and pin-striped trousers, Ajamu was living his dream of a life 'erotic and unapologetically about fun, pleasure

Credit: Ian Townson Archive/Bishopsgate Institute

and kink' that stimulated his curiosity into the roots of human potential. As a student at Leeds University he started a magazine and called it 'BLAC', an acronym for Black Liberation Activist Core. After seeing an advertisement in the *Caribbean Times* for a 'National Black Gay Men's Conference', he knew that he had to go. The conference held in Camden changed everything, and by the following year he had moved to London. Black queer blues parties and cultural life made the decision to make this his home an easy one, and thus began his journey to become one of Britain's most loved queer Black photographers.

Taking the name 'Ajamu X' in 1991, meaning 'he who fights for what he believes', Ajamu's soul-fire would continue igniting conversations about race, class and gender bringing to life the words of the late author and activist bell hooks: 'Surely our desire for radical social change is intimately linked with our desire to experience pleasure, erotic fulfilment, and a host of other passions.'

Back when Ajamu X was still just a tiny queer with big dreams, on a bright Spring day in 1974, his queer ancestors stood proudly behind these gates where the South London Gay Community Centre once stood. Fifteen queens, some wearing appliqued kaftan flowing dresses, frizzy hennaed hair, varnished fingernails and patterned shoes are getting ready to go to Camberwell Magistrates Court.

Their crime? The South London Gay Community Centre had refused to pay local taxes because none of the rates were used to provide amenities for gay people in the wider community. The brick walls of this building housed a vision that demanded freedom for all. The building was squatted by people who were determined to come out into the clear light of day and establish an undeniable and irreversible presence of gay people in the area. 'Gay Liberationists Take Over Bookshop!' the local press exclaimed. The presiding judge had difficulty in persuading the plaintiffs that they should 'know their place' and behave accordingly.

Behave according to what? During its brief existence that began in March 1974, the Centre acted as a focal point, bringing together gay people from many different backgrounds through social activities and political action. Their flowing dresses were the leading edge in challenging rigid masculine identities, as relationships of solidarity were built among revolutionary groups. This included squatters groups setting up Black gay housing projects that still exist today and the 'Claimant's Union' that supported those entitled to welfare benefits, helping them to make successful claims. By 1976, the Brixton Faeries had helped form a housing cooperative on Mayall Road, parallel to Railton Road, defying homophobic stereotypes within the Black community.

Together, they picketed shops that refused to sell the *Gay News*, and they campaigned in solidarity with Black, lesbian and women's groups, breaking down the isolation of gay people in a friendly environment.

Step into the centre on any given day and you would find a hive of activity including modern dance classes, a wrestling group, discos, campaign trainings and advice on creating radical communal housing, radical families and sharing sex partners, all in order to smash the structures of an oppressive system and start anew. With pioneering places and spaces like the Centre, it is little wonder that in 2021 the Brixton business district has been twinned with New York's Harlem's 125th Street, linked 'through their shared place values, rich histories and diverse communities', in a first of this kind of twinning.

4. *SISTER LOVE, SISTER LOVE, SISTER LOVE* – BRIXTON BLACK WOMEN'S CENTRE, 65 RAILTON ROAD

Not content with simply overturning social, racial and housing inequalities, the soul-fire at the heart of Brixton had set up an entirely new economy and today the face of a very special someone represents it. Behind this black door was the home of Olive Morris. Olive squatted the building with Liz Obi in 1974, establishing a base to set up the Black Women's Centre and support the local squatting movement.

Olive Morris was a tireless organiser and fighter against racism, sexism and other forms of oppression. The great feminist and lesbian teacher Audre Lorde, an inspiration of Olive's, reminds us in her love letters to partner Pat Barker between 1969 and 1988:

> Why am I angry? Who am I angry at? And what can I do to change it? And of course, the minute I start thinking along this vein, I get even more angry. From the monumental thought of overthrowing the system and ridding my life of capitalism, racism, sexism, classism, to the smallest nuisance ... Sister love, sister love, sister love. We are not talking anything simple or easy here ...

With this wisdom, in the early 1970s Olive became a member of the youth section of the Black Panther movement and a founding member of the Brixton Black Women's Group. Committed to critical thought and action, Olive co-wrote a piece titled 'Has the Anti-Nazi League Got it Right on Racism?', in which she criticised the strategy of prioritising the fight against fascism, while largely ignoring the impact of institutionalised racism in the police and the educational system, arguing that we need to oppose racism wherever it is found.

Why do I care? Well, as a white queer Jew whose ancestors fled the Nazi Holocaust to seek sanctuary in London, I am indebted to the fierce words and intersectional action(s) of people like Olive, for making this great city a home for us all.

Over the coming years, Olive's passion, combined with her anti-colonial, internationalist approach to activism, led to her partaking in solidarity delegations to Jamaica, Italy, Northern Ireland and China. But while her heart was ablaze, her body began to weaken.

Olive became ill during a trip to Spain in 1978. Diagnosed with non-Hodgkin's lymphoma, she died on 12 July 1979, aged just 27 years old, at the local St Thomas's Hospital, and was buried in Streatham Vale cemetery. Today, a Lambeth council building at 18 Brixton Hill is named after her and so too is the community garden and play area in the Myatt's Fields area. In Brixton the Remembering Olive Morris Collective began in 2008 to publicise her legacy and contribution to political struggle with awards in the form of bursaries to young Black women. Today, Olive Morris's face, chosen by popular vote, is found on local currency the 'Brixton Pound', set up to support local businesses.

5. *MY NAME IS MRS MOLD* – THE GEORGE, 82 RAILTON ROAD

'My name is Mrs Mold. I've grown so cold – forgotten how to smile. Managed to keep the gays out for good but could only keep the Blacks out for a while.' So sang the Brixton Faeries in the play *Mr Punch's Nuclear Family*. It was here, at the very whites-only George pub during the 1970s, that you could hear a pin drop even on Saturday nights thanks to the notoriously bigoted landlady 'Mrs Mold'. She refused to allow either LGBTQIA+ or Black people to enter or drink. In response, the Brixton Faeries that were spawned by the South London Gay Liberation Theatre Group back at the Community Centre would demonstrate defiantly outside. 'Coming out' wearing 'Glad to be Gay' and 'Yes, I'm Homosexual Too' badges on their chests, holding hands and doing each other's make-up, they forced the zealot Mrs Mold back into her damp building, alone. She was eventually charged under the Race Relations Act (1965) for barring Black people, but succeeded in banning gay people.

Luckily Mrs Mold was just a blip in this building's backstory of Black queer power bringing glory to all. Look up at the Black plaque above you. In 1956 it housed one of the first Black women's hairdressers in London and was called the Winifred Atwell Salon. Trinidadian-born Atwell was undoubtedly one of Britain's most popular entertainers and with her undisguised cheerful personality and well-played honky-tonk ragtime music she brightened up many a 'knees up' in the fifties. In fact, when Atwell reached number one in 1954 with 'Let's Have Another Party', she became the first Black musician in this country to sell a million records and is still the most successful female instrumentalist to ever have featured in the British pop charts. It's a fully instrumental song, so there are no lyrics to share but please play it now wherever you are, it will bring you oodles of joy.

6. *I'M BISEXUAL, YA KNOW!* – PEARLS SHEBEEN, 103 RAILTON ROAD

If you listen closely, you can hear the faint thrum of bass coming up from the basement. Here you'd find a 'shebeen' – an unlicensed bar – that began in the mid-1970s, filled with dancing Black bodies intimately entwined in a gay way that they could never dream of expressing outside. Regulars flooded in from the gay squats nearby. Underneath the decadence, these spaces provided a deep duty of care, strangers connecting to find shelter, food and safety, a real testament to the enduring, revolutionary love practised for each other. And behind the bar, standing proud, is the woman behind it all: the Black bisexual queen of Brixton, Pearl Alcock.

At the time, Pearl's shebeen was the only gay bar in Brixton, which meant it attracted Black men from all around London who wanted to relish in a queer space where you could avoid the racism prevalent in the predominantly white gay scene and as Dirg Aab Richards remembers, 'get a half-pint of Heineken for 50p'. Richards, a long-time friend of Pearl's, says she was a 'big smoker', a 'kind and generous' person and always 'full of laughs'. She was authentic, spiritual and expressive of her Caribbean roots. She 'always left an extra plate out to give thanks' when she made food, and she was very much out and proud. 'I'm bisexual, ya know!' she proclaimed to new friends on arrival.

Unfortunately, the good times didn't last. With the election of Margaret Thatcher as prime minister in 1979 and the coming of a heightened moral panic over 'traditional moral values', the police started a clampdown on shebeens that later became known as 'Operation Swamp 81'. Casting zero doubt on institutionalised racism at the heart of the police, the reference to 'swamp' was inspired by Margaret Thatcher's speech about being 'swamped by alien cultures'. This harks back to arch-fascist and Conservative MP Enoch Powell's infamous 'Rivers of Blood' speech in 1968, in which the blood from racial tensions swamp 'decent' and 'moral' community life. Ever since, the mantra 'Self-defence is no offence' has echoed in the community to express the right to live without fear of racist attack. When it is an offence to simply be yourself, there is no other option but self-defence.

The 'Sus Laws' implemented throughout Operation Swamp meant that the police could arrest anyone they deemed suspicious, requiring neither a victim nor any physical evidence to justify their allegations. When they were eventually overturned as an abuse of power, was the community free from this unrelenting cruelty? No, the Sus Laws didn't die, instead they changed form and were reincarnated as the government's 'stop and search' tactics as used by the police today.

During the 1980s, people 'hanging out' on Railton Road and other sensitive spots were repeatedly stopped, searched and arrested. To avoid risking that herself or her customers experience the violence of an inevitable police raid, Pearl closed the doors in 1981. Like Olive, Pearl was never one to give up, and she continued with an open heart and set up Pearl's Cafe next door.

Pearl catalysed space for deep transformation like no other. It is difficult to replicate such space today, especially as gentrifying forces dig their claws into Black communities. She stood up to the powers of erasure, from the vilification of Thatcherism to persistent misogynoir (racism and sexism targeted at Black women), all while making brilliant art and beaming love and generosity to the people around her. She was mercurial, glamorous and entertaining with a cheeky sense of humour. Pearl's star continues to shine, because when you live a life through generosity, you will never truly be forgotten.

7. BRIXTON DYKES ON THE RAMPAGE –
121 RAILTON ROAD

Picture the banners covering the front of the building: 'Stop the Gentrification!', 'Defend squatters rights!' and 'Resist the Lambeth Mafia!'

Restless after transforming number 65, Olive and Liz were back. Even when giant cranes with wrecking balls turned up to intimidate squatters into leaving their homes, they weren't giving in. Olive and Liz knew that a reduction in vacant homes leads to more community transformation, so in 1973 they inspected the area and found a suitable property to live in right here. Within a year, 121 Railton Road became a hub of political activism and hosted community groups such as Black People against State Harassment, as well as housing Sabarr Bookshop, one of Britain's first Black community bookshops. Over the coming years, the annual DIY punk Queeruption festival was based here, Food not Bombs distributed free vegan and vegetarian food for the neighbourhood, and Community Resistance Against the Poll Tax, Anarchist Black Cross and the Troops Out of Ireland movement were among the other community liberation programmes active within these walls. The classic *Squatters Handbook* was written here. 121 Railton Road remained a social centre until it was closed in 1999.

Ian Townson from the Brixton Faeries reflects on the importance of squats for queer community in those days:

In essence, without squatting we would have remained isolated as gay people living in our individual shabby bedsits or flats or houses. Squatting enabled us to come together collectively to break down that isolation and produced some of the most productive political campaigning and radical theatre, not to mention a shot at non-bourgeois, non-straight ways of living.

Shocking Pink was distributed here, a magazine standing defiantly against patriarchy and capitalism, promoting hard-edged demands for control over women's bodies. It pioneered advocacy for fertility treatment, contraception and abortion on demand, free 24-hour childcare facilities and socialised housework, all written with a combination of feminism, humour, irreverence and anarchy. Louise Carolin recalls:

> It was an empowering experience of being a young woman and doing something creative, you could get something done, express yourself and feel that commonality with other girls, even girls that you'd never met who were reading it in remote bits of Wales.

It also spawned 'the new generation of commercial gay magazines', including *Diva*, the biggest lesbian magazine in the UK today.

One of the resolute and riotous revolutionary dykes inhabiting these walls was Atalanta Kernick. As she told me years later:

> Getting to 121 was a bit like the Holy Grail for me. There was a space for bands to perform. On the ground floor, there was an actual bookshop, meeting space and on the first floor a cafe. On the top floor there was a food Co-op and at another point, therapists took over the front rooms. Solidarity organising was abundant as we used to go to Stoke Newington and Tottenham police stations to demonstrate against police brutality and obviously around the homophobic legislation 'Stop the Clause 28' and the economically exploitative 'Poll Tax'. All

these catalysed righteous anger across Britain which we mobilised around as well. At one point, one of my flatmates was one of the most wanted people in Britain for the Stop the Poll Tax demos. Anarchist feminism was really important because we were intersectional before you know, the word existed.

After Gay Pride 1988 in Jubilee Gardens, some of the crew laid their 'Brixton Dykes on the Rampage – No One Fucks Us Over' banner painted in red dripping blood-style lettering to rest back at home at 121. On the stage here, the 'Sluts' were ready to wow the crowds of sex workers, faerie queens in miniskirts and butch dykes in biker jackets and leather chains. Local Dyke club nights 'Chain Reaction' and 'Venus Rising' influenced queer rave culture from Finland to New York City. They organised a plethora of workshops held at the Wild Women's Weekend Festival which was at the squatted housing benefits office (HBO) around the corner on Effra Road. These included campaigning for greater awareness of AIDS in the lesbian community, sex-positive 'find your cervix' workshops, and training in electrics and plumbing. 'Beyond the parodies, our own songs included the indigenous rights (anti) bicentennial in Australia, songs about Clause 28 and against the benefit sanctions regime. And sex of course, with our finale number "Wild, Hot and Wet"', Atalanta shares with a smile.

8. *YOU NEVER KNOW WHEN IT IS GOING TO EXPLODE* – RACE TODAY, 165–167 RAILTON ROAD

Explosive life didn't stop at 121. A few doors down at number 165 is the first blue plaque in honour of a Black man in Lambeth.

Credit: Jacob Joyce

C.L.R. James was a visionary Trinidadian historian, Marxist, political activist and author of the seminal book *Black Jacobins*, chronicling the power of the Haitian Revolution to overthrow colonisers. Acutely prescient, in one of the last interviews before his death he said 'You never know when it is going to explode. The revolutionary movement is a series of explosions when the regular routine of things reaches a pitch where it cannot go on'. James wrote here between 1981 and 1989, fired up from the heat rising beneath the floorboards below, the temporary offices of the Black Panthers and the GLF.

James's nephew Darcus Howe edited *Race Today* from 1973 to 1988, a monthly magazine shedding light on the social forces affecting Black and Asian people in Britain, and chronicling their forms of collective resistance and struggle. The collective that ran the magazine included Caribbean, African and South Asian members, several of whom had been active in the British Black Panthers, a Black power organisation that fought for the rights of

Black and Peoples of Colour in the country. The Black Panthers' main offices were not fixed, but moved around Brixton by necessity to avoid police raids.

The GLF were directly inspired by the US Black Panther Party after co-founder Huey Newton's speech on 15 August 1970 in New York City:

> Whatever your personal opinions and your insecurities about homosexuality and the various liberation movements among homosexuals and women (and I speak of the homosexuals and women as oppressed groups), we should try to unite with them in a revolutionary fashion. There is nothing to say that a homosexual cannot also be a revolutionary. And maybe I'm now injecting some of my prejudice by saying that 'even a homosexual can be a revolutionary'. Quite the contrary, maybe a homosexual could be the most revolutionary.

Two white activists, Bob Mellors and Aubrey Walter, were in America and after learning from Huey and the Street Trans Action Revolutionaries (STAR), who led the Stonewall Uprisings, they came back to the UK to 'chart their own course'. The Gay Liberation Front (GLF) started in the London School of Economics in 1970 and two years later founded the first Gay Pride in Britain that catalysed similar movements across the world. Huey may have had a point.

Like the *Gay News* or the GLF *Come Together* newspaper, *Race Today* forged a holistic approach to activism that weaponised journalism as a powerful campaigning tool. They were in alliance with the People's News Service down at 119 Railton

Road, featuring stories the establishment press refused to print. This symbiosis, coupled with the Collective's consistently global outlook, reached a pinnacle in 1981 with the 'Black People's Day of Action' – the largest demonstration of Black people in the UK up until that time. Fuelled by rage and grief after the New Cross Fire in January 1981, several groups, with the Collective at the forefront, began to mobilise in order to demand justice. These events were recently explored by Steve McQueen in his trail-blazing documentary series *Uprising*, and captured by Menelik Shabazz in his landmark film *Blood Ah Goh Run*.

Everything *Race Today* wrote had 'some root in doing something'. One of the Collective's greatest but lesser-known achievements was their role in collaboration with the 'Bengali Housing Action Group'. Together they found empty houses for families who could not stay in their homes for fear of racial attack, resulting in the development of the largest contemporary housing squat in Europe, without which the East End queer Bangladeshi community wouldn't be thriving today.

Icebreakers, a radical gay group, also worked their magic in these rooms creating a telephone service for isolated LGBTQIA+ people, to 'support the breakdown of a rigid gender division in order to liberate gay men and women and establish a new society'. Born out of the GLF 'Counter-Psychiatry Group', they focused on analysing and attacking the psychiatric establishment's wholesale acceptance of religious prejudice and its use of electric shock and drug programmes on gays and lesbians. 'Icebreakers phone line was open 7.30 to 10.00 p.m. every night of the year,' shares Nettie Pollard today, who was active in the group. 'We talked to people who felt isolated as fellow oppressed people and seeing ourselves as oppressed is what is needed to counter our self oppression.'

The address is now home to the Brixton Advice Centre, specialising in the areas of civil law most relevant to disadvantaged communities.

9. *PLATFORMING AFRICAN QUEERNESS* – ROTIMI FANI-KAYODE, 151 RAILTON ROAD

Ajamu X's camera clicks today are influenced by a vast array of musical genres, erotic fiction and other artists in the area. One influential photographer was Rotimi Fani-Kayode, who lived and died here between 1955 and 1989. He pushed the boundaries of his own art, exploring sexuality, religion, racism, colonialism and the tensions and conflicts between his homosexuality and his Yoruba upbringing. His images have lifted the spirits of QTIPOC people throughout the world since, for evoking a sense of fleeting beauty that fuses racial and sexual politics with religious eroticism, platforming African queerness in all its glory.

10. *BRIXTON FAERIES THEATRE COMPANY* – ST JUDE'S COMMUNITY CENTRE, 213 RAILTON ROAD

'Oooooh my, what's this?' You might hear such words in second-hand shops across the city in the mid-1970s as they were rummaged for fabulous outfits by the likes of proud Brixton Faerie Jim Ennis, known as 'Wendy Wattage' for his tailor-made 1978 white-ruffled two-piece dress. Ian Townson remembers those days fondly:

Jim Ennis was persuaded, against his better judgement I think, to clobber up as Queen Elizabeth II and John Haycock dressed in a long white frock. Julian Hows wore his very own special creation which included a huge, bulbous Chinese lantern as his head dress. There are great photos of us all sitting and standing on the roofs of the gay squats.

Credit: Townson archive/Bishopsgate Institute

Promoting 'radical self-identity', the Brixton Faeries Theatre Company was formed here at St Jude's Community Centre in 1974. 'The practice was very much to outrage and challenge the eternal verities of bourgeois conventions that were deeply embedded in the lives of "Norman Normal" and "Clarissa Conformist",' reminisces Ian Townson cheerfully.

Gay theatre was on the rise, as Brixton Faerie Terry Stewart recalls:

> Disco was still all the rage and it seemed like we were never going to stop dancing. Gay Sweatshop Theatre Company was pumping out great shows, as were Bloolips and Hot Peaches, the American theatre group. We were cultured, radical and ready to take on the world ... Nothing was going to stop us, not the local council, not the police, not the judiciary and certainly not the public opinion.

Show highlights included *Mr Punch's Nuclear Family* – based on the traditional Punch & Judy children's show, exposing the myth of the nuclear family as a haven of peace and tranquillity as the 'patriarch' strangles his wife and bludgeons his gay son to death. *Out of It* was a play written in the light of the increasing rise of fascist activity and Christian fundamentalism, and against psychiatric 'cures' for homosexuals. *Gents* was about 'cottaging' – its celebrations, its pleasures but also the dangers of queer bashers and police agent provocateurs. Straight in the bullseye for radical gays giving respectable gays a bad name. The list of pioneering Gay Sweatshop plays continues. Three decades after the publication of *This Island's Mine*, which beautifully explored the creation of positive representations of homosexuality in a hostile environment, or Noël Greig's *Poppies*, which unpacked how we can stop toxic masculinity from leading to nuclear war – the lessons are still, hauntingly, relevant.

Ian continues mischievously:

We drew our inspiration from many different sources. Pantomime allowed us the latitude for playfulness and clowning around. Agitprop and street theatre pressed us more in the direction of immediacy in getting our politics across to the audience in a succinct and instructive way. Radical drag and elements of more traditional camp drag acts on the 'straight' gay scene gave us the ability to branch out into fantasy land and indulge in ironic and challenging views of 'straight' life.

11. *BRIXTON GAYS WELCOME ANTI-FASCISTS –* BROCKWELL PARK

In a rare break from fanning the flames of Gay Theatre and debaucherous discos, in 1978 the Brixton Faeries watched proudly as 150,000 demonstrators for that year's massive Anti-Nazi League demo passed by their squats. Waving them on in full drag the marchers went under the giant pink 'Brixton Gays Welcome Anti-Fascists' banner that stretched across Railton Road.

The dynamism and energy were electric as black and white, straight and queer people came together to confront racist ideology in Britain, turning up to watch Elvis Costello, Stiff Little Fingers, Aswad, the Clash, Sham 69 and Misty in Roots.

On the same day, thousands of anti-fascists were demonstrating in Bethnal Green, East London, and the racist National Front were resisted there too, as local Victoria Park had hosted another huge 'Rock Against Racism' festival earlier, in April 1978. After the fascists sent death threats to the musicians, they also tried to cut the power to the stage, but people power reigned. While people were climbing trees for a view of the main stage, the backdoor stage entrance burst open and out came Sham 69 singer Jimmy

Pursey with an impassioned outcry: 'No one's gonna tell me what I can and can't do, I'm here 'cos I support Rock Against Racism'.

How does the community harvest all this queerstory today? How can society at large learn from the truth behind creative and collective uprisings for total human transformation, before they are pacified and stereotyped as 'riots' or as mere responses to the status quo? Look no further than the magnificent mural covering the bricks on the whole side of the last building before Brockwell Park appears on the right. The mural depicts some of the seismic social shifts against prisons, racist police brutality and gentrification. Don't wait outside though, because inside Ajamu X might have a new world-class exhibition for you. Working away in his studio here, Ajamu X continues to celebrate the lives of Queer Black communities across the world from Scotland to São Paulo, New York and South Africa.

The faggots, dykes, poofs and queens, tormented by the anti-gay laws that were exported by British colonialism across the world, have come home to roost and Brixton is all the better for it. Today you can find Ajamu X facilitating workshops on desire, vitality, erotic fulfilment, bondage basics – and all the techniques, safewords, consent and control needed within.

Continue mincing to Herne Hill station and have a tinkle on the piano here, ragtime style, singing the lyrics of Winifred Atwell's 'Bewitched': 'I'm wild again, beguiled again, a whimpering, simpering child again, bewitched, bothered and bewildered, am I'. Because, after all this collective organising, what could the future hold? The bricks emblazoned with pink signs dotted across these streets have the answer – that there is formidable unity in community.

As the writer Reni Eddo-Lodge reminds us: 'Faced with collective forgetting, we must fight to remember.'

WHERE'S THE PUB? BRIXTON HOUSE, 385 COLDHARBOUR LANE

The new Brixton House on Coldharbour Lane is the birth child of Oval House, a hotbed of artistic activism and fomented revolutionary thought, including the British Black Panther Party, Black Theatre Co-op and the Theatre of Black Women, and more recently the 'Sex Workers' Opera', where Sex Workers take back the stage to tell their own stories in their own words. Raise a glass to Cherry Groce and everyone resisting police brutality, and enjoy nourishment for the mind, body and soul here in abundance.

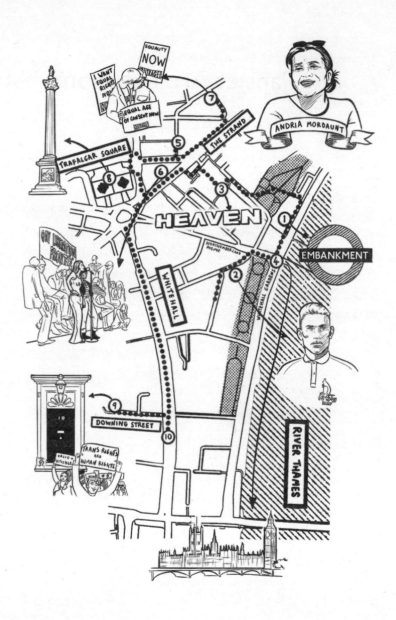

3

The Pansies Are in Bloom
Trafalgar Square

Sit yourself on top of the lions and pause before we start this
tour. Hold your heart and soak in the thousands of dreams that
have been hard fought for and won here. Trafalgar Square is the
heartbeat of democracy and people power in London Town. It
provides a history of change so rich that you will want to stand
up and shout your dreams up into the sky, so that one day, they
can come true too. So clear your throat, take a swig of water and
get ready to shout!

START: EMBANKMENT STATION

1. Oh! And Another Thing! – *Victoria Embankment Gardens*
2. A Secret Society of Homosexuals – *The Authors' Club, 1 Whitehall Place*
3. The Gay Ultradisco – *Heaven, under the Arches, Villiers Street*
4. We Are Not Going Back into the Closet – *The Thames / Houses of Parliament*
5. We Are All in the Gutter, but Some of Us Are Looking at the Stars – *Oscar Wilde Statue, 3 Adelaide Street*
6. Why Wank for Five Years? – *Lyons Corner House, 460 Strand*

1. *OH! AND ANOTHER THING!* – VICTORIA EMBANKMENT GARDENS

Take a moment before we start and step into the beautiful Victoria Embankment Gardens. Peaceful, eh? Yes, until you spot the cameras on every corner recording your every move. Outside of China, London is the most surveilled city in the world and is notorious for its strict containment of public spaces. Right now, you are surrounded by the institutional epicentres of surveillance. New Scotland Yard, the headquarters of the Metropolitan Police, is within walking distance by the Houses of Parliament. These are the folks responsible for mass surveillance on all protest groups to keep the status quo and the establishment intact. A bit further down still is the headquarters of MI5, the UK's prime security agency who work hand in hand with the government against domestic counter-intelligence.

If anyone knows a thing or two about countering intelligence it is legends like Antony Grey and Eric Thompson. Their work for homosexual liberation is at the crux of critical legislation which has influenced life all around the streets you are about to embark on.

In 1959, Antony and Eric were two gay men who took the chance to rent flats in the same building, when Antony was 32 and Eric was 25 years old. Their companionship grew from social and financial pragmatism into a deep mutual trust and a commitment. Sounds fairly innocent? Think again – after all, this was at a time when homosexuality was deeply forbidden by the law and stigmatised in the public eye. Living together under the watchful eye of the police and state apparatus was a deeply brave act. It was not easy then for two men to unashamedly share one flat with two bedrooms, as landlords were very hostile to grown men sharing, either from their own prejudice or from fear of police harassment. Eric, as the younger man and in safe employment as a civil servant, supported Antony behind the scenes, in his ground-breaking campaigning work for homosexual legal reform that would change the course of history. Most daring of all, neither when at work would tolerate an open verbal assumption that they were straight.

Back at home in their flat in West Hampstead, the street was so rife with fellow homosexuals, such as their good friend Esme Langley (the founder of the lesbian magazine *Arena 3* and of the women's Minority Research Group), that they nicknamed it 'Queer Street'. Avid readers and lovers of men, their activities behind closed doors weren't easy to cover up, and they soon discovered that the neighbours rightly concluded that they were gay.

In those days, rather than challenging the roots of homophobic crime, the police busied themselves with targeting spare bedrooms and intercepting phone lines, spitting out slurs like 'pansies', 'poofs' and 'filthy sodomites' as they carried out their raids.

Anytime there were signs of the police in the street, whether because of a car accident or a local burglary, Eric and Antony knew they had only a few minutes before the police might knock at the door. Hiding books, shoving reports in drawers and messing up all the beds, they had to make sure that each bedroom showed signs of occupancy. Like a pair of synchronised swimmers they moved into prompt action. No words needed.

Eric remembers that time vividly:

Before the Sexual Offences Act in 1967 that led to the partial decriminalisation of homosexuality, if we saw the police coming it was a race in the dark against time to distribute clothing and bedding between rooms to create the illusion that we were 'only' flatmates. They would react to two men who not only shared a flat, but far worse, a bed. We could quite easily have been arrested, maybe even imprisoned, if the police thought otherwise.

You would be wrong to think that they were panicking. Eric and Antony had been here many times before and took the necessary precautions. Reflecting the essence of the British 1950s, they were full of outward conformism, but behind the scenes utterly bold. They were always ready to take the necessary precautions if they saw police on the street investigating local situations or questioning witnesses. 'Both of them, like every homosexual and straight person of their generation, had lived through a hot war on British soil', recalls their friend and fellow Gay Liberation Front (GLF) activist Andrew Lumsden.

The Second World War had opened up possibilities towards female emancipation, the welfare state and nationalised health-care. On the other hand it also opened opportunities for widespread moral panics and witch hunts. The infamous 'Red Scare' personified by US Senator Joseph McCarthy led to shrieking denunciations and fear-mongering which targeted all left-wing people and movements as alleged communists and socialists, terrorist(s) threat who were spied upon and arrested for political subversion and even treason. In the same period, another moral panic, the 'Lavender Scare', specifically targeted homosexuals and the oppression of gay people suddenly became much more overt and intensified, with the police actively going after people, creating lists and raiding bars. In the context of that overt oppression as well as expanded freedoms in that period, you can see the beginnings of organised gay activism in America, like the Mattachine Society, Daughters of Bilitis and the Gay Liber-ation Front. In the context of the Civil Rights Movement, gay activists started becoming more militant and daring.

After finishing his studies in history at Cambridge University, Antony left, committed to 'do whatever I could to fight the iniq-uitous laws which had destroyed the genius of Oscar Wilde and brought untold misery to many thousands of otherwise blame-less men' and he meant it. Within a few years, in the early 1960s he became the secretary of the Homosexual Law Reform Society (HLRS), the campaigning body set up to persuade Parliament to implement the Wolfenden Report and decriminalise sex between men. He was invited to America to connect with and learn from parallel movements there, which emboldened his astute, resolute behind-the-scenes lobbying back in Britain.

Reflecting on the submission of the Wolfenden Report in 1957, which paved the way for the Sexual Offences Act in 1967, Antony said:

I did not become secretary of the Homosexual Law Reform Society merely by accident. I had in fact known since I was a teenager that I intended to do something significant about my own plight as a homosexual person, and that of my fellows. During the first half of this century, homosexuality in Britain was shrouded in a conspiracy of silence. Harsh laws compounded social ignorance and homosexuals' fearfulness. It was the 'silent years' between the 1890s and the 1950s [that] saw a great deal of homosexual behaviour, most of it discreet and undetected.

The decriminalisation that came with the Sexual Offences Act changed all that, by allowing people to glimpse a world where they could declare themselves homosexual. However, from defiant queens to terrified, closeted married men, after the Sexual Offences Act, life didn't suddenly become all sunshine and rainbows. Many who discovered homosexual feelings within themselves, especially the sensitive young, often weren't equipped with the code-switching language and signifiers to build connections that others had learnt before them. Indeed, even 'Antony Grey' was a pseudonym. He avoided using his real name (Edgar Wright) in public to avoid causing his parents embarrassment by association with the cause of homosexual rights, a benevolent hypocrisy of which he was conscious.

After the Sexual Offences Act, a bright social spotlight was suddenly switched on, bringing public speculation about everyone's sexuality. For those who did not already have a sense of subterranean community or psychological support, this new pressure to 'come out' imposed a heavy burden. On one occasion during a break in the House of Commons from introducing the Sexual Offences Act, Antony was asked by a civil servant, 'How do you know these people?' He smiled and then got on the train home. To avoid detection in public, when passing each other in the Parliament corridors Antony and Eric would say to one another, 'Oh! And another thing!' – their code for 'I love you'.

2. *A SECRET SOCIETY OF HOMOSEXUALS* – THE AUTHORS' CLUB, 1 WHITEHALL PLACE

George Cecil Ives was born on 1 October 1867. In 1892, Ives met a charismatic poet and playwright here at the Authors' Club in London who introduced himself as Oscar Wilde. By this time Ives had accepted his homosexuality and was working to promote the end of the oppression of homosexuals, what he called the 'Cause'. Ives lived at 196 Adelaide Road near Primrose Hill in Northwest London with his non-traditional family of former lovers and their wives and children. It was a communal domestic and artistic space, welcoming both live-in and day students, and hosting famous dinner parties with guests including Vita Sackville-West, Benjamin Britten, Peter Pears and Maggi Hambling, creating an atmosphere which 'was robust and coarse and exquisite and tentative…faintly dangerous', an early example of brave communal queer living.

By 1897, Ives' gut instinct was that the Cause would not be accepted openly in society anytime soon and therefore need to go underground. And so, he founded here the Order of Chaeronea, a secret society for homosexuals. The name insinuates a pre-determined bond of sexuality rather than a voluntary dynamic, a homosexual connection of such depths that Ives saw the Order's rituals as acknowledging rather than instigating, with a monumental lineage stretching back 2000 years. In 338 BCE the 300 members of the 'Sacred Band of Thebes', a network made entirely of friends and lovers, were annihilated by the army of Philip of Macedonia. An elaborate system of rituals, ceremonies, initiations, seals and codes were used by the members. The Secret Society became a global organisation and Ives made sure to take advantage of every opportunity to spread the word about the Cause. It was a historically rooted family which demanded his allegiance as well as his other families, his household, his birth family and so on. Writing his vision with a quill pen on parchment paper, could he know where it would lead?

3. *THE GAY ULTRADISCO* – HEAVEN, UNDER THE ARCHES, VILLIERS STREET

If 'love is as love does … an act of will – namely, both an inter-vention and an action' as the great late author bell hooks states, where can the force of love take us? What does the hope, spilling out of trapped emotions after nightmares, unfurlings of hot desire and the pounding thud of expression, no longer encapsulated in a ruffled spare bedroom duvet, look and feel like?

Welcome to Heaven, the 'gay ultradisco' nightclub' on Villiers Street, a street so laced with queer seduction it is even named after King James I lover, George Villiers, the 2nd Duke of Buckingham, in the seventeenth century. One of the first major queer spaces to open in 1979 after the passing of the 'Sexual Offences Act' of 1967, here many from the sexual liberation movements took a break and danced the night away. Daytimes were spent in continuous back-breaking meetings, protests and the creation of alternative spaces to close the void of the 'partial' aspect of the law – the different age of sexual consent for homosexuals, and the discrepancies of acceptance across the whole 'LGBTQIA+' community. These non-stop activists deserved a good boogie.

Heaven founder Jeremy Norman was not new to the game. The year before he had established the Embassy nightclub in Bond Street, immortalised in the set of Sylvester's 'You Make Me Feel Mighty Real' video. With Heaven, he aimed even higher. At the time of its opening, Heaven was the biggest gay club in Europe. Costing a staggering £300,000 to renovate, it boasted 5000-watt sound, overhead tweeters and bass horns built into the floor, plus a hi-tech light show complete with lasers, lightning-effect and planet-shaped neon spotlights and high-power floodlights. The *Evening Standard*, reviewing Heaven's opening night, was clearly impressed: 'Heaven's biggest headache could be in deterring London's non-gay discophiles who could end up trying to pass for gay to get past the elegant bouncers at the disco's equivalent of the Pearly Gates.'

Heaven's arrival coincided with new directions in disco. After the 1960s soul and swing, the beats got faster, mixing became essential and electronics replaced live instruments. Gay disco and hi-energy became the soundtrack to the parallel scenes that took over Heaven and gay Earl's Court. Between the beats, live shows sent ripples of laughter and roars of queer hunger throughout the crowds. In 1982, the visionary American poet Allen Ginsberg bemused punters by getting up on stage at the 'Amateur Talent Night' to read from 'Please, Master', a deliriously sadomasochistic love poem that still is one of the most sexually explicit poems ever written:

Master push my shoulders away and stare in my eyes, & make me bend over the table, please master grab my thighs and lift my ass to your waist, please master your hand's rough stroke on my neck, your palm down to my backside.

He may have been one of the most famous 'beat generation' poets in the world, but in Heaven, he still came second. Here you have to reach for the stars.

The 1980s at Heaven saw Spandau Ballet and Boy George in concert, new romantic, goth and acid house. Drum and bass launched us into the 1990s with DJs such as Fabio and Grooverider, while pop stars like Cher also rocked the stage. Fast forward to 2022 and the crowds are still going wild as local girl turned superstar Adele turns up unannounced as a surprise guest to judge strippers and dancers at 'Porn Idol', even taking a turn herself on the stripper pole.

The liberation taking place on the dancefloor, however, didn't stop the tabloid press from producing homophobic headlines, in which the *News of the World* condemned the place as 'more like hell' in 1981. The level of visibility that Heaven brought was unprecedented. 'Prior to the arrival of Heaven, gay clubs were only found underground in pub cellars', recalls Mark Elliott, current general manager, 'Heaven was the only venue of its scale in the last few years before the arrival of the AIDS epidemic. Inevitably, young people now don't realise the importance of a single institution, but there is an appreciation among those in the know.'

Rewind to 1982 and you are dancing your ass off to Donna Summer's 'Love is Just a Breath Away', your throat hoarse after screaming the lyrics to Culture Club's 'Do You Really Want to Hurt Me?' and dreaming of that hottie across the dancefloor whipping you into their arms and all over your bed at home later. Time to rejuvenate because you really don't want a hangover to stop you coming back again tomorrow. You head to the bar.

'Please can I have a large bottle of water and one for my mate?'

The handsome barman leans over to hear you more clearly.

'Two large waters please darlin''.

A pause ... Maybe he can't hear among the banging tunes?

He walks away and your eyes wander after him and suddenly, a thud and he collapses before your eyes at the side of the bar.

What ... the ... Hell ... is ... going ... on?

Meet Terry Higgins.

Terrence (or Terry) Higgins was born in Pembrokeshire, Wales on 10 June 1945. Alienated as a teen because of his sexuality, he left the small-town life and moved to London, like thousands across the island did and still do. Terry worked as a reporter in the House of Commons by day and as a barman and a DJ by night. His talents led him to perform in New York and Amsterdam throughout the 1970s, but he always loved coming home to his favourite London stomping ground Heaven, until one night when he collapsed.

Ian Johns, another Heaven regular, recalls a conversation he overheard in the cloakroom queue at around that time:

I was standing in Heaven, talking to some guys talking about herpes and I was going, 'Well, I don't want to get that, it never goes away.' And someone said to me, 'Oh no, there's a new one now. There's a new VD, a venereal disease that is affecting people who are gay men in America, where you just keep getting flu and then you die.' And I'm going 'Ah! You can't die from VD.' And then we slowly started hearing stories. And then suddenly, you heard about a friend of a friend, then a friend, then an ex and it escalated from there really ...

Rupert Whitaker, Terry's partner, was with him in hospital. Rupert was fully aware, and deeply scared of what the few reports were referring to as the 'Gay Cancer' which then became known as 'Gay Related Immune Deficiency' or GRID. Casual homophobia of the time laid bare; there were no 'heterosexuality-related conditions' that affect primarily heterosexuals and there still aren't.

On 4 July 1982, aged 37, Terry died from pneumonia and the related opportunistic infection neural toxoplasmosis, at St Thomas Hospital on the South Bank. He was one of the first people in the UK to die from an AIDS-related illness. AIDS – Acquired Immune Deficiency Syndrome – was first recognised as a medical condition in the US in 1981. Later that year Dr Tony Pinching diagnosed the first case in the UK, in a heterosexual woman, at St Mary's Praed Street Clinic in London. DJ and writer Stewart Who? remembers the quick change in the atmosphere over the following years:

> AIDS was the shadow that stalked the creative brilliance of London's scene. Lesbians were nursing gay friends, because as a community we had to come together. We were under siege. So many of my beautiful and spirited disco friends became worries, then memories. They'd be out every night of the week; preening, gurning and laughing... then gone. It wasn't wise to ask questions, as people would be evasive, or worse, tell the truth. 'That one died, dear', they'd whisper, sucking on a Marlboro Light. 'Such a shame. His family were vile. They banned gays from the funeral. You didn't sleep with him did you?'

Devastated, Rupert and friends harnessed their grief to create understanding among the confusion and to make sure Terry's life and tragic early death was not lived in vain. That's when, in a flat in central London, the Terrence Higgins Trust (THT) was born.

Out of heartbreak, THT's mission was to personalise and humanise AIDS in a very public way and to prevent others from having to suffer as Terry had. 'At first, it was to raise funds for research but then we realised much more was needed, and more immediately', Rupert recalls of these initial, intense months. The alchemy of grief led this small group of committed volunteers to focus all their energies and try to build relationships and work equally with gay men, lesbians, haemophiliacs, sex workers and drug users to raise funds for research and awareness of the still unknown illness. Rupert never forgot about Heaven though. In the subsequent years, it had opened its doors in the daytime to serve the needs of the community as the AIDS epidemic became a turning point for gays and lesbians in Britain. The following year, a public meeting about GRID was co-organised by THT and the London Lesbian and Gay Switchboard (now known as Switchboard LGBT+ Helpline), the biggest LGBTQIA+ telephone helpline at the time to respond to the rising deaths and the simultaneous, deadly Government bigotry and inaction.

As mentioned previously, in 1986 homosexuals were seen as 'swirling in a cesspit of their own making', in the words of Greater Manchester Chief Constable James Anderton, who later claimed God told him to say it. The rise of the 'moral majority' vilified people diagnosed with AIDS, and the wider gay community. Headlines at the time included 'Gay – and Wicked' (the *Sun*), and 'Britain Threatened by Gay Virus Plague' (the *Mail on Sunday*). The combination of misunderstanding of the HIV virus and AIDS, and an influential and homophobic right-wing press helped to create a culture of intolerance, homophobia and fear among the British public at the exact time that thousands of innocent people were becoming HIV+ and were dying unnecessarily – or being murdered, as I now realise.

4. *WE ARE NOT GOING BACK INTO THE CLOSET* – THE THAMES/HOUSES OF PARLIAMENT

Walk back through Embankment Station and look out to the gushing Thames, and over to your right.

In 1988, a year after Terry died and when prime minister Margaret Thatcher made the infamous speech at the Conservative Party Conference in Blackpool in which she said that 'children are being taught they have an inalienable right to be gay', I started school. That speech launched Section 28, known up to that point as 'Clause 28', which banned the 'promotion of homosexuality' by local authorities in the UK. Parallel policies were established across the Commonwealth countries as far away as Australia. Section 28 dug its sinister claws into every aspect of life; there was nowhere to learn and nowhere to turn. It wasn't repealed until 2003. Inalienable means 'not subject to being taken away from or given away by the possessor'. The significance of this cannot be underestimated. The clause was fascistic in its essence of depriving people of their self-determination and of our collective agency. Fitting, as Thatcher also tried to condition us that 'There is no such thing as society'. Like fascist regimes before, Thatcher's movement knew that critical consciousness through education was a threat, and in the run-up to Section 28's passing, protests against LGBT-inclusive education were held across the country. The Haringey Parents' Rights Group, for example, organised a burning of Danish children's book *Jenny Lives with Eric and Martin*, which told the story of Jenny, her father Eric and his partner Martin.

Millions of children began a torturous 'education' where we would never hear about LGBTQIA+ life or the realities of HIV in school, or the need to look after or protect ourselves as queer people, or anything so silly and dignified. At the time my only frame of reference was from watching the falling 'AIDS tombstone' adverts stating 'Don't Die of Ignorance', or HIV+ *EastEnders* character Mark Fowler speeding off on his motorbike after seeing 'AIDS Scum' graffitied on his wall. These were the images that defined a generation.

So I would slink out on the night bus to Soho and suck off a stranger in Heaven after blagging my way into the VIP area, or wake up next to some guy called Barry in Bedfordshire at 6 a.m., just in time to leg it to school. Hiding in the train's toilet, STD-rich but financially poor, it wouldn't be long before I hit the jackpot and got HIV. I pondered killing myself before the state could knock me off first. I could barely spell AIDS, let alone understand what it meant. Queer self-respect was banished in schools. And when I did eventually make it to school, I wasn't fully there because I was so stoned out of my head; the dysphoria was so dizzying, getting stoned seemed the only natural thing to do.

What was the point in going to class? The mental arithmetic of homosexual existence didn't add up; there was no language allowed for my identity in English, so I'd be better off learning Latin; the only flame I would feel in chemistry was unrequited love for the straight boy intent on beating me up; and, as for biology, don't ask – it wasn't until 1990 that the World Health Organisation (WHO) declassified homosexuality as a disease. There were no teachers to console me at lunchtime; Section 28 forbade such emotional support. So I would be in detention, on report, and social services would be called. It wasn't until I was diagnosed as HIV+ a few years later, that all the rules changed and I turned to AIDS activism for my true education instead.

Thousands of miles away from my classroom, in the LGBT+ Centre in New York in 1987, well-known activist and playwright Larry Kramer took to the mic. He began his speech by asking everyone on one side of the audience to stand up. 'At the rate we are going, you could be dead in less than five years', he bellowed. Kramer argued that gays would die in large numbers unless they became much more visible and increased pressure on the Federal Drug Administration (FDA) to expedite the testing and approval of AIDS drugs:

> If my speech tonight doesn't scare the shit out of you, we're in real trouble. Plague! We are in the middle of a fucking plague – half of you are gonna die – you're all gonna be dead in six months now, what are we gonna do about it?

Two days later, 300 people established the AIDS Coalition to Unleash Power (ACT UP). Its motto: 'United in anger and committed to direct action to end the AIDS crisis, along with the broader inequalities and injustices that perpetuate it.'

Smart, sassy, sexy people took to the streets of New York, San Francisco and also across the pond here in London Town, screaming outside Government buildings and occupying stock exchanges chanting 'ACT UP! Fight Back! Fight AIDS!' Simon Watney, a prolific activist, writer and critic, was active in both ACT UP New York and London chapters and recalls:

> If you were to fly over New York City at the time at night, there would be a great flare of light that you would see. AIDS has been like that in the United States since the early 1980s. That was not the case in Britain. In Europe we also have the advantage of socialised medicine, from the cradle to the grave and we assumed, we hoped, that we will be looked after. But there is a horrifying logic in the socialised medicine systems of

Western Europe that says we will lay on the social workers, get you the meals on wheels, get the social security sorted and pay the mortgage if you are lucky. The logic behind all this is 'HIV = AIDS = death'. You are on a conveyor belt, it's a very comfortable conveyor belt, but there is no sense of anyone wanting to stop the conveyor belt and that's where activism comes in. The logic of losing so many people took us to places we never thought of.

With a daredevil spirit, Andria Mordaunt's courage took her to streets where many would never go, to the Bronx in New York in the late 1980s, and back home to the streets of Hackney, where HIV was killing so many drug users. In 1988 she became the drugs counselling officer at THT, recruited for her pioneering work in setting up 'Mainliners', the UK's first support group for HIV-affected drug users. It was during those years that Andria was most involved with ACT UP, when the onslaught of dying co-workers and friends was non-stop and relentless. Andria's efforts to support harm reduction for drug users included campaigns for access to clean needles, condoms and heroin substitutes as the best way to prevent HIV in injectors and slammers.

During this time, at the height of the AIDS intensity, a series of meetings were organised to discuss the Section 28 threat. This helped pave the way for the formation of 'Stonewall', now the UK's leading LGBTQIA+ charity, which launched on the first anniversary of Section 28 passing into law, 24 May 1989. Heated debates electrified activist meeting rooms across London Town, hours before the heat of sweaty bodies hit the Heaven dance-floor, with so many people becoming ill in those days there was no time to hold back. Lisa Power, a founding member of Stonewall, remembers:

> We were in a position where all we could do was get out and march. We wouldn't negotiate with the Tory government, and for me that was the lesson that came out of Section 28 in the long run. We needed to affect the legislation as well as mobilise the community.

'We are not going to get back in the closet, or hide, or be ashamed of the way we are,' stated Angela Eagle, Labour MP for Wallasey, while choking on tears in a 2019 Parliament debate on Parental Involvement in Teaching. 'Nor are we going to allow a generation of pupils who are now in school to go through what pupils in the eighties had to go through because this Chamber let them down.' Two years earlier, Angela became the first MP to come out voluntarily as a lesbian and made damn sure the doors didn't close behind her. She advocated for gay partners to be given equal immigration rights, inclusive sex and relationship education to be mainstreamed in schools, and today she is intent on 'banning the abhorrent and abusive practice of conversion therapy' targeting the Trans community. Angela, like millions of others creating lifelines for freedom and safety for all people, will never forget Section 28. Indeed, Westminster Council, responsible for the area we are standing in now, have had to change their ways. In 2018, they had to reject plans to install a statue of the former prime minister Margaret Thatcher opposite the Houses of Parliament as it could attract 'civil disobedience and vandalism', so they went for Plan B. In 2022 a bronze statue of Thatcher was lowered into place in her hometown of Grantham, Lincolnshire instead, placed on a ten-foot plinth surrounded by fencing and CCTV. It has been egged regularly ever since. God bless those chickens.

If 'Heaven is a Place on Earth', as Belinda Carlisle sang in 1987, what do we have to do to get there? Walk back through the station, past Heaven and up Villiers Street, and with every step you take and every move you make, take strength from Gabrielle's lyrics in 'Dreams Can Come True', also performed at Heaven in 2013: 'Dreams can come true, look at me babe, I'm with you, you know you gotta have hope, you know you gotta be strong.'

We all need to dream of a world beyond bigotry, like Eric, Antony and the pioneers of Heaven, Terrence Higgins Trust (THT), Aids Coalition to Unleash Power (ACT UP) and Stonewall did and still do. With every step we take, every move we make, let's dream even bigger.

5. *WE ARE ALL IN THE GUTTER, BUT SOME OF US ARE LOOKING AT THE STARS* – OSCAR WILDE STATUE, 3 ADELAIDE STREET

Could Eric and Antony have predicted that the stars shining through their flat window could carry such force? Stop and say hello to the ultimate dreamer, poet and playwright Oscar Wilde, leaning backwards under the London spring sunshine and winter fog, inscribed with words from his play *Lady Windermere's Fan*, 'We are all in the gutter, but some of us are looking at the stars'.

The statue's presence is thanks to another visionary, artist and LGBTQIA+ activist Derek Jarman, who noticed that there was no public memorial to Oscar Wilde in the very city where he lived and his plays were most performed. Jarman and others (including poet Seamus Heaney and actors Dame Judi Dench and Sir Ian McKellen) formed a committee led by TV producer Jeremy Isaacs to make it happen, and the statue was erected in 1998. In the beginning Oscar was smoking a much-loved cigarette in this sculpture by prolific lesbian artist and fellow chain smoker Maggi Hambling. In its first few months, Oscar's cigarette was repeatedly removed, 'the most frequent act of vandalism/veneration to a public statue in London', and so it turns out that the cheeky chappie's spirit lives on.

At Oscar Wilde's gross indecency trial in 1895 at the Old Bailey he famously used the words 'the love that dare not speak its name' as a euphemism for homosexuality. We need to speak that love's name and publicly commemorate more of our queer dreamers, like Jarman, who never got to see the realisation of his vision for an Oscar Wilde memorial as he died of AIDS-related complications in 1994. Statues commemorate our past, celebrate our daily brilliance and guide our visions for the future. Thankfully, today, many statues honouring history based on greed are being torn down, and it's time to replace them. Out of the privatisation of grief and our isolation from each other, the possibility of beautiful collective transformation is at our fingertips.

6. *WHY WANK FOR FIVE YEARS?* – LYONS CORNER HOUSE, 460 STRAND

The twinkling non-binary traffic lights you see around the Square give a tiny inkling of the profound LGBTQIA+ freedom struggles that have taken place here, where dreams have turned into concrete action. Trafalgar Square is still the beating heart of rebellious London, where tourists pose in front of the stunning lions proudly overlooking the sheroic lineage of ordinary people throughout history celebrating the people's right to protest.

Eric, Antony and the HLRS let some queer genies legally out of the bottle, but not all of them: there were still different ages of consent between homosexuals and heterosexuals. Back on 28 August 1971, the first lesbian, gay and trans demonstration was instigated here by the GLF Youth Group and supported by the London Gay Teenage Group from the Campaign for Homosexual Equality. They demanded that the age of consent for homosexuals be reduced from 21 to 16, ending the homophobic discrepancy between them and heterosexuals. The GLF knew that actions spoke louder than words: several months earlier hundreds had turned up at Highbury Fields confronting police entrapment and catalysed the first LGBTQIA+ demonstration in Britain, on 27 November 1970.

The sun was shining and hundreds of marchers turned up, pulling themselves up to the lions all around Nelson's Column. 'We were visible, colourful, loud, inventive, flamboyant and very, very funny', recalls Michael James, former drag queen and member of the GLF. 'We were herded by police towards Trafalgar Square's lion statues. There was nowhere to go but up.' Caught by the police, he was carried 'like a pig on a stick through the crowd', who 'shook their fists at me and chanted "Kill him".' Then the GLF went and had a party in Hyde Park and did a lot of kissing under the noses of the police who rapidly disappeared and they carried on enjoying themselves in the park playing games.

Carla Toney didn't realise she was about to make herstory that day either:

In 1971 I was 24 years old, the 'brothers' were up on the plinth, but there wasn't a single woman up there. Then I heard my name called from the plinth, 'Carla! Where's Carla?' Wearing an orange t-shirt with 'LESBIAN' emblazoned on the front, I turned to my friend, Rosie Dadson, and asked her to please come with me and we climbed up on the plinth. Rosie was wearing a purple wig and held my hand. All I said was, 'Gay is good! I'm a lesbian and I'm proud!' and the crowd erupted into cheers. When Rosie and I came down from the plinth, a young girl came up to me. 'I want to be a lesbian, too', she told me. 'All you need is courage', I replied.

Carla's speech became the first public address by a lesbian since partial decriminalisation and it had profound effects, not least in challenging the sexism in the male-dominated queer community.

Placards that day included 'Why wank for five years?', 'Gay is good', 'Gay is angry', 'Lesbians come out', 'Gay Liberation Front Youth Group', 'I'm homosexual, I'm under 21, I'm angry', and my favourite: 'Take a deep breath – the pansies are in bloom'. High off the energy of people power, after the demo these trail-blazers descended on the Lyons Corner House, where they were promptly turfed out for being too loud, raucous, out and proud.

Memories of police officers in blue uniforms and swarms of wailing sirens around the square that day bring home the reality that police tactics of intimidation and harassment to squash our right to protest is nothing new, and continues today. In 2022 the

Police, Crime and Sentencing Act threatens the very freedom to protest, whereby 'causing disruption will be unlawful, as will stopping traffic'. People are becoming fearful of potential jail sentences and threats to 'remove citizenship' against those that engage in civil disobedience. So we can take hope in the knowledge that here at Trafalgar Square we stand in the footsteps of thousands of movements that rose up, and inspire us today to keep fighting. As Andrew Lumsden from the GLF reminisces about the first Pride, 'It wasn't about changing the law, it was about changing ourselves. Just like you are changing yourselves today.'

Through people power, maybe heaven really is a place on earth.

7. *DROP YOUR TROUSERS, DROP YOUR LAWS* – CHARING CROSS POLICE STATION, AGAR STREET

As queers we've always swum close to the enemy, having a 'funny'/'fuck you' relationship with the police to expose the social power dynamics that we'll need to overturn in order to achieve our dreams. Centuries of police entrapment have been carried out through the practice of 'pretty police', whereby creepy pseudo good-looking undercover police bubbling with jealousy try to arrest us. Back in 1994 this practice had escalated, and on 7 May queers responded with the 'Teenage Turn-In' here at Charing Cross police station. A few months before in February, Parliament had lowered the age of consent for gay men from 21 to 18. OutRage! demanded equal age of consent with heterosexual couples which was then sixteen.

Prolific throughout the 1990s, OutRage! LGBTQIA+ civil rights group were often organising two demonstrations a week even when so many members, including teenagers, continued to fall ill and die of AIDS complications without access to healthcare. They had already organised mass 'kiss-ins' demanding an end to laws against procuring, importuning and soliciting. Chants of 'Cruising is not a crime!' 'Drop your trousers, drop your laws!' and 'Repeal the anti-gay soliciting laws!' ricocheted off of London's walls of power. It was now time to take the righteous anger to the scene of the real crime, London's epicentre of 'pretty police' arrests. The 'Teenage turn-in' encouraged sixteen-to-eighteen-year-old gay teenagers to hand themselves in, challenging the police to arrest them for having underage sex as part of the 'Age of Dissent' campaign. The equalisation of the age of consent was finally achieved in 2001. Turns out dreams really do come true when the pansies are in bloom.

8. *ACT UP! FIGHT BACK! FIGHT AIDS* – TRAFALGAR SQUARE

In 1989, nearly ten years after the first reported case of AIDS in Los Angeles, there was still no effective government policy. By 1992, AIDS would become the biggest killer of men aged between 25 and 44 in America. Not only were people dying in great numbers, but the association of a killer plague with queer perverts became fixed in the public mind. One night Andria and friends from ACT UP came up with a plan to draw attention to the crisis. A team of 'queer construction workers' came to give Nelson's Column a makeover ... with a giant condom. Fifty-five metres long, the crew had spent weeks sewing together a vast

Credit: Bishopsgate Institute

piece of thick cellophane, heaving it out of a van before sunrise to sneak it up there.

'How the hell did you get it up there?' Andria asked the construction crew, her spine tingling as she giggled, watching the condom unrolling down the column. 'Easy when you have friends in construction, Andria!' her friend John replied, and the sheer audaciousness of it all calmed Andria's pulsing heart.

A few weeks later and hundreds of people are lying on the ground holding placards stating 'Action equals life'. It's June 1989 and ACT UP London are staging a 'die-in', in protest against the press's attacks against the LGBTQIA+ community and its misrepresentation of AIDS-infected people. The mass die-in was one of the most potent methods of protest used by ACT UP. Protestors carrying crosses, some that bear the group's

Credit: ACT UP

call to arms, 'Silence = Death', lay on the ground in complete stillness as though dead, creating a haunting, poignant and suitably dramatic statement. For Andria, however, this was no mere performance. 'For me, it was just really painful because my life partner was actually dying of AIDs. He is literally lying on the floor pretending to be dead and we're all doing this act of protest. It's so powerfully symbolic, but it's real as well.

People were desperate. Andria recalls:

A nurse from the Broderip Ward at the Middlesex Hospital in Fitzrovia, which was the first ward dedicated to the care and treatment of people affected by HIV/AIDS in the UK, was speaking from the lions. She was holding back the tears explaining about funding for HIV+ treatment being taken away, and then after a priest came to the mic. As soon as God was mentioned, half the crowd turned around and walked away. How could we believe in a god who would let this happen? We didn't have space to grieve, just another death, another death and another.

In the following years, HIV/AIDS protests happened in America and here in the UK too, sometimes every day, where ordinary people dedicated their lives to activism and came together to demand public action against pharmaceutical greed and government inaction. Gay men, lesbians, trans people, drug users, migrants and their allies organised ACT UP and took on issues of homophobia, racism and sexism that no one else would touch – indeed, some people literally wouldn't touch people with HIV. They drove AIDS right up the political agenda until 1996 when combination therapy medication became available. In this way the activists saved countless lives and set the stage for a different kind of movement in the future, from the dancefloors of Heaven to the Trafalgar Square floor they were unstoppable. 'Witnessing the solidarity between lesbians and the AIDS struggle at the candlelit vigils in Trafalgar Square was huge', ACT UP activist Ian Johns recalls with a tear in his eye.

When Andria's life partner died from AIDS in 1995, she founded the John Mordaunt Trust, a peer support and advocacy project for daily drug users, to honour John's memory. Since the 'die-in' she has gone all over the world promoting drug reform in communities across the world and to meetings at the United Nations, with her focus being the self-organisation of ex and current injection drugs users.

The social bonds created through the courage to act by ACT UP and the HIV movement of the 1980s and 1990s had its roots in the work of the Gay Liberation Front (GLF), who set the stage here at Trafalgar Square 20 years before, which in turn was directly born out of the Stonewall Uprisings in 1969. The playbook for direct action around AIDS – and often the activists themselves – came straight from the GLF, who provided the template and toolkit for effective activism. Through exploring the genealogy of protest that led us to the current moment, we release stories of human scarcity and can begin to thrive – as individuals and as movements hungry for collective social change.

Could those attending the funerals, vigils, and die-ins in Trafalgar Square in the 1980s and 1990s have imagined that 30 years later, there would be a revolutionary pill that is up to 99 per cent effective in preventing the transmission of HIV? In 2016 Andria was back here in the Square joining demonstrators decked out in blue, the colour of a 'pre-exposure prophylaxis' (PrEP) pill, scrawling blue chalk graffiti over the pavements of Westminster. Speakers lambasted NHS England's refusal to get behind the most valuable new tool in the fight against HIV in two decades. PrEP has since been approved and rolled out for free among sexual health centres and the nightmares of the past have created a dream of sexual freedom for the future, but still, every World AIDS

Day on 1 December, Andria, like so many in London, remembers the dead to fight for the living. Under the watch of South Africa House on the corner of the Square, we remember that an apartheid in global healthcare has taken more than 36 million lives and that 1.5 million people across the world were diagnosed with HIV in 2020 due to continuing pharmaceutical greed and government inaction. In 2022, the Trans community faces flagrant prejudice by healthcare providers, subsequently leading to higher HIV rates and a far-reaching scarcity of access to vital services. For World AIDS Day that year, marching around the Square are activists from Catwalk for Power, Resistance and Hope, a project born to amplify HIV+ women and HIV+ migrants' voices, chanting 'Amandla! Awethu!' ('The power is ours!') – dreaming, and acting, until there is healthcare for all.

9. WE'RE HERE, WE'RE TRANS, WE'RE FABULOUS – 10 DOWNING STREET

'When Trans people are under attack, what do we do? Stand up, fight back! We're here, we're Trans, we're fabulous, don't fuck with us!' So chanted thousands marching to the 10 Downing Street gates on a crisp morning in April 2022. British prime minister Boris Johnson has just announced that he would not ban conversion therapy for the Trans community, resulting in a new Section 28 that creates instant barriers to healthcare for Trans people. It is now 1 July 2022, the 50th anniversary of the Gay Liberation Front starting radical Pride all those years ago. ACT UP activist and performer in the trailblazing trans-femme sisterhood girl band the Trashettes, Dani Singer is preparing to welcome the crowds to the steps of St Martins in the Field Church back at the Square, where it all began. Wearing an incredible leopard-print skirt, pink-satin top and sequinned police hat, they say to me, 'Understanding myself to be queer and trans was the most fantastic curve ball in my adult life, and I feel so deeply euphoric to be part of my beautiful queer community', as they turn and beam at the crowd.

As an activist with the AIDS Coalition to Unleash Power (ACT UP) London Chapter. They have hosted 'HIV/Hep C Blind Date', a dating show for people living and learning to love again with HIV, stripped naked in pharmaceutical giant Gilead's headquarters in Holborn demanding pre-exposure prophylaxis (PrEP) be released for all people to have sex without fear of contracting HIV and spearheaded campaigns for HIV+ migrants to have access to treatment. Dani continues:

More recently I've become rooted in abolitionist principles, which has only deepened my connection to myself, and my intuitive ideas about how to navigate The Way Things Are. Marrying up everything in my life – identity, career, passions – has been something of an adventure, but I think I've arrived at somewhere pretty exciting.

10. *WE REMEMBER … THE PINK TRIANGLE –* THE CENOTAPH, WHITEHALL

It's Remembrance Sunday in 1971, and fifteen members of the GLF are wearing pink triangles and putting a wreath on the Cenotaph. The card on top of the flowers reads:

In memory of the countless thousands of homosexuals branded with the pink triangle of homosexuality who died in the gas chambers and in the concentration camps of Europe, who have no children to remember them and your histories forget, we remember – The Gay Liberation Front.

Surrounded by the police, they were told they must remove their badges as they were 'too political'.

Is the past ever really the past? Is choosing to commemorate one war over another coincidental? Is mass-grief ever apolitical? Can we ever still our rocking hearts and continue to dream of a world beyond AIDS?

Dreaming begins with a permanent AIDS memorial being built right here, in the heart of London, so that the pansies of the past can continue to give us strength to fight for the living.

We are in the middle of an unfinished revolution. The late Eric Thompson (1934–2022) reflects:

Remember that in the early 1930s Berlin was the gay capital of Europe and look what happened by the end of 1930s. What is required for a healthier, happier twenty-first century is nothing less than a sexual revolution. The journey to liberation isn't as smooth as we want – we have to keep active. I am glad that history is being remembered, it is very important. People should know their history for the pathways ahead.

WHERE'S THE PUB? HALFWAY TO HEAVEN, 7 DUNCANNON STREET

Since 1991, this little gem has been, in their own words, 'jam-packed with fabulous, flamboyant cabaret, seven days a week, brought to you by the best in the business. Offering fun, love, light and laughter to regulars and newcomers alike, the friendly staff are always ready to welcome you into Halfway to Heaven's warm embrace.' Have a ball, raise a glass and repeat after me 'ACT UP! Fight Back! Fight AIDS – Until there is healthcare for all!

4
The Fags Have Lost that Wounded Look
Piccadilly

'History is not the past, it is the present. We carry our history with us. We are our history', James Baldwin. I've never understood why anyone hates pigeons. Pigeons are the mascot of rebellious, defiant, who-gives-a-fuck London Town. Treated as vermin, they mischievously peck at the feet of those who look down their nose at them. Every day they persist and take over the Piccadilly streets and sky above us. They have seen it all. They know too much.

To look is an act of choice and like our feathered friends, the queer community have gone from being treated like vermin to developing a rebellious, defiant, who-gives-a-fuck attitude too. Now we are visibly everywhere and the city belongs to us – but how did this happen?

Welcome to Piccadilly, where change is in the eye of the beholder.

START: PICCADILLY CIRCUS

1. Queens with Handbags – *Piccadilly Circus*
2   Walk on the Wild Side – *Statue of Eros*
3. Homosexuals and the Law – *32 Shaftesbury Avenue*

1. *QUEENS WITH HANDBAGS* – PICCADILLY CIRCUS

It's a quiet December morning in 1972. The moon is rising and the frost is cracking here underneath the bow and arrow of Piccadilly Circus's Statue of Eros. Sit yourself down on the cascading steps surrounding it. A flock of pigeons are searching for scraps waiting for the morning commuters to start scurrying around town. As London stirs into another day, a handful of London black cabs and red double-decker buses are circling around to pick up early morning workers. You spot a smiling young man cycling past with a paper tied to the back of his bike. Ted Brown is a 22-year-old trainee typesetter and aspiring journalist. Buzzing through Ted's ears are the lyrics from Lou Reed's just-released 'Walk on the Wild Side'.

As a child, Ted knew deep down that life was a pendulum. Sometimes it swings towards all those demanding change and sometimes it swings back to the status quo. Curiosity burned in Ted's soul as he thought 'if there is still one person whose existence is wiped out of the picture, how can we fight for them? How can we stoke the fires in our hearts that maintain the necessary vigilance for us all to build a world where we can all be seen?' Every circular motion Ted pedalled on his bike helped him meditate through this, but the answers were not obvious yet.

Just a few years earlier, in June 1969, Ted had 'read about queens with handbags fighting with the police at a bar in New York'. He had to catch his breath: 'Just hearing about other homosexuals taking action together was incredible. I remember doing cartwheels all around the living room.' Marsha P. Johnson and Sylvia Rivera's brick-throwing moment sent ripples across the Atlantic straight into Ted's beating heart. From that moment on, the Street Trans Action Revolutionaries (STAR), Gay Liberation Front (GLF), Black Panthers and others organising together to fight for gay liberation and inclusion, creating shelters and social space, supporting Trans people in prison and empowering marginalised people not supported by the mainstream, blew his mind wide open. No longer believing that homosexuals can only be victims, Ted was ready for other ways to make sense of the world.

Even though Stonewall happened in New York, thousands of miles away, this watershed moment sowed vital seeds. Back on his bike Ted began to question, how can we flip the script from being wounded sinful beings to being empowered to organise society in a completely different way? His eyes opened to something that, finally, could relate to his story and provide answers to the question: how can we here in London Town begin to be seen too?

For Ted and for all of us hungry to be seen, looking is an act of choice. Long before London became a thriving queer metropolis and a beacon for LGBTQIA+ community around the world, it was a very different place. Ted knew that there must be places where gay people met, he had seen the clubs with blacked out windows. He knew we were viewed merely as wicked perverts, escaping from the condemnation of straight society. He got that memo. There existed a scattering of stories of centuries of arrests including by the Society for the Reformation of Manners. Formed at the end of the seventeenth century, the Society set out to entrap homosexuals, with the aim of the 'suppression of bawdy houses and profanity'. Below Ted's cycle wheels, in the Piccadilly station underground passages, innocent people had long been trapped by the police while cottaging in the toilets. Indeed, the whole neighbourhood had been under scrutiny for centuries, as illustrated by the stark headline in the 29 July 1721 edition of the *Ipswich Journal*:

A Club of Sodomites discovered in Leicester Square to the Number of 50, who meet almost every Night at a Coffee House near that Place, and those Abominable Wretches publicly call one another by the Name of Dolly, Molly, Betty, Bridget, Grace etc. and perform such ghastly Actions in that Lewd House, as is not fit to mention.

Like brave moths to a dangerous flame, since the early 1900s Piccadilly Circus and neighbouring Leicester Square, have been one of the first places for covert homosexuals to gather. Many spent evenings cruising the London Pavilion and Criterion theatres and music halls, making out in the dark during a show until theatre managers cottoned on and sharply turned up the lights. If nerves became too much, they took a breather with middle-class gay Londoners; the clerks, shop assistants, workmen, civil servants and the metropolitan intelligentsia could be found at the Lily Pond cafe. The queer-only section in Lyons Corner House or the all-male Long Bar at the Trocadero provided delights too. Rewind back to the eighteenth century and the sexually aroused and seduced would sneak off under the moonlight to a 'Molly house', a private room or tavern for homosexual liaisons, to shed each other's armour and see each other closer.

In 1957, the Parliamentary Wolfenden Committee published a report, recommending that 'homosexual behaviour between consenting adults in private should no longer be a criminal offence', and for the next ten years, against so many barriers, the movement for homosexual freedom fought on. The Sexual Offences Act of 1967 then led to the partial decriminalisation of homosexuality in Britain, allowing men over the age of 21 to have sex in private – how very generous of the government.

Often right under the police's nose, courageous people were living a different story from those society chooses to tell, distinct from what we are led to believe. While all homosexuals were still under threat, around Piccadilly Circus were a sprinkling of straight spaces where gay people could meet undercover and connect, at least until the police would invariably clamp down. The police would press blotting paper against faces in an attempt to find residue of rouge if they suspected anyone of being gay, and arrest people en masse. Ted had been listening excitedly to the debates in Parliament, but he didn't want to exist in private. The time was ripe for a liberation movement.

2. *WALK ON THE WILD SIDE* – STATUE OF EROS

Ted yearned for a different story, one of love, closeness and companionship. Can we glean lessons from Cupid, the ancient Greek symbol of Selfless Love, seen here at the top of the fountain? Maybe the statue's architect has some wisdom to share. Unveiled in 1893, Architect Frank Gilbert spent five years considering how to celebrate the life of Lord Shaftesbury, a philanthropist and social reformer, the namesake of the adjoining Shaftesbury Avenue. Shaftesbury had campaigned against many injustices, such as child labour conditions in factories and mines. The statue was modelled on Gilbert's assistant, a fifteen-year-old from Shepherd's Bush named Angelo Colarossi. Gilbert wrote in 1903:

If I must confess to a meaning or a raison d'être for its being there, I confess to have been actuated in its design by a desire to symbolise the work of Lord Shaftesbury; the blindfolded Love sending forth indiscriminately, yet with purpose, his missile of kindness, always with the swiftness the bird has from its wings, never ceasing to breathe or reflect critically, but ever soaring onwards, regardless of its own peril and dangers.

A love that is allowed to unfurl, nurture and grow – would Ted ever be able to feel love's sensuous touch? Not if he listened to the tyrannical Shaftesbury Memorial Committee, who after the unveiling stated, 'The fountain itself is purely symbolic, and is illustrative of Christian charity'. But now we know that right here in London's beating cultural heart, stands a reminder that love is all encompassing, a force to change the world and Ted knew that it had to start with him.

Ted had a feeling Dorothy, his mother, might understand, as the injuries of a divided society had shaped her life too. In racially segregated America, Dorothy had been involved with the National Association for the Advancement of Colored People (NAACP). The NAACP are known for focusing on racial equality but their concerns were far wider, covering issues of class, wealth, nationality, gender and even sexuality. A theme which ran throughout their campaigns was, 'until all of us are free, none of us are free'. This mantra would become the driving principle for the GLF that would soon rock Ted's world. Dorothy was listed by the Federal Bureau of Investigation (FBI) as a 'troublemaker', a powerful trait that seemed to run in the family. In an attempt to escape the discrimination they faced in the US; together Dorothy and Ted travelled by ship to the UK in 1959. 'Through the NAACP my mother learned, and passed on to me, the knowledge that there are people of every culture who will fight for freedom', Ted recalls, smiling, and continues:

> My main experience of life as a Black gay teenager in the 1960s was a time when homosexuality was genuinely 'the love that dare not speak its name', a quote from a love poem read at Oscar Wilde's trial that is still a euphemism for homosexuality. There were no 'out and proud' role models. If ever it was mentioned it was in terms of sickness, crime, or evil perversion.

Gay life was extremely restricted and sex was deeply disapproved of and highly illegal with severe penalties. My sex life involved occasional trips to the two gay pubs I knew at the time, the Vauxhall Tavern and my favourite, The Coleherne in Earl's Court, though neither of them was particularly welcoming to Black gays. A lonely life dawned before me.

This loneliness would drive him to connect with other visionaries whose isolation drove them to create seismic change. In his school library Ted read in the *Oxford English Dictionary* that homosexuals were 'perverse' and 'a negative interpretation' of human psychology; he thought 'Well, if this is a negative interpretation there must be a good interpretation'. It was the grief over a friend's suicide that drove him to come out to his mother. 'I had to tell somebody. And she cried on my shoulder. I cried on her shoulder. She said: "Well, you're going to have to deal with the racism, and also society's hostility to homosexuals."' Today Ted turns to me decisively:

My queer icons were and still are: Bayard Rustin for his courage and great achievements, being out as a proud Black gay man, simultaneously contributing very significantly to the Black Civil Rights along with Dr Martin Luther King Jr; Barbara Gittings, who founded the first lesbian organisation in the USA, the Daughters of Bilitis, in 1955; James Baldwin for writing important literature on the gay and the Black experience; and Harry Hay, who founded the homophile Mattachine Society in 1950. Although they all could have adopted the furtive closeted lifestyle of most queer people at the time, they publicly, bravely challenged homophobia in the face of intense hostility and minimal support.

'We need, in every community, a group of angelic troublemakers,' Bayard Rustin stated. 'Our power is in our ability to make things unworkable. The only weapon we have is our bodies. And we need to tuck them in places so wheels don't turn.' Bayard Rustin stated, and these words struck Ted. 'Who are these angelic troublemakers back in London Town and how can I connect with them?' young Ted wondered, and was hell-bent on finding out. 'Come on, follow me, let's learn from them!' Ted calls to us today, his eyes smiling widely – it's time to stand up from underneath Eros.

Optimism is a political act. As the great civil rights leader and Black Panther Angela Davis teaches, 'You have to act as if it were possible to radically transform the world. And you have to do it all the time.' Being trapped inside ourselves can lead to an intensely distorted view of the world. However, in order to transform the world, we have to firstly see ourselves within it, instantly turning a negative into a positive. Why, you ask? Because for centuries, it is the everyday acts of queer support, identification, subversive communication and the meeting of eyes in a crowded central London hotspot that says, 'We are one'. So here, in the centre of Piccadilly Circus, do a cartwheel in honour of Ted, just like he did when the Stonewall Uprisings set his young heart on fire. Cruise two minutes up Shaftesbury Avenue and stop outside number 32.

3. *HOMOSEXUALS AND THE LAW –*
32 SHAFTESBURY AVENUE

When Ted still was a child, it was here on the second floor at 32 Shaftesbury Avenue, where the first office of the Homosexual

Law Reform Society (HLRS) was established on 29 May 1958. The HLRS mission? To change the law and place homosexual culture legally, visibly and beautifully at the heart of society. The Stonewall Uprisings of 1969 sparked Ted's life-long activism with the GLF. It was the HLRS that would generate legislative freedom that entirely changed the cultural landscape and created the space for this activism to occur within it. Picture, in a very dark and dingy room, a table stacked high with scrapbooks full of clippings on topics including murder, 'freaks', theories of crime and punishment, transvestism, the psychology of gender, homosexuality, cricket scores and personal letters to newspaper editors. Peering out from behind this mess is academic A.E. Dyson, reading responses to the letter he published a few months before in *The Times*, calling for reform of the law.

Fast forward to the 1990s and the good vibrations of the HLRS office upstairs reverberated through time and permeated Bar Rumba below – my favourite drum and bass club as a teenager. Oblivious to the building's history, this is where I danced the night away with a hot guy called Gary in the tidiest spearmint-rhino Nickelson puffer jacket before getting kicked out for shagging in the toilets. Today it is a tourist toy shop selling cardboard pictures of the queen, so let's take a moment to delve into the powerful history of this address in a challenge to the monarchy and its foot soldiers in government.

The HLRS was born out of centuries of monarchic and establishment bigotry, campaigning to overturn anti-gay legislation. Under the Criminal Law Amendment Act 1885, any homosexual activity between males was illegal. After the Second World War there had been an increase in arrests and prosecutions, and the Wolfenden Report was published on 4 September 1957. It proposed that legislation reconsider the crimes of both homosexuality and prostitution after a succession of well-known men were convicted. The pamphlet *Homosexuals and the Law* was written by Peter Wildeblood, who had been one of the high-profile victims, and it was sent to Ministers of Parliament (MPs), by the HLRS in preparation for their first debate. However, it became clear that the government had shelved the report and was not planning to implement any reform. 'I am not going down in history as the man who made sodomy legal', the Lord Chancellor, Viscount Kilmuir, said at the time.

Instead of submitting to continued Government persecution, the efforts of the HLRS bounced powerfully from this building's walls and on the 12th May 1960 over 1000 people attended the organisation's first public meeting in Caxton Hall by St James's Park. Oppressed people turned up en masse to transform society's view of them, from being mere objects to subjects taking a stand to liberate themselves. This led to the 1964 founding of the Campaign for Homosexual Equality (CHE), that supported the HLRS to enact the 1967 Sexual Offences Act and worked for the removal of laws against gay sex between men. After the Act, the HLRS melted away and the CHE continued the struggle. By 1972 CHE was the largest LGBT organisation this country had ever seen, with 6000 members and over 100 local groups around the country. Their aims were only partially achieved in the 'Sexual Offences Act' in 1967 because it didn't accommodate for the different age of consent for gay men having sex (21) versus the heterosexual age of consent at sixteen. Partial too, as homosexuals were still not able to fully participate in society as the most fundamental pillars of a democratic society – education, healthcare, the judicial system, welfare and more – institutionally discriminated against homosexuals, and in many ways still do.

Indeed, there was no mention of the brutality experienced by the LGBTQIA+ diaspora communities who landed in the UK as a result of the British Empire's exported homophobic legislation across the world. We cannot forget that the borough we are standing in, Westminster, is home to the monarchy. These are the 'pioneers' who brought 'civilisation' to the world – which is of course completely false. There is nothing less civilised and more barbaric than exporting versions of Henry VIII's 1533 Buggery Act throughout the British Empire, a global system of racist, colonial dispossession. The Empire tried to annihilate the deep liberatory potency of queer people across the planet as healers and visionaries. This attempt ultimately failed, of course; our powers are too strong.

Each family within the lesbian, gay, bisexual, transsexual, queer, intersex, asexual demographics and communities beyond continue to tread a unique track towards freedom. To start with, 'dangerous lesbians' shook the establishment's bigots in the run up to the Wolfenden Report. Albertine Winner, the first female deputy chief medical officer at the Department of Health, wrote in *Homosexuality in Women* in 1947: 'There are two categories of female homosexuals … the woman who tends to prefer the society of women … and a much more dangerous type, the promiscuous Lesbian who … may cause great harm and unhappiness'. Clearly Albertine was intent on missing out on all the fun.

What about lesbian recognition with integrity, let alone freedom? Parliament first attempted to criminalise female homosexuality in 1921. But the law was not established for fear that it might encourage females to indulge in practices they would never otherwise have thought of. Therefore, lesbian cruising has never been illegal. Seven years later, Radclyffe Hall's ground-breaking novel *The Well of Loneliness*, which depicts female same-sex love, was published, and subsequently banned. Within a deeply patriarchal British society, how could women not be reliant on men? And what's worse, being explicitly oppressed or being written out of herstory, or rather excuse me, history altogether?

Even the very bricks and mortar that make up the borough's royal buildings in this neighbourhood tell a different story. Around the corner on Pall Mall in Marlborough House, a stone's throw from Buckingham Palace, a queer herstory unfolds. In 1711, Anne, queen of Great Britain, ended a long-lasting intimate friendship with Sarah Churchill, Duchess of Marlborough (hence the building's name). Anne and Sarah had invented pet names for themselves during their youths, which they continued to use after Anne became queen: Mrs Freeman (Sarah) and Mrs Morley (Anne). Effectively a business manager, Sarah had significant control over the queen's activities, from her finances to deciding who would be admitted to the royal presence. Alongside Abigail, Baroness Masham, she was one of the 'queen's favourites', and wielded power similar to that of a government minister. When their intimacy soured, she blackmailed Anne with letters exposing their affection, and indicted her of perverting the course of national affairs by keeping lesbian favourites. Ouch, how heartbreak hurts.

4. *REPEAL SECTION 28* – PICCADILLY CIRCUS

More recently, the 1980s witnessed an unleashing of iconic lesbian direct action. Sick and tired of the invisibilisation of lesbian power, and inspired by the 1970s era of women's and gay liberation activism, the 'London Lesbian Avengers' sprang into 'Visibility Day Actions', and quickly gained a reputation for their high-profile protests or 'zaps' that confronted lesbophobia everywhere. All the while lesbians donated blood in their thousands to people with HIV and AIDS, and supported people of all genders and sexualities to get access to treatment. From chaining themselves to the editor's desk at the *Sunday Times* in protest against lesbophobia, to challenging misogyny within the LGBTQIA+ community, they continued pushing lesbian visibility towards the light. Outside Buckingham Palace in 1989, four lesbian activists chained themselves to the Palace Gates and invaded the queen Victoria monument opposite. They proudly asserted that funnily enough, lesbians do exist and have long made a sheroic contribution to humanity.

Just a few footsteps from the HLRS offices in June 1995, their 'piece de resistance' took place. If you turn left from 32 Shaftesbury Avenue and back to Piccadilly Circus you can see the spot where there stood a classic double-decker red London bus, parked at the centre of the intersection. Dripping down its side, the bus was splattered with pink paint and a giant black and pink banner was held by two activists on the roof, stating 'Repeal Section 28'. Another open-top bus tour of the West End by 50 Avengers marked the seventh anniversary of Section 28, which stated that a local authority 'shall not intentionally promote homosexuality or publish material with the intention of promoting homosexuality'. A megaphone taped to the side of the bus was used to address passers-by. 'Yes, you in the brown coat, hello, we're lesbians ... we can spot your homophobia', playfully shouted Ms Sutcliffe, one of the prime movers of the group. A kiss-in was held by the statue of Rodin's *The Kiss* at the Tate Gallery; in a branch of Laura Ashley they mocked the pretty dresses and thrust their leaflets on customers; and in the Marks & Spencer lingerie department they distributed more information and mucked around with the underwear.

Looking back at Ted, he is holding his bike, smiling knowingly. Queer visibility hasn't happened overnight, it has been fought for and won through millions of bedrooms and interactions in public life. This battle has left a treasure chest of tools that we can draw upon to fight the current examples of homophobic legislation we

face across the world today, such as Florida's 'Don't Say Gay' bill or Russia's 'Gay Propaganda Law'.

Whether the authorities recognise it or not, our fight to maintain pleasure in our interconnected existence is as precarious and volatile as the passion for visibility in our hearts. As the Lesbian Avengers bus leaves the Circus and a trail of pink smoke floats in its wake, remember this is what makes the struggle for queer freedom so damn beautiful.

5. PUTTING THE 'CAMP' BACK INTO CAMPAIGNING – THE 'WINK-IN', STATUE OF EROS

Founded on 10 May 1990, OutRage! was a radical, non-violent, direct action LGBTQIA+ movement addressing equal parenting, homophobic attitudes among the police and throughout society, and more. Their name derived from the continuous feelings arising out of reading daily bigotry in the papers and a steely determination to subvert rage through panache. They set about to turn despair into creativity and put the 'camp' back into campaigning. Catalysed in reaction to the murder of a gay man, Michael Boothe, on the 10th May 1990, three gay journalists – Keith Alcorn, Chris Woods and Simon Watney – called a public meeting at the London Lesbian and Gay Centre in Farringdon, attended by 30 LGBTQIA+ activists. Inspired by the US-based Queer Nation, they adopted a 'cell structure' to organise and plan their actions. Outrageous acronyms for each 'cell' group animated this energy and became popular within OutRage! Highlights included 'PIG' – the Policing Intelligence Group; 'PUSSY' – Perverts Undermining State ScrutinY; 'FROCS' –

Faggots Rooting Out Closeted Sexuality and 'LABIA' – Lesbians Answer Back In Anger. The fundraising group evolved into 'QUID' and finance transformed into the adorable 'QUANGO' – Queer Accountants Never Go Out. The prize for the most intricate name goes to the group which initiated a protest at an anti-censorship festival at the Southbank Centre. The group's acronym became 'SHAGPILES' – Screaming Homos Against Gutless Prissy Icky Lawmakers Enforcing Celibacy! Iconic.

'OutRage! was very creative. It was a completely different way, from writing an article, of narrating a political idea and one which I found I was actually very good at. It developed my skills of knowing how to manipulate the media, which I still use', remembers activist Keith Alcorn fondly. OutRage! created pandemonium in the straight media and within queer communities, from the high-profile outing of MP's and bishops, to their attacks on hypocrisy in the Catholic Church.

There is a lot of power in a seductive wink ... and you are about to find out why. It was here at the Statue of Eros that OutRage's iconic 'wink-in' action took place on 5 March 1992. A banner unfurled over the statue reading 'Queer Is Cool' as a young man climbed up and kissed Eros modelled as we know, by Shepherds Bush's finest – Angelo Colarossi – on the lips.

Blowing whistles, banging drums and sporting t-shirts with in-yer-face slogans, these self-styled queers with attitude at the wink-in provided a fun forum to flout the law. They demanded that the police cease arresting lesbians and gay men for cruising, chatting up, winking, smiling and exchanging names and numbers, and an end to laws against procuring, importuning and soliciting.

Hundreds of people took part, many couples kissing and listening to the piercing pride-fuelled chants of 'Cruising is not a
crime!', 'Drop your trousers, drop your laws!' and 'Repeal the
anti-gay soliciting laws!' A collection of elaborate props included
giant displays of telephone numbers, large winking eyes on
sticks, and even the ... er, erection of a children's toy Wendy
house to conceal 'bonk-ins' involving more than two people at a
time. Martin Maynard from OutRage! remembers the day:

> Looking back at it now, being arrested for giving someone your
> phone number seems a little ridiculous, but I can remember
> when people were done for it. Some of the phone numbers
> that were held up on big boards were government ministries,
> Downing Street and things like that. It was terribly theatrical.

Among the spectacle of the action, a flyer is handed out. The
anonymous manifesto *An Army of Lovers Cannot Lose* was first
distributed at the Pride March in New York two years previously,
and had made its way to London around this time. It called for
the reclamation of the word 'queer'. It reads:

> Being queer is not about a right to privacy; it is about the
> freedom to be public, to just be who we are. It means everyday
> fighting oppression; homophobia, racism, misogyny, the
> bigotry of religious hypocrites and our own self-hatred.
> (We have been carefully taught to hate ourselves.) And now
> of course it means fighting a virus as well, and all those
> homo-haters who are using AIDS to wipe us off the face of the
> earth. Being queer means leading a different sort of life. It's

110

not about the mainstream, profit-margins, patriotism, patriarchy or being assimilated. It's not about executive directors,
privilege and elitism. It's about being on the margins, defining
ourselves; it's about gender-fuck and secrets, what's beneath
the belt and deep inside the heart; it's about the night. Being
queer is 'grassroots' because we know that everyone of us,
every body, every cunt, every heart and ass and dick is a world
of pleasure waiting to be explored. Everyone of us is a world
of infinite possibility. Let's make every space a Lesbian and
Gay space. Every street a part of our sexual geography. A city
of yearning and then total satisfaction. A city and a country
where we can be safe and free and more.

We have OutRage! to thank for catalysing this lip-licking queer
satisfaction here in London.

A year and a half earlier, on 5 September 1990, OutRage!
descended for a 'kiss-in', again here at the Eros statue, pioneering
the fight against police repression which had since become more
acute within the context of the AIDS pandemic. Fierce, funny,
camp and sexy, they continued their merry mission to embarrass
the Metropolitan Police by drawing attention to the victimisation
of gay men for engaging in consensual sexual behaviour.

OutRage! activist Lisa Power, caught up in the excitement,
recalls: 'I remember the actor, Richard, climbing up Eros – the
bloody thing swayed! And he did crack it, they had to repair
it. Even the police said "Bloody hell!".' The actor was Richard
Sandells, member of Gay Sweatshop theatre company and one of
the founding members of the arts against Section 28.

Lynn Sutcliffe relives the experience gleefully:

I'd never kissed my girlfriend in the street before, and it was so exciting being able to do that, people cheering and clapping. Because I've done a lot of work in the theatre, I liked the way OutRage! were using theatrical devices. I thought to myself, 'Oh, I can contribute to that sort of thing' and so I started to go regularly after the kiss-in.

OutRage! co-founder Simon Watney adds:

Every time we have demos we bring our gayness with us and are affectionate with each other, to platform gay and lesbian visibility and to confront homophobia and AIDSphobia. The reason we chose this place is that it is right in the centre of London, no one would miss this. The original idea of the kiss-in was to challenge the law so we were expecting arrests. Instead we actually set a precedent whereby the inspector in charge of the West End Central Division stated that people wouldn't be arrested for showing affection in public. Someone I was fond of even shimmied up to kiss me on the statue of Eros.

OutRage! completely changed the game, legally and artistically. This sense of effective fun continued when, following the example of 'urban glamour assaults' in America, the affinity group WIG (Work it Girl) organised 'urban drag' from here a few months later. 'Following the simple premise that queers are everywhere, WIG planned a shopping trip down Oxford Street in drag to bedazzle fellow shoppers with queer fashion', remembers Alan Jarman. James Kierny was there too and relives the moment: 'I had one of those very tight skirts that billowed at the bottom. We went and had a make-over in Selfridges, had tea in Fortnum and Masons upstairs – that was queer visibility at its best.' This creative fury sustained the group's activism for ten years. They captured the righteous anger of queers who knew that they were vulnerable to violence, and they changed the face of Britain forever. This led to many legislative victories such as equalising in 2001 the age of consent for heterosexuals and homosexuals (to sixteen years old in England, Scotland and Wales, and seventeen in Northern Ireland).

Queer culture is a vibrant culture and a declaration of enlightenment. The Homosexual Law Reform Society, London Lesbian Avengers and OutRage! were exciting and effective. Protest is more than just trudging around with placards, which I've done many times, often trying to impress a boy I've fancied. It is about taking ownership of our lives, being assertive, imaginative and often hilarious, diffusing hostility, overcoming apathy and promoting an interest in collective action. Visual protests like the wink-in made activism an art form, securing press headlines, raising public consciousness and provoking vital public debate around anti-LGBTQIA+ discrimination. Today, Simon Watney catches his breath and smiles at me, 'You know, Dan, you can't put a gag on London as a city of pleasure. There has to be pleasure, romance, the erotic charge, canoodling walks down the River Thames. A city without pleasure is a monstrosity.' Well, Simon may not be putting a gag on London but I won't be throwing mine away anytime soon.

6. *FEASTING WITH PANTHERS* – THE MEAT RACK, 44–46 REGENT'S STREET

Here at the 'Meat Rack', under the bright lights at Piccadilly Circus, lie the roots of London's queer erotic charge. Scratch beneath the surface of what is now Boots pharmacy ('promoting health and wellbeing') and you are standing on a mountaintop of powerful, phenomenally daring queer creatures who knew how to promote and sell beauty long before Boots existed. For centuries, the 'Dilly Boys' who worked at Piccadilly Circus, London's principal location for selling sex, attracted to this place the desires of thousands. Young gay men who had been thrown out of families and were likely homeless, would stand here at the junction of Regent Street and Piccadilly Circus, waiting for 'straight looking' men who would come and pay them for sex.

The numbers of young people working as sex workers in a homophobic, economically unequal system, can be hard to visualise today, as online escorting has replaced many street sex workers. But throughout most of the twentieth century, slouching here on the railings in seductive tight trousers on this notoriously dangerous patch, you would have been sure to meet the neighbourhood's iconic rent boys.

Imagine it's night-time. Focus your eyes in the dark to witness centuries of unfolding dramas of sex workers reclaiming rights as workers. Courageous people seeking protections in defence of their lives. Ted was born into the civil rights movements that erupted out of centuries of slavery and dispossession. This movement went on to expose the FBI's COINTELPRO programme of surveilling, infiltrating, discrediting and disrupting domestic American political organisations that would keep the masses in chains. Have no doubt that cultural erasure, police entrapment and systematic establishment cover-ups have taken place here too in abundance. Closeted politicians shriek that prostitution is evil but under the moonlit sky, the perspective of those they pay for their services tells a very different story.

'Feasting with panthers' was Oscar Wilde's steamy reflection as a regular client of the Dilly Boys, written in a love-letter from prison in Winter 1897. 'A curious, very young but hard-eyed creature' made him feel as if 'an icy hand had clutched his heart'. To make clear that he was a customer, Wilde wore a green carnation, and was known to the boys for paying over the going rate, taking them out to dinner and giving the prettier boys silver cigarette cases, which they could sell on. Moralistic pearl-clutching about the area, so rife with Dilly Boys and brothels, led to the Gross Indecency Law being introduced by Henry Labouchère in 1885, in which homosexual offences received a two-year sentence with hard labour, and all gay sex was criminalised.

Fast forward now to 1973 when Ian Johns, a homeless seventeen-year-old, was living in a car and in desperate need of sexual liberation, and money. He recounts to me today:

I just remembered once I was wearing a pair of bright green loon pants, low waisted and really tight fitting with huge bell bottoms at the Dilly when a guy shouted from a car, 'Look at that boy's gorgeous bum!!' I was rather embarrassed.

Ian was hungry to create a world where he could see himself within it and so Soho 'became the centre of queerness really':

I'd rent just because I had no money. So I got a tenner. I'd get a bed for the night and a little bit of love as well. But I do remember once going back with a Billy Bunter [meaning 'punter' in the language of the Dilly Boys], who said to me in the cab back to his plush flat in Kensington. 'Are you not worried that someone might take you home and hang you from the rafters?' I think the only positive thing I ever saw about being queer as a teen was with my parents, watching Charles Aznavour singing 'What Makes a Man a Man', which is absolutely beautiful.

'You're not like all the others', said one 'Billy Bunter' to Ian. He was referring to how hardened many Dilly Boys became, or were forced to become. For safety against attacks and arrests, the Dilly Boys spoke in Polari, a coded gay language, beautifully illustrated in the 2015 short film *Putting on the Dish*, directed by Brian Fairbairn and Karl Eccleston. Most common in the 1950s, Polari is 'verbal drag' that harnesses the power of camp as a vital form of protection, with users referring to themselves as 'Mary-Ann', 'pouf', 'fairy' or a 'tapette'.

Often described as 'lawless', the Dilly Boys weren't the only ones defying the law. The dangers have always been real, and those drawn to the Meat Rack all risked something: blackmail, prison, rape, rip-off and death. The worst of the dangers came to light in 1982, when human bones were found blocking the drains of a London house, leading to the arrest of the gay serial killer Dennis Nilsen, who prowled the Meat Rack for his victims. Dilly regulars also included predators looking for young strays and runaway boys. While the boys called their abusers 'punters', the men who abused them referred to them as 'chickens', pimping them out for child sex abuse rings that included celebrities and the politically powerful. These power dynamics only compounded these brave workers' tenacity to continue. Yet even today, sex workers aren't often recognised as workers deserving of rights and protections like any other.

In September 1975 Charles Hornby was among five men convicted in a high-profile child abuse investigation which centred on the Playland amusement arcade near Piccadilly Circus, and involved the sexual exploitation of homeless boys. A pillar of the establishment, Hornby was a wealthy socialite, a Lloyd's Bank underwriter and an old Etonian, 'who on occasion had Prince Charles among his dinner guests'. Hornby got a much shorter sentence than the working-class defendants in the case, even though he was convicted of attempting to pervert the course of justice by approaching witnesses to change their stories. The other four, described by the press as 'nobodies', later had their sentences reduced in mysterious circumstances. One of them, David Archer, alleged that Hornby was far from being the only VIP involved in the Playland scandal, with a large account of 'millionaires and titled and influential people' involved: 'I believe there was a tremendous cover-up to protect these people.'

During the 1980s, the decade infamous for Conservative politicians introducing the lethally homophobic Section 28 law, the acquisition of homosexual sex workers during Conservative Party conventions in luxury hotels ran rampant. Queer-bashing and the proliferation of AIDS were results of the Conservative government's homophobic policies at the time. Britain's MI5 security service even had their own dedicated unit which monitored the sexual antics of Conservative MP's, called the 'Dolly Mixtures'. It was set up on the 'personal orders' of Margaret Thatcher to avoid embarrassing Tory sex scandals.

117

The following year, Manchester police launched Operation Spanner after finding a video of men they believed were being tortured to death. These men were enjoying themselves in privacy (i.e. in each other's homes), and thought what they were doing was legal. Judge Rant said in court that he'd nearly fainted on seeing the film, which was so violent and disgusting. He must have lived a very sheltered life. The defendants went to prison for years on ludicrous charges like 'aiding and abetting an assault upon themselves' while their barrister said the tapes were clearly showing adults having fun. At the time the chief constable of Manchester was Margaret Thatcher's friend James Anderton, an evangelical Christian prone to making outrageously reactionary homophobic remarks. 'Why do homosexuals freely engage in sodomy and other obnoxious sexual practices knowing the dangers involved?' James spat venomously in May 1987 – maybe he should have asked his constabulary and the politicians they protect for the answers. He could have even asked his daughter when she came out a few years later in defiance of his horrific homophobia.

Queer-bashing and sexual abuse was often perpetuated at the hands of the police too. Dilly Boy Alan Kerr remembers multiple assaults after being escorted towards Vine Street police station:

They would start pushing and pulling you to make it look like you were causing them trouble. They would use this as an excuse to punch you in the stomach; always in the stomach; up against the wall outside the station. They never bruised your face as you might be going up before the Bow Street magistrates.

The litany of examples of police, political and press collusion to cover up displays of political shame at the Meat Rack wouldn't fit on the giant Piccadilly Circus billboards, even in the tiniest of fonts.

Can we untangle ourselves from the web of centuries of systemic police violence? Can we imagine how society can re-allocate resources to alternative forms of public safety and community? Can we abolish the police, as slavery was abolished?

We can be brave – queers have always had to be. So if there is one place to start the process of abolishing and transcending the police, given their track record, surely, it should be at Pride.

7. *PLEASE SIR, CAN I HAVE SOME MORE?* – SAVOY TURKISH BATHS, 92 JERMYN STREET

Time to step away from the exposed streets and the cold nights to somewhere warmer, and as sizzlingly scandalous. Here stood the Savoy Turkish baths, opened in 1910, an all-male establishment that was one of three London baths open all night, and frequented by homosexuals intent on appreciating their bodies outside of the glare of public intrusion.

Welcome to the street of hot desire. Picture red-faced, steamed up people coming out of these buildings' doors. The women-only baths were situated at 12 Duke of York Street directly around the corner. In the early twentieth century communal baths were essential for the sanitation of the working masses but one of the attractions of the Savoy baths was the many famous people to be seen. They were one of the few places a closeted gay actor, of which it would be fair to say there have been quite a few, could feel reasonably safe from the police. This brought scandals like the one when Rock Hudson was thrown out for importuning in 1952 and when writers Christopher Isherwood and W.H. Auden had a threesome with renowned composer Benjamin Britten in 1937. 'Very pleasant sensation. Completely sensuous, but very healthy. It is extraordinary to find one's resistance to anything gradually weakening', Britten wrote in his diary of his experience at the baths. Even Harold Macmillan, the British prime minister (1957–63), went there, as film-maker Derek Jarman documented: 'as a young MP, Harold Macmillan – who was expelled from Eton for an "indiscretion" – used to spend nights at the Jermyn Street baths; anyone who went to them would have been propositioned during the course of an evening. I went there myself on two or three occasions.'

On 17 April 1941, a Nazi parachute bomb exploded above the original baths at number 76 Jermyn Street. It was the same bomb that ended the life of the popular jazz vocalist Al Bowlly, famous for singing 'Goodnight Sweetheart' and 'Love is the Sweetest Thing', and who at the time was reading a cowboy book in bed in the adjacent Duke's Court apartments. Meanwhile the exclusively male Savoy Turkish Baths at 92 Jermyn Street remained open all night long. Actor Alec Guinness, star of many classics from Ealing comedies to *Oliver Twist* (in which he played Fagin), was a regular there too, although he wrote in his diary, 'it all revolted me'.

Apparently it revolted him so much, he kept on going back. Oliver Twist's words 'Please sir can I have some more' have never tasted so good.

8. *THE BOYS IN THE BAND* – EMPIRE,
5–6 LEICESTER SQUARE

Eyes glued to the screen, it was here at the Odeon cinema, as it was previously called, that Ted saw a special film. Instantly, he knew that his life would never be the same again. In 1970, the cinema shone with loud, bright lights outside at night, while inside, Ted was watching the landmark gay film *The Boys in the Band*. The cinema was quiet and just over half full. Just going to watch the film was an act of coming out in itself.

The film ends with the line 'If only we didn't hate ourselves so much'. Within the small selection of movies in which gay people appeared at the time, most were rife with mawkishness and self-oppression, all mixed with an affirmative sense of what it means to be an outsider or even an outlaw. For Ted, *The Boys in the Band*, despite its shortcomings, was the first Hollywood film where homosexuals showed that they love each other. The character Emory's camp behaviour was looked down upon and his abuse of Black character Bernard, left Ted angry. 'They don't look homosexual' Ted heard in the film and thought 'I am that, but where are the others like me?' Ted walked out of the screening and was handed a leaflet declaring 'Gay is Good!' 'Come Together!' outside in the brisk Autumnal evening breeze.

The man handing the flyer was part of a group that was protesting against the film's 'doomed homosexual' narrative, and the leaflets were inviting people to join the Gay Liberation Front (GLF). A few days later Ted went searching down the corridors of the London School of Economics (LSE), to change the course of queerstory. 'Walking into that first GLF meeting – just seeing

gay people together, without shame, just being openly gay –
that was as astonishing as walking on the surface of the moon.'
Just opening the door to the meetings would have been nerve-
wracking. As Ted recalls:

I go in that door in fear and anger. Fear of the unknown, for
I'm sure that my life changes here. Anger, which is like a hand
in the back shoving me through the door, because Great Britain
has reduced queer people to living in an open prison. Central
to this was the act of Coming Out, making yourself visible.
The Gay Liberation Front became the only space we'd ever
had, where for the first time we could break the silence and
finally talk openly about our lives and what had happened to
us personally when growing up.

The GLF originated in the US shortly after the Stonewall
Uprisings that began on 28 June 1969 in New York City. Young
Brits Bob Mellors and Aubrey Walter were at the Black Panthers'
Revolutionary People's Constitutional Convention the following
year in Philadelphia, which famously strengthened connections
between revolutionary movements of the time. Soon after, they
returned to the UK to found a transatlantic branch of GLF. It was
at the LSE that the just-knighted Sir William Adams, the school's
director, knowingly let his basement be used by homosexuals
planning a revolution. The weekly gatherings involved raising
critical questions, a constant unveiling and intervention into their
reality. They immersed themselves in community education as
the practice of freedom rather than the practice of domination.
They saw beauty in homosexuality and sought to take ownership
of the term, reshape it and offer society a different vision of the

future. The seventies dawned, glistening with hope and a new idea of love.

Here Ted met Andrew Lumsden, a charismatic young whippersnapper journalist, who explains excitedly:

In the early days there were under 20 there but word went down the telephone and into the bars: hot women, hot men and hot ideas! We reached out and lesbians and gay men from Scotland, Ireland, Rome and Paris came with delight to meet with us.

A first demo in the name of Pride and announcing the end of shame, was held on 25 November 1970 in Highbury Fields to protest the arrest of a young man by police on mere suspicion that he was cruising.

Times were starkly different. 'Gay' was a brand-new term that encompassed both men and women, which came from the old word for a prostitute. 'British media would not use the word "gay". In the UK it was a reference to sex workers, until it went transatlantic and became super radical and defiant', Andrew outlines. People that weren't heterosexual were more commonly referred to as homosexuals by the media and in society. Andrew chuckles at me today:

We were a peculiar scientific aberration. Trans, non-binary and intersex identities were decades away from being recognised. We were all queers, in the pejorative sense. Although the word has today been reclaimed in a celebration of non-compliance to expected ways of being, thinking or loving, back then queers were considered perverts and sexual deviants ... and we were.

While the politics of 'coming out' were central to the GLF, identity wasn't the main driving force. Ultimately the mission was, and still is, to gain absolute freedom for all oppressed people(s). Their demands and activities included mobilising against discrimination in the workplace, in education and by the medical establishment, and to cultivate ways to communicate and have public displays of gay affection. General meetings happened every Wednesday and specific groups formed including a Women's Group, Street Theatre Group, Communes Group and The Youth Group for the under-21s fighting for a reduction in the age of consent to catalyse sexual freedom for young people. A Counter-Psychiatry Group included analysing and attacking the psychiatric establishment for use of electric shock and drug programmes on gays and lesbians who did not fit within society's constraints, or who were found guilty of breaking the law. Graffitiing 'People not Psychiatry' and 'Gay Is Good' in Harley Street, the heartland of the medical establishment, brought relief and joy. The Counter-Psychiatry Group started 'Icebreakers', a gay help service with revolutionary aims, gave talks to doctors' surgeries, wrote the pamphlet 'Psychiatry and the Homosexual – a Brief analysis of oppression' and organised a major conference aimed at the psychiatric profession at the LSE theatre in December 1971.

'I went to meetings frequently, five or six times a week and I always went on demonstrations. GLF was bursting with energy! It was always exciting, challenging and often fun', lifelong GLF activist Nettie Pollard recalls devotedly today. An action group organised political 'zaps', a boisterous performance art tactic that ignited early LGBTQIA+ activism. Deceptively simple, it involved sudden, loud, brief action. GLF organised public dances in local town halls and 'Gay Days' in parks too, with games galore, kiss-ins, spin the bottle and sing-a-longs to emerging gay folk classics such as GLF activist Alan Wakeman's 'Everyone Involved – A Gay Song'. A breath-taking amount of mobilisation in a tiny amount of time.

Finding the GLF finally allowed Ted to see a future for himself. In activist spaces he would find a clear purpose, friendships and a life-long partner. Within a year Ted harnessed the spirit of his civil rights educators and helped organise the very first ever gay demonstration through central London, organised by GLF's Youth Group that took place on 28 August 1971. Soon Ted had moved into one of GLF's communes, which were popping up in Notting Hill, King's Cross, Muswell Hill, Bethnal Green and the women's commune in Faraday Road, Ladbroke Grove. 'Not only was I living with other gay people, I moved in with Noel, the man who I still love and became my civil partner.' Ted smiles; it is becoming a more permanent fixture across his face.

9. *GROOVY GARDEN PARTY* – KINKY GERLINKY, LEICESTER SQUARE EMPIRE

Turn around now and you'll see a door to the basement, an Alice's Wonderland where many of the GLF crew would later let off steam. This was the portal that led to the Leicester Square Empire ballroom and Kinky Gerlinky, the biggest glam-drag ball in Britain. Launched in 1989, for four years it was the West End's most proudly hedonistic club night at the intersection of queer culture, fashion, music and the avant-garde. With icons like Boy

George and Vivienne Westwood in regular attendance, the party was a gleeful subversion of the idea of celebrity, where every reveller was a star for a night. Stilt walkers voguing in hoop skirts and fake police outfits would delight the crowds at the legendary themed parties, like the 'Spirit of Xmas Past', 'Models' Ball' and the 'Groovy Garden Party', dancing to classics like 'You Spin Me Round (Like a Record)' by Dead or Alive.

Swivel around again and face the Square. Picture yourself here on a Saturday night in 1989. During the AIDS pandemic the government was complicit in entrenching homophobia when it should have been saving our lives. It wasn't just Kinky Gerlinky that lifted the spirits, the Square was filled with queer havens. Theatre-goers would emerge from their shows to witness the illuminating extravaganza of debauchery and decadence moving through Leicester Square. Taboo took place at the Maximus disco a few doors up from the Empire, attracting all those suburban-kids-gone-wrong at the epicentre of the 1980s scene. Exuberant, opulent and highly theatrical, many of the talents would be wearing lampshades on their heads just to get in. Leigh Bowery, Taboo's host and grand marshal of London's wild and glam scene until his death of AIDS in 1994, took fashion to new and wild places. 'Things will never be like that again', says Boy George today:

One of the prices you pay for liberation and tolerance is that you sacrifice individuality. Taboo thrived in a period of right-wing politics, the Thatcher/Reagan years is proof of a basic human need to have something to kick against. That's what made it such fun. It completely upped the ante and convinced us that we were somehow being terribly, terribly naughty.

Are you planning something naughty soon? I do hope so.

10. *GAY NEWS* – 3A NEWPORT PLACE

Take the next left onto Little Newport Street under the gorgeous red lanterns indicating the start of Chinatown, where the queer Chinese community are emerging from the shadows too, to chants of '我们酷儿，有爱，有力量' ('Queer love, queer power') as members join Pride protests. Only a few places have been known to provide sanctuary for the Chinese queer community, such as the Long Yan Club, primarily catering for middle-class middle-age gay men. But times are changing, Orientation UK is a new social group for Chinese gay men established in 2022, the year of the tiger, and Queer China UK is launching 'Queerness of Chinatown', a multifaceted project to discover and record queer Chinese stories in the past and present through oral history archives, documentary, photos and 'Queer Chinatown through Zine Making' exhibitions.

On your left is another seemingly mundane building just like the one that hosted the Homosexual Law Reform Society, where we began. Behind this blue door, number 3A Newport Place, is where GLF activist Andrew Lumsden lived between 1968 and 1973, and this is where Ted's interest in journalism was sparked. Andrew knew that the GLF ideas had to reach beyond the LSE walls and came up with the idea of a paper. 'This is what we need to do and this is how we can do it', Andrew said after reading about the GLF following the Stonewall Uprising:

Without a clue what 'Gay Liberation Front' might mean – knowing only, through newspaper reports, of a National

Liberation Front of Vietnam, I couldn't wait to get to wherever this Gay Liberation Front might be. Quietly mocking the section of the Times for which I wrote, called Business News, I decided such a newspaper should be called *Gay News*, an in-joke at the expense of the existing media. A gay-controlled newspaper. That would be the answer.

Gay News was the first LGBTQIA+ publication since partial decriminalisation in 1967, first sold at Pride, and it became the world's biggest homosexual newspaper in the world through the 1970s. It was a copy of *Gay News* that was strapped to the back of Ted's bike where we began our tour. Every world-changing movement starts somewhere.

Following *Gay News*, the GLF media group created the *Come Together* newsletter. Early editions were put together in activists' flats and assembled using collaging techniques combined with hand-drawn artwork, cartoons and sketches. Andrew recalls longingly, smiling:

During those months, after a day at work at the *Times* and often an evening with Gay Liberation Front, I thought in my room in Soho just how busy GLF was. We were all so busy, we were falling into bed, our own or somebody else's.

11. *THE FIFTEEN-FOOT CUCUMBER –*
FOYLES BOOKSHOP, 107 CHARING CROSS ROAD

Little did Ted know that the leaflet he picked up outside the cinema would lead to watching a '15-foot papier mâché cucumber' being pulled from the arse of one of his fellow GLF activists. It was time for Foyles bookshop to be 'zapped' as part of a series of hilarious actions throughout 1971 against David Reuben's 'counselling' book, *Everything You Always Wanted To Know About Sex (But Were Afraid To Ask)*.

On 13 February 1971, the GLF were out in force leafleting outside Foyles as part of a spectacular campaign launch that alerted the press to one of the most homophobic texts in recent history. The day before the activists met outside W.H. Allen publishers in Essex Street, the heart of London's law district, opposite the Royal Courts of Justice. The book claimed to tell candid facts while avoiding moral judgement. In the sections on gays and lesbians it contained references to light bulbs, cucumbers and the use of wire coat hangers for abortions. Using unscientific methods of denial and assertion to 'prove' that homosexual relationships cannot be happy and are almost invariably short term and impersonal, Reuben even states that 'A masturbation machine might do it better', and his only remarks about female homosexuality are under the chapter heading of 'Prostitution'. Andrew recalls:

> It would put off any vulnerable person seeking a gay life and we're all appalled by what faking it, not coming out, does to us. The publishers inside were astounded! Then they asked us to come and discuss the matter inside. Clearly they weren't used to demonstrations then.

The demonstration was covered by *Peace News*, the *Guardian* and the *Evening Standard*, and soon the GLF were alerted that the book was to be printed in paperback. On 30 October 1971 GLF activists Barbara Klecki and Lindsay Levi stopped outside. Barbara reached under Lindsay's coat with the hook of a coat-hanger and out popped a raw liver, a mock 'abortion in the street', satirising dangerous parts of the book. They didn't wait outside either and headed in to take the books off the shelves. As Peter Tatchell recounts: 'There were a couple of small raiding parties which went into Foyles and a couple of other bookshops to put stickers on the covers.' Several arrests were made as police chased people in and out of the various entrances of Foyles.

The GLF launched their climactic action on 10 December 1971 at Pan Books, the paperback publisher of the title, at 33 Tothill Street, SW1. Hobbling up to the publisher's entrance, Denis Lemon of GLF – the first editor of *Gay News* and a central part to the GLF Street Theatre Group – pulled out the giant cucumber from his behind, with the guidance of others in the street theatre group.

GLF activist Peter Tatchell played a crucial role on the day:

We did get inside the head office and this huge cucumber was duly presented to the staff. When the police arrived their reaction was a mixture of belligerence and amusement. They knew what we were doing was illegal but they didn't quite know how to handle a fifteen-foot cucumber. So to speak.

Leaflets were distributed to the bemused onlookers, announcing:

This is what you read in the Pan book: that you 'thrive on danger', that you 'rarely know the names' of those you love, that 'random and reckless selection of partners' is your trade-mark, that 'mutilation, castration and death' are 'sadly all part of the homosexual game'.

The leaflet went on to urge readers to action:

Well, you say, what can I do about it? Tell people. Warn them off it. Try MPs and the usual channels. Write to yours. We cannot, on this leaflet, suggest that you take more positive action. Unfortunately. That is your own decision. It depends on how much you care. We care.

The book wasn't withdrawn, but the stickers plastered all over the inside of it up and down the country remained. If you find a copy today the stickers would say: 'Warning. This book does not represent the majority of medical and psychiatric opinion'.

12. *OUT OF THE CLOSET, INTO THE STREETS –* CHARING CROSS ROAD

A few months later a curious Ted was on a mission that would lead him to help organise a mass kiss-in, the UK's first gay pride in 1972, that marched from Trafalgar Square through Soho to Hyde Park. Here on Charing Cross Road, Ted and approximately 500 jubilant LGBTQIA+ people, many in drag, would be holding placards high above their heads, bearing slogans like 'Homosexuals are Nature's Children' and 'Gay is Angry', and chanting proudly, 'Out of the closet, into the streets!' No carnival floats, no corporate signs, not even a rainbow flag. The date chosen was

1 July, the nearest Saturday to the anniversary of Stonewall – a conscious homage to the rebellion's first spark. The street may be emptier now, but Ted's still here, smiling, holding in his heart the queer footprints of the first pride.

These demonstrations captured the transition from the private to the public, from fearful homosexual to revolutionary gay, a full participant in a broader movement for liberation. Civil rights alone were inadequate. For fellow GLF activist Nettie Pollard, the goal is as ambitious today as it was then:

> I believe the only way forward is to join with others, not for a seat at the top table, but to abolish the top table. It means working with other marginalised groups such as trans, refugees, homeless, sex workers. Any revolution must be economic but if it is to last there must be a transformation in how all humans relate to each other and the planet. It's so exciting to see what's happened since. I hope lots of young people are going to be involved but I'm not giving up. Andrew grins 'As evangelical conversion therapy, Gay Liberation was great. But remoulding the world inside one's head is difficult enough; it is far harder to revolutionise the world outside'. As Allen Ginsberg of New York GLF announced, 'The Fags have finally lost that wounded look!'

Ted is now in his seventies. Throughout his lifetime he has organised against institutional homophobia, including the formation of Black Lesbians & Gays Against Media Homophobia, successfully fighting against Buju Banton's viciously homophobic song 'Boom Bye Bye' and confronted media attacks on Black gay footballer Justin Fashanu. Today we are seeing vital moves in the sporting world to honour the LGBTQIA+ community across the world. Seventeen-year-old Blackpool midfielder Jake Daniels cited Justin Fashanu as an inspiration when he came out in 2022, the first openly gay male player in England since Justin in 1990. Ted tilts his head:

> I vividly remember as a twelve-year-old reading an article headlined 'How to spot a possible homo'. They could say and do whatever they wanted to LGBTQIA+ people and not face any challenge. We now feature in television, radio and media much more, however, by necessity the work continues.

So much progress has been made, but now more than ever the political is personal. We must ensure that those who started Pride continue to be cherished. Noel, the love of Ted's life, whom he met 50 years ago in the communes, like many Pride pioneers, was pushed back into the closet in a so-called elderly 'care home'. 'Are you a gay man? Do you like gay men?', Ted recalls two staff members taunting his partner, before dragging him into his room. Shortly afterwards, Ted discovered bruises and what appeared to be a cigarette burn on his partner's hand. His life partner died on 26 December 2021. Other residents asked Ted 'not to let the staff know that they were lesbian, gay or trans' for fear of 'suffering the same' abusive treatment.

Homophobic abuse in care homes is on the rise. Compassion in Care, a charity campaigning for an end to such treatment, received 50 reports of homophobic abuse in homes between 2017 and 2019, and many more since. Although the majority of care staff do not abuse queer people in their care, almost half of the reports received relate to queerphobic abuse in care homes. The experiences of older LGBTQIA+ people is often marked by heteronormative assumptions, which can include preventing visits from partners and aesthetics dominated by images of straight families, religious symbols and royal family memorabilia. Christianity often has a strong presence even in secular care homes. On Sundays, celebration days or at the end of someone's life, priests often visit homes, a deeply distressing experience – especially when elderly residents are encouraged to 'repent their previous sinful lives'.

Geoff Hardy, Ted's lifelong friend and GLF activist, was also determined to keep fighting for queer liberation. In 2021, they shared the megaphone while protesting outside the Department of Health and Social Care near the Houses of Parliament. They were there to demand a care system that respects the experiences of queer people as they age.

Geoff turned to the crowd with a determined look and asked, 'Because when you're fighting for your own life, why would you give up?'

13. *ALL NIGHT GAIETY* – THE CARAVAN CLUB, 81 ENDELL STREET

Get yourself to our final stop by crossing Cambridge Circus and stroll towards Covent Garden. If you wanted to let your hair down after a hard day's graft in 1930s London, you would be heading to the Caravan Club, 'London's Greatest Bohemian Rendezvous'. The club closed long ago, but the entrance to the alley down which number 81 is located is prominently marked. During the blackouts of the Second World War, London was for many queers the biggest and best dark room in history. Known as 'the most unconventional spot in town' promising 'all night gaiety', 'dancing toe Charlie' and my favourite cruising-anecdote 'periodical night trips to the Great Open spaces', sweat dripped off the wall and those inside danced their socks off as if every night might be their last.

'Unconventional' was a euphemism for a gay bar. Just like the Molly houses of 200 years earlier, the Caravan Club fell foul of undercover police surveillance and raids. On a balmy summer's night in 1934, anonymised complaint letters signed off by 'A Citizen', 'An Englishman' and 'pro bono publico' ('for the public good') led the police to sit with binoculars and notebooks in the turret of the Shaftesbury Theatre diagonally opposite, planning a raid. The police saw it as their moral and civic duty to shut down places that are 'only frequented by sexual perverts, lesbians and sodomites. It's absolutely a sink of iniquity.' Sounds delicious to me, where do I sign up?

103 people were arrested that night. Among the evidence seized were love letters, found as ripped up fragments under furniture. This included a letter to Billy, one of the owners of the Club, from Cyril the Lionheart. The letter said, 'My Dear Billy, I didn't intend coming to the club last night only I felt that I must see you. I have only been queer since I came to London about two years ago, before then I knew nothing about it.' Only too aware of the implications if it was found, Cyril's love letter ended with 'please be a dear boy and destroy this note'. We are now at the

end and let us wonder together on this quest for collective visibility, instead of '*coming out*' what are we '*coming into*'?

WHERE'S THE PUB? COMPTON'S, OLD COMPTON STREET

Head back towards Charing Cross Road and get yourself a well
deserved tipple as you remind yourself that an army of lovers
cannot lose. Here's to you Uncle Ted! Choose from the array of
dazzling options in Old Compton Street – as well as Compton's
there's Ku Bar, G-A-Y, the Yard Bar, CIRCA and many more!

5
A Cache of Diamonds
Whitechapel

Whitechapel has a treasure chest of stories connecting across class, religious, gender, sexual and racial lines. For centuries the community have defied the knocks on our doors by authorities intent on rooting out debauchery, lust and the organisation of modern democratic and public queer life. Don't let the narrow streets in our pilgrimage across Brick Lane give you the wrong impression – the impacts of queer life here are so huge, that they are felt across the world.

START: SHOREDITCH HIGH STREET STATION

1. Bethnal Rouge Acid Drag Commune – *248 Bethnal Green Road*
2. The Cock Exchange – *Intersection of Bethnal Green Road and Pollard Row*
3. If I Can't Dance it's Not My Revolution – *Bethnal Green Working Men's Club, 42–46 Pollard Row*
4. The Society for the Reformation of Manners – *The Glasshouse, 118 Bethnal Green Road*
5. Shimmering Queer Love – *Hunky Dory, 226 Brick Lane*
6. Phil Mitchell, Gay Icon – *Bender Defenders, 168 Brick Lane*
7. Banglatown – *Raj Mahal Sweets, 57 Brick Lane*

8. We Are Dust and Shadows *–Brick Lane Mosque, 59 Brick Lane*
9. Deeds, Not Words *– Toynbee Hall, 28 Commercial Street*
10. A Post-Capitalist World *– Freedom Bookshop, 84b Whitechapel High Street*
11. Miss Muff's Molly House *– 45 Whitechapel Road*
12. We Exist *– Altab Ali Park, Alder Street*
13. The Rainbow Tree *– East London Mosque, 82–92 Whitechapel Road*
14. Who Makes Profit? Somebody Knows *– Parfett Street*
15. You Messed with the Wrong Faggot *– Whitechapel Station*

Where's the Pub? *The (New) Joiners Arms, 116–118 Hackney Road*

1. *BETHNAL ROUGE ACID DRAG COMMUNE –* 248 BETHNAL GREEN ROAD

Julian, pass the torch, would ya darlin? If we could just prise this brick from this wall … or actually wait … what about under that floorboard there … those damn rhinestone diamonds have got to be stashed somewhere around here … but I can't see anything! And stub that joint, I'm gonna pass out down here!

—Andrew Lumsden, Gay Liberation Front (GLF)

This address is now a Western Union bank, but back in 1973 you might have found Andrew, Julian Hows and the Radical Feminists (or 'RadFems'), who were an artistic collective within the GLF, scrambling around the basement at the 'Bethnal Rouge Acid Drag Commune'. The sign on the front door here announces:

Dear Brothers + Sisters, Bethnal Rouge, a commune of gay people, have taken over the former Agitprop bookshop. The shop will continue with the emphasis on gay's, women's + children's books and periodicals. There's plenty of room here for people to relax, chat and have coffee, so come on round. Love Bethnal Rouge Collective P.S. Tube: Bethnal Green (Central) Bus: No. 8.

Formerly the anarchist Agitprop Bookshop, it was rumoured to have once been owned by a banker to the Kray brothers gang and that there was a wall safe hidden downstairs. If only they could find it!

Nothing was ever found, but they did have a lot of fun trying. Andrew remembers, with a twinkle in his eye, 'We were dancing to tracks from the *Andrews Sisters*, *Velvet Underground*, *Hunky Dory*, *Gold Diggers of 1933*, *42nd Street* or Marilyn Monroe's rendition of "Diamonds Are a Girl's Best Friend", every drag queen's delight!'

If you ask me, there is treasure to be found in the streets of Bethnal Green and Whitechapel – streets that reek of scandal, mischief, naughtiness and a grubby defiance that change can happen. Personally, I wouldn't be writing this today if my Jewish grandparents fleeing the Nazis in the Second World War hadn't been welcomed here, one of the most multicultural and multifaceted neighbourhoods in London, just like many other new communities have been throughout history.

This is one of the most economically deprived boroughs in London Town. In stark contrast, it neighbours the looming ice wharfs of London's financial centre where bankers' daily earnings equate to the annual wages of most in this community. Sandwiched between the financial hub of the Square Mile and Canary Wharf, it is being increasingly consumed by luxury flats for city workers, squeezing out social housing and heavily influencing patterns of consumption, surveillance and control.

But the whole really is more than the sum of its parts, and no community reflects this more than Tower Hamlets. The jackfruits bulge in pride of place at the market stalls, saris in all colours glisten from the shop fronts and the tugs of war across class, race, gender, ability and sexuality have initiated processes of change that have had imprints on a global scale.

Across the road, punters at the Old George pub freaked out when the acid drag queens first arrived, but their piano-playing dynamism and singing skills led to some degree of acceptance and lots of laughter. There was never a dull moment inside the squat either. Andrew recalls:

The bathroom was filled with Peanuts cartoons from the *Observer*, rather endearing, this in the revolutionary Agitprop premises. We painted a mural at the far end of the ground floor and upstairs had drapes and hangings everywhere, mattresses strewn around the floor, and various people came to live there and visit. We even took the door off the loo because we didn't believe in privacy, everything had to be done in public.

I might try that in my flat today. Housemates – you have been warned.

Many of the Queens had met through the first intense roller-coaster years of Gay Liberation Front (GLF) activism, diamonds placed on the roadmap to this country's developing queer freedom today. Electrifying interventions in the homophobic status quo included Britain's first LGBTQIA+ demo against police entrapment in Highbury Fields in 1970, and the GLF Youth Group action against the unequal age of consent (1971) that led to the first Gay Pride (1972), both events taking over Trafalgar Square.

By late 1973, however, the movement's energy was fracturing and the treasure hunt's shine began to fade. Inevitable growing pains set in, as they do for all movements on a quest for fundamental transformation. Some participants began to question the notion of an acceptable gay culture, benign toleration and being smiled upon by 'straight' capitalist society, while others demanded a subversive sexuality.

GLF activist Michael James recalls, 'We didn't take the label "RadFems". It got thrown at us one night in an argument ... "You radical femme acid queens!" ... it was something from outside. We never used words like that.' Legendary Queen Bette Bourne remembers: 'We would say "get a frock on dear" whenever they were ranting away. You see, drag is as old as the hills.'

Michael James continues:

It started with jellabas and kaftans and long hair and flowers ... then we discovered glitter ... and then nail varnish. Later, some of us – a quarter of the men, I'd say, at some time or other – would get a nice new frock for the next Gay Lib dance. Then a few people began wearing it to meetings. It just evolved.

Subversive political drag continues today with the local Glory cabaret venue, drag superstar collectives like Lese Majeste, Sink the Pink and many more are all doing the Queens of Bethnal Rouge proud.

2. *THE COCK EXCHANGE* – INTERSECTION OF BETHNAL GREEN ROAD AND POLLARD ROW

'Vroooooooooooom!'

Wow! What's that? Zooming away from London's financial centre, in a green Morris Minor convertible, are three adrenaline-fuelled activists in a getaway car. The Red Lesbian Brigade, a militant breakaway group from the GLF, are sprinting from the London Stock Exchange. In the early hours of 11 June 1971, right under the noses of security guards at the centre of Britain's financial heist, where everyday money, gold and diamonds are traded to support mainly rich, straight, white men, the world's financial elite, a battle plan for a new world order was underway. Walking past the main door of the building they sprayed 'Sod the Cock Brokers' in three-foot-high red letters, and beside it the intertwined symbols for women in black paint. Mary McIntosh was there and remembers, smiling, 'We painted the Stock Exchange or as we called it the "Cock Exchange", at the time it was in temporary buildings with hoardings up outside which were very easy to spray on. I was doing the driving rather than the painting and we were pretty terrified'.

All across London, the Women's Liberation Movement and the women of the GLF were taking action. 'One of the first actions of Women's Lib', says Angie Weir, 'was to occupy Wimpy Bars because no woman was allowed in after midnight as they were assumed to be prostitutes.' After the all-night sit-ins at Wimpy

Bars all down Oxford Street, ten lesbians, sick and tired of the anti-liberation stance of the Gateways Club, a lesbian hotspot in Chelsea since the 1930s, that had banned political flyers and compounded by frustrations from the male dominated spaces within the GLF, took the situation into their own hands, literally.

The radical lesbians were emboldened after taking over the GLF's magazine *Come Together* for its first women's issue in 1971, in which they came out to their families with articles that unpacked feminist queer potential, such as 'Revolution In The Head – Or In The World'. Sarah Grimes recalls why she wrote it:

> [It] was a personal confessional piece. I was thinking about why it had been so hard to come out before GLF and it was to do with the image of lesbians, of not having any charisma, any glamour, any creative ability or genius. Lesbians were silly, crass. There wasn't a role model equivalent to Oscar Wilde. There were two counterpoised articles – 'Revolution In The Head – Or In The World'. That was two different points of view which we allowed to coexist, individualism and internal revolution versus seeing that as just the first step to external revolution.

The trail of adrenaline-fuelled laughter and car fumes blasting down the streets leaves us in a cloud of smoke. Can the Red Lesbian Brigade and the Bethnal Rouge RadFems antics impact our quest for queer freedom today?

3. *IF I CAN'T DANCE IT'S NOT MY REVOLUTION* – BETHNAL GREEN WORKING MEN'S CLUB, 42–46 POLLARD ROW

The pumping tunes blasting out of 42–46 Pollard Row do justice to the spirit of Russian anarchist Emma Goldman's mantra, 'If I can't dance, it's not my Revolution'. Goldman 'promised [myself] never to go back to the East End, yet [I] would invariably return' after her visits to Whitechapel back in the 1890s. At this address since 1953, the Bethnal Green Working Men's Club has been the place to be for wild, racy, pioneering good times. Dancing and singing in front of its giant heart onstage, you can relish in performances from famous Bangladeshi trans dancer Shelly Rahul Abdin or sign up to join Odbhut Queer Bangla Group organising parties for the Bangladeshi and South Asian LGBTQ community since 2017.

Save some energy for tomorrow, though, because during the day the Rainbow Tree, the biggest Bangla LGBTQIA+ platform in the world since its inception in 2022, continues its mission of queer Bangladeshi empowerment. They host queer tours of the neighbourhood, picnics, parties, movies, shows and coordinate queer counselling, job signposting and protest placard making sessions. Emma Goldman may have told the local masses about 'The Futility of Politics and Its Corrupting Influence', but the Rainbow Tree hasn't given up yet. Their placards in rainbow coloured Bangla and English translations state 'An attack against one is an attack against all – the slaughter of Black people must be stopped! By any means necessary!' and 'Liberate all Black lives', pricking up the ears of the Bethnal Rouge Acid Drag Queens and the Red Lesbian Brigade activists from across the road. All of these movements and the placard statements are intimately connected with the visions and the slogans of the Black Panther Party, whose co-founder Huey Newton declared in Philadelphia in 1970 after the Stonewall Uprising:

[T]here is nothing to say that a homosexual cannot also be a revolutionary. And maybe I'm now injecting some of my prejudice by saying that 'even a homosexual can be a revolutionary'. Quite the contrary, maybe a homosexual could be the most revolutionary.

Damn right.

4. *THE SOCIETY FOR THE REFORMATION OF MANNERS* – THE GLASSHOUSE, 118 BETHNAL GREEN ROAD

The fact that the Glasshouse, a new permanent LGBTQIA+ bookshop, cafe and community centre, even exists is a treasure that the queers in seventeenth-century Bethnal Green could only have dreamt of.

'Knock knock, are you there? It's a warden from the Society for the Reformation of Manners', those queers of an earlier era might have heard banging on the door in the middle of the night. Like debt collectors but for morality, 'The Society' was formed in the borough in 1690 with the aim of the 'suppression of bawdy houses and profanity'.

Debauchery had to be rooted out, particularly among the lower classes. A network of moral guardians spread across the UK, stewarding streets to gather the names and addresses of offenders against morality, all collaborating with one another to persecute and arrest queers for fear of the brimstone of Sodom and Gomorrah.

To a great extent the Society was itself responsible for stimulating the growth of the gay subculture. The church sermons and tracts, as well as the attention from the raids and trials, were in fact great publicity. Gay men became aware that a fair number of them were about town – and that they could pick each other up for lustful encounters underneath the moonlight at the cruising grounds helpfully identified by worthy clergymen. See? Wherever oppression encroaches, our community rises, in every way imaginable.

Knowing that Tower Hamlets was so wicked that The Society for the Reformation of Manners and its consequent queer sexual revolutions began here, makes me smile from ear to ear. Fitting, as the etymology of 'Bethnal Green' comes from the Anglo-Saxon for 'happy corner'. The battleground for love starts in language, always at our disposal even when all our other rights are removed. '*Te amo puella*', the Romans would say; '*Je t'aime mon coeur*', the Huguenots would purr; '*Kh'hob dikh lib, mayn zisinke*', Yiddish lovers exclaim to their sweethearts across Brick Lane; and today 'আমি তোমাকে ভালোবাসি প্রিয়তমা' or '*Āmi tōmākē bhālōbāsi priẏatamā*' are the Bangla words expressing queer love in street whispers and screamed on dancefloors today.

5. *SHIMMERING QUEER LOVE – HUNKY DORY*, 226 BRICK LANE

Ian Bodenham and Ian Johns know a thing or two about the magnificence of queer love. Dancing to David Bowie's 'Oh! You Pretty Things' in the same step as the Bethnal Rouge Queens 50 years before, you can find them here at Hunky Dory, the crème de la crème of East End vintage stores they co-manage. In an array of dazzling vintage outfits they continue to polish the diamonds in each other's hearts. In 1984 after bumping into each other and locking eyes at pubs, clubs and on the tube, finally they plucked up the courage to ask each other out and have been together ever since. 'Love starts as infatuation with someone's qualities, looks and voice and everything. Then it mellows and becomes deeper. It's more touching, than it is to be set on fire', Ian Bodenham reminisced from their journey today.

These templates of queer love are unimaginable for many and were at one time for Ian Johns too, outlined in a letter to his teenage self. In 1973 he was a sex worker at the Meat Rack, the haunt of picking up 'man-meat' mentioned in Chapter 4:

I know life is pretty shit for you right now, you're only seventeen and it's 11.30 p.m. on the meat rack, you are homeless, it's cold and raining and you need a bed for the night and some love from somebody, any man who will take pity on you. I can tell you one day soon you won't feel so bad about yourself, so you met a kind older man tonight who made you feel loved, and gave you a tenner and made you breakfast, but soon you are going to meet your Queer family, you will be popular, you will be invited to parties, you will be driven around London in a sports car with the warm wind in your hair. You feel shit about being a Queer now, but soon you will celebrate it and march through London with thousands of others filled with pride. You will meet a man and fall in love, it's hard to believe right now, but you will marry him. Life will be good, very good. Believe me mate, it's going to get better, so much better soon.

Queer love is precious, shimmering, like the people wearing sequinned jackets dancing around Brick Lane on a Friday night, or queuing for a smoked-salmon bagel the following morning. Hard fought for, we have to defend it.

6. *PHIL MITCHELL, GAY ICON* – BENDER DEFENDERS, 168 BRICK LANE

On 25 April 2016, Xulhaz Mannan and Mahbub Tonoy, two pioneering LGBTQIA+ activists and journalists, were murdered by religious extremists in Dhaka, Bangladesh, for promoting LGBTQIA+ rights. Mazharul Islam was next on the hit list so he fled to London. Alongside Tashnuva Fardousi and hundreds more queer Bangladeshis in the neighbourhood, they continue to build power in the community through the Rainbow Tree network.

In Bangladesh, India and across Asia, centuries before homosexuality became illegal as a direct inheritance from the British Indian government's Section 377 of 1860, the barbaric history of homophobic colonisation has resulted in millions of dispossessed people clawing their way to survival, crawling through trenches, gripping onto the edge of boats and being trapped in prison cells that knows no parallel in homosexual history. Their quest for

Credit: Brenda Goodchild

dignity has fuelled journeys across separated lands to build a new freedom, a new love story. Sadly, Maz would face violence in his new home, too. In 2019 he was beaten up by homophobes after walking home from a 'stand up to LGBTQIA+ hate crime' demonstration in Soho, an irony so cruel it's enough to make our queer ancestors turn in their graves. Maz was the tenth friend of mine to be beaten up in just two short weeks, all attacked while alone, unable to fight back. This is the same dominator culture, the fear-inducing rigid maintenance of a society premised on hierarchical superiority, which has resulted in a 57 per cent increase in homophobic hate crime in Tower Hamlets since 2017. 148 queer people in 2019 attacked (and that's just reported cases), queers dreaming of belonging, their lives deemed unworthy.

Queer Night Pride demonstrations were organised in response to the 150 per cent increase in attacks since Brexit in 2016, with marches in the streets of Hackney and Tower Hamlets. Brexit, that genius plan that has emboldened racists and made our shop shelves dearer. One day around that time I was cycling down Brick Lane, minding my own business (yeah, right), when a brainwave shot through me. *EastEnders*, London's iconic soap opera, had captured the press with its episode the night before. 'Phil Mitchell a "gay icon" after punching a homophobe' was ringing in my ears, and outside the Oceanic Creations jacket wholesalers shop I hatched a plan. Queer self-defence classes had been set up in response to the racist National Front's presence in the neighbourhood in the 1980s, and the Guardian Angels of New York patrolling the subways against bigots in the 1990s in sunglasses and bomber jackets looked so cool. So here, outside the shop selling an array of bomber jackets, was born Bender Defenders: a new street defence movement confronting rising hate crime against queer people, to empower people to own their bodies and the streets. With icons from *EastEnders*, including Pat Butcher, Ash Kaur and Phil Mitchell as the 'Patron Saints' emblazoned across the jackets, they never fail to turn heads in this part of London Town.

Training sessions offer more than just Muay Thai and other martial arts techniques, they're designed to provide a sense of catharsis for attendees who might often feel under attack. As coach Luca says, 'This can be your space to release anything that happened to you. I call it brutal mindfulness. You can't zone out; you have to be there for yourself; you have to be there for your partner. You have to remember combinations; you have to be quick.' Each class is themed around different LGBTQIA+ icons, from Octavia Butler and Kitty Tsui to Divine and local Drag Race UK legend Bimini Bon-Boulash, to uplift attendees. 'Alongside helping people with fitness, we see the Bender Defender sessions as supporting good mental health and helping to improve people's confidence by providing valuable life skills', Bender Defender Tara explains. 'Sessions are taught in a light-hearted, fun way, and the classes offer a real sense of community.' Join them at the gym around the corner every Saturday.

7. *BANGLATOWN* – RAJ MAHAL SWEETS, 57 BRICK LANE

Don't leave Brick Lane hungry. Next to the plaque in tribute to Haroon Shamsher, the music revolutionary behind ground-breaking Bangla music collective *Joi*, stop off for some mouth-watering Asian deserts. Mithai is always difficult to resist and a sumptuous meal is incomplete without sweet dishes like gulabjam, rashmalai or gajjar halwa.

Satisfied, we can appreciate even more how the heritage of food adds one more powerful facet to the diamonds of these streets. A diamond is a prism after all. Stand here in the middle of the unique Brick Lane, once you shine a light through one side of this rare jewel, a million colours come out, beaming through time and across cultures.

At the other end of Brick Lane at Aldgate stands the crumbling remains of the London Wall. From its birth, London was an international city, founded by immigrants. Long may it continue. A defensive wall was built here by the Romans around the strategically important port town of Londinium around 200 CE, where men would be oil wrestling naked to 'prove their manliness' and friends would eat grapes off each other's bodies, long before homosexuality became a crime. Fast forward to the eighteenth century when the French-speaking Protestants, loosely referred to as Huguenots, arrived here from religious persecution and civil war on the continent. In the shadows within their many craft-making workshops, queers may have expressed their feelings for each other through weaving a special silk throw or a lace garment for seducing a date, cutting diamonds or polishing watches for a wealthy lover. Then came the wave of Jews during the 1880s as tens of thousands landed here fleeing the pogroms in Russia. By 1900, over 95 per cent of the now world-famous Petticoat Lane market were Jewish immigrants wildly clapping hands and stamping feet after work, perhaps some of them to surreptitiously impress lovers under-cover, beneath the watchful eyes of thousands in Yiddish theatres, cinemas and dancehalls here.

Today, Whitechapel is officially recognised as the 'Banglatown' electoral ward. The LGBTQIA+ community here are chiselling away the homophobic castaways of the British Empire's legacy, in the very place where the persecution began. Prior to 'Section 377', LGBTQIA+ relationships were featured in Asian literature, myths and Hindu temple art.

In fact, long before the British colonial authorities labelled the Hijra as a 'criminal tribe', they were mythological, deeply creative people, disrupting the gender binary that can be found in the Kama Sutra written in the second century, excelling at the 'principles of love' and teaching the world about sexuality, eroticism and emotional fulfilment in life. 'Aravani' আরাবনী, is a trans woman who was assigned male at birth, 'Aruvani' আরুভানি is a trans man assigned female at birth, and 'Jogappas' জোগাপ্পাস are the gender-fluid population, receiving huge social reverence described as a divine possession by the Goddess Yellamma. Today, Hijras are officially recognised as a third gender in the Indian subcontinent, a far cry from the Conservative politicians making laws prescribing conversion therapy for Trans people in Britain. How can these politicians sleep at night? Probably well, because they haven't read the Kama Sutra.

8. *WE ARE DUST AND SHADOWS* – BRICK LANE MOSQUE, 59 BRICK LANE

Look above you at the top of Brick Lane Mosque, up the towering steel minaret to the sundial at the top. The inscription *Umbra Sumus* means 'We are dust and shadows', beaming a calming effect to us below. We are all tiny specks in the grand scheme of everyone's search for belonging walking these streets. Home to three successive religions, this Georgian Grade II listed building was erected in the 1740s by the Huguenots and in 1890 became a Synagogue. Inside there is still a Hebrew prayer plaque on the wall. Now it is home to the Muslim community and the LGBQTIA+ population too from the Muslim LGBT Network, from which the co-ordinator Ejel Khan shares, 'My sexuality is now public, but has never been a problem. All Mosques should be open to all. Local members of our organisation regularly attend Friday prayers there.'

Today's war on the dispossessed includes the xenophobic Hostile Environment policy targeting those with the audacity to enter a country whose own empire was, in many cases, the root cause of why they left their original homes in the first place. Former prime minister Boris Johnson had ramped up the bigoted rhetoric as far back as 1998, describing gay men as 'tank topped bum boys', Black children as 'piccaninnies' with 'watermelon smiles', and said that Muslim women's clothing makes them look like 'bank robbers' and 'letter boxes', egging the police and street thugs to ratchet up their harassment. Alongside the shadowy figure of the 'Muslim Migrant', portrayed as a threat and contributing to nationalist sentiment in the rise of Brexit, another stereotype here is being overturned. Queer Muslims are courageously building a presence here and across town, despite encountering structural racism and heteronormativity everywhere they turn.

9. *DEEDS, NOT WORDS* – TOYNBEE HALL, 28 COMMERCIAL STREET

On 4 October 1936, 300,000 people including local Jews, Irish dockers, trade unionists and communists came together and successfully stopped fascist Oswald Mosley and his Blackshirt henchmen from marching in neighbouring Shadwell, popularly known as the Battle of Cable Street. On this day, the course of British history was changed forever. In an era of rising fascism and antisemitism, former Member of Parliament (MP) Oswald Mosley and his supporters, planned to march through the East End, targeting the Jewish community. Despite public outcry and a petition submitted to parliament to stop the march, the government allowed it to go ahead. Today here at Toynbee Hall, we can benefit from a wide range of educational programmes that celebrate the world-changing anti-fascist battles without which life for queers, women, disabled, the poor, Roma, Muslims and Jews would have been very different. In the shadows of the financial district's skyscrapers, Toynbee Hall opened its doors in 1884, exemplifying working-class solidarity and promoting empowering solutions among the oppressed in a community where today 44 per cent of people in Tower Hamlets still live in poverty. The Conservative Party and their austerity regime are at the root of lethal precarity today, and so the community's centuries-old toolkit in response has never been more necessary.

In 1919 the 'father craft' movement began here, running classes in household and caring skills that encouraged men to be more actively involved in childcare, a rare trailblazing feminist education initiative aimed at men. George Ives, who had met Oscar Wilde at the Authors' Club at 1 Whitehall Place in Central London, took classes here in 1892. By this time Ives had accepted his homosexuality and was working to end the oppression of homosexuals, with what he called the 'Cause'. By 1897 Ives understood that the Cause would not be accepted openly in society and must therefore have a means of underground communication. Thus he created and founded the Order of Chaeronea, a secret society for homosexuals. In his words, 'Equality was a far too limiting agenda. We never wanted equal rights within the social status quo. We saw society as fundamentally unjust, and sought to change it, to end the oppression of queers – and of everyone else.'

At the same time the East London Suffragettes were supporting women's liberation across the UK, that included Black, differently abled, queer and working-class women, escalating their 'long march to freedom' through 'deeds, not words'. Post boxes were booby-trapped with enveloped cloths soaked in kerosene, windows were smashed, bombs planted and brave women handcuffed themselves to railings, went on hunger strikes and threw themselves under the king's horses, all in the name of women's right to vote. At the time, Suffragette Ethel Smyth, smitten with Emmeline Pankhurst, wrote in her diaries in 1892 that she 'conceived an ardent affection' on meeting her, and 'wonder[ed] why it is so much easier for me to love my own sex than yours'. Alongside Toynbee Hall, the former Women's library in the Whitechapel washing houses on Old Castle Street across the road archived this vital queer herstory. They collected imagery and iconography of the Suffrage movement including symbols and signifiers of lesbian existence, culture and intimacy which is now housed at the London School of Economics (LSE). This legacy continues to inspire queer people and women in the neighbourhood today who are still fighting for a voice, as refugee and migrant women go on hunger strikes against illegal detentions, imprisonments and the raids of their homes. You can see a beautiful memorial to Suffragette Sylvia Pankhurst, a profoundly effective activist, socialist and visionary, nearby on the side of the Lord Morpeth pub on Old Ford Road in Bow. This is where Sylvia and other local Suffragettes lived, worked and ran a cost-price kitchen to feed women suffering from the rise in food prices at the beginning of the first world war, survival tactics still needed today.

10. *A POST-CAPITALIST WORLD* – FREEDOM BOOKSHOP, 84B WHITECHAPEL HIGH STREET

Welcome to Freedom Press and the Freedom Bookshop, a hive of radical political literature and activism that can be found at the end of the tiny Angel Alley. Contradictory to the stereotype, anarchy is not disorder. Anarchy is an ecosystem that is arrived at through the philosophy of anarchism. Mutual aid. Without rulers. Living together. Working things out together. Lining the walls outside the bookshop are pictures of Emma Goldman, Karl Marx and other visionaries who marched through these streets telling us to create the world anew. Emma Goldman (1869–1940) campaigned on many causes including anti-war, feminism, freedom in love, birth control and taught that 'the most vital right is the right to love and be loved'. She was ahead of her time, speaking in defence of the rights of homosexuals as the most radical, 'the problem most tabooed in polite society'. After coming back from a fiery speaking tour she stated: 'It is a tragedy, I feel, that people of a different sexual type are caught in a world which shows so little understanding for homosexuals and is so crassly indifferent to the various gradations and variations of gender and their great significance in life.'

Founded in the 1880s, Freedom Press has long distributed essential knowledge to the masses, challenging Franco's coup in Spain and the Blackshirts at the Battle of Cable Street. In this building throughout the 1970s, activists from the Gay Marxist Group would be diligently engaged in group study of Marx's *Capital* – to oppose not merely homophobic oppression, narrowly defined, but exploitation, fascism and economic inequality at large, not least because these injustices always put queers in the line of fire.

Under capitalism, the majority of people, including most LGBTQIA+ people, are living with a measure of insecurity, where our ability to survive economically is always in danger. You know those periods where you never seem to be able to get out of your overdraft, or when you are one step away from having your savings wiped out, being unable to pay your rent or having to use food banks? Capitalism has created the material conditions for this precarious existence. Can we imagine a post-capitalist world where exploitation is the past and queer freedom is the future?

11. *MISS MUFF'S MOLLY HOUSE* – 45 WHITECHAPEL ROAD

What has NatWest bank got to do with queer liberation? Weren't they bailed out during the 'banking crisis' that entrenched austerity throughout Britain resulting in mass youth homelessness, in which LGBTQIA+ people make up a third of young people living vulnerably and on the streets? Yes, but just like at Western Union, where we started at 248 Bethnal Green Road, with a little bit of digging through the corporate trash, here is another queer gem to be found.

On 5 October 1728 at this site, a bit closer towards Old Montague Street, 'nine male ladies' were arrested in full masquerade ball outfits. In eighteenth-century London, Miss Muff's Molly House was one of the most notorious Molly houses, as previously mentioned in Chapter 4. Here men could meet in secret to socialise and have sex, providing people with the opportunity to explore fetishism and transvestism. Jonathan Muff, otherwise known as 'Miss Muff', was the proprietor. He took huge risks, as sex between men was a capital offence. Miss Muff's notoriety finally ended that night, 'charged on Oath with committing the detestable Sin of Sodomy'. The arrested did not submit sheepishly, often putting up a show of resistance when they would be stopped and searched, their faces dabbed to expose make up.

'Molly' or 'moll' was a slang term for a homosexual man, and also for a lower-class woman or a woman selling sex. Men disguised themselves as witches, bawds, nursing maids and shepherdesses, while women dressed as hussars, sailors, cardinals and boys from Mozart's operas. Considering that the population of London was only about 600,000 in the 1720s, having even just a dozen molly houses at that time is a bit like having 200 gay clubs in the 1970s. So, in some ways, our iconic sodomite-ancestors within eighteenth-century molly subculture were as prolific as any modern gay subculture, and their legacy lives on today in the Drag Queens of Bethnal Rouge and the Odbhut performers at Bethnal Green Working Men's Club.

Leave the bank, step out of the underworld of 'wickedness' and cross over to Altab Ali Park.

12. *WE EXIST* – ALTAB ALI PARK, ALDER STREET

On the same site as a fourteenth-century church that gave Whitechapel its name, Altab Ali Park was named in 1998 in memory of a 25-year-old British Bangladeshi clothing worker. Altab Ali was murdered here on 4 May 1978 by three teenage boys as he walked home from work. This was during the time of the racist National Front (NF) terrorising the streets and one of many racist murders in the East End. This catalysed Bengali youth movements into action, building unity across the community showing that they were 'here to stay, here to fight'. Today young Black people are ten times more likely to be routinely pulled up by the police in controversial 'stop and search' programmes for which they don't even have to be suspected of having committed a crime. Black youths are watched in schools to 'expose radicalism', and much of the NF's wider political strategy has become mainstreamed in the Conservative government's agenda. But in this corner of London, there is peace to be found.

Along the path down the centre of the park read the words, 'The shade of my tree is offered to those who come and go fleetingly', a fragment of a poem by Bengali poet Rabindranath Tagore. Every year on the anniversary of Ali's death, thousands descend here to the beating heart of Banglatown to draw a line in the sand against racist hatred and to say loud and clearly 'we exist'.

Around the corner in the Tower of London, resting on a plump purple pillow nestles the Koh-i-Noor diamond, along with the Crown jewels, the star attraction of Britain's colonial wars. The gem represents not just the exoticism of the British Empire in the East, but a prime trophy of British military prowess as the empire set about expanding its territories in India. Diplomatic missions calling for its return are refused, and so on 25 March, Bangladesh Independence Day, the crowds in Altab Ali Park swell. At each one 'The Rainbow Tree' activists gather and branch out into the wider community. Many are not 'out' and so take necessary respite in the shade of the tree but others like Tash and Maz attend, waving rainbow flags on behalf of the 'British Bangladesh LGBTQIA+ community' to say, loudly and proudly, that 'we exist too'.

13. *THE RAINBOW TREE* – EAST LONDON MOSQUE, 82–92 WHITECHAPEL ROAD

Millions of Muslims uprooted from their native homes landed in the capital of the British Empire at the turn of the twentieth century, needing a place to call their own. After a meeting of Muslims and non-Muslims at the Ritz Hotel in 1910, the London Mosque Fund began. Fast forward to its latest incarnation in 1982, and here stands a beautiful white terracotta welcome sign above the door, beneath the giant dome of the largest Mosque in the UK. East London Mosque houses prayer halls as well as classrooms, a fitness centre and a radio station. Personally, as a proud pro-Palestinian Jew, I cherish the conversations with my neighbours here about our tumultuous, humbling and interconnected histories, illustrated by the Hebrew on the old Synagogue around

Credit: Odbhut/The Rainbow Tree

the back just next door. However, not everyone welcomed the opening of the Mosque and the *Adhan* (the call to prayer), broadcast live five times throughout the day. The noise-complainers clearly focused their anger here and forgot about our local dual carriageway a few streets away, blasting traffic noise 24/7, all year round.

Since the Finsbury Park Mosque attack in June 2017, when a white terrorist drove a van into worshippers, there has been a noticeable increase in hate mail and harassment by fascist group Britain First, and extra protection is now installed outside to prevent attacks by vehicles. While wrenching out homophobia in religion will not happen overnight, Tash, Maz and the Rainbow Tree activists are looking to the future. They are intent on developing communication to support the Mosque to tackle racism, discrimination and hatred of all forms while also continuing to provide lifelines for many queers kicked out of their homes. This includes organising anti-fascist demonstrations, meetings and working in local tension monitoring groups such as Rainbow Coalition Against Racism, LGBT+ against Islamophobia and Rainbow Hamlets.

14. *WHO MAKES PROFIT? SOMEBODY KNOWS –* PARFETT STREET

Houses stand empty while homelessness grows
Who makes profit? Somebody knows!

So wrote Bangladeshi families, squatters, artists and the queer activist community in 1973, around the back of the Mosque. It was here in Parfett Street, in these tumbledown back-to-back houses, that some of the queens from Bethnal Rouge minced over from the commune to, including Julian Hows. As he recalls, 'When we got evicted we came here, to one of the few back-to-backs left in the East End'. In giant white letters across the whole estate front they were not holding back, defiantly displaying their anger at a racist, homophobic and capitalist system. Supported by the Brixton-based *Race Today*, they were able to provide safety through housing for Black and Oppressed communities here. Without roots, without queer housing and our other fundamental human needs for shelter, protection, energy, food and water, our communities can never thrive. Led by Bengali women against racist attacks and for secure homes, this has since become London's largest Bangladeshi social housing project.

15. *YOU MESSED WITH THE WRONG FAGGOT –* WHITECHAPEL STATION

My placard reading 'You messed with the wrong faggot' holds pride of place on my bedroom wall. I held it with delight at a local Queer Night Pride march organised alongside the Muslim LGBT+ Network founder Ejel Khan. When they are not busy organising 'Queer, Muslim and Proud' kiss-ins at the seat of top-down power in Parliament Square you can find Tash, Maz and Ejel here at Whitechapel station on their weekly stall encouraging young Muslims to be more open about their sexuality, generating support for LGBTQIA+ worshippers and demanding that all Mosques acknowledge and support them. Ejel explains:

165

I always feared that Muslims and non-Muslims alike would view me negatively for being both Muslim and gay. I thought that no one would understand me. I wish I had come across something like this during my darkest moments as a young gay Muslim. No one deserves to be alone. We will not be driven back into the closet.

Ejel touches my hand today, and cracks a joke: 'The only meat that goes in my mouth is Halal and circumcised!'

WHERE'S THE PUB? THE (NEW) JOINERS ARMS, HACKNEY ROAD

You could go next door to the Blind Beggar pub at the corner of Whitechapel Road and Cambridge Heath Road, where notorious 'bad gay' gangster Ronnie Kray, when not stashing diamonds under local floorboards, murdered one of his victims. Instead let's go to the newest gem of the East End. The 'Friends of the Joiners Arms' successfully campaigned to save this pub, my favourite late-licence, radical, debaucherous queer pub on Hackney Road. Targeted for luxury flat developments, the campaign set a precedent that a building cannot be demolished if it is of importance to the queer community. That our cities are not simply for corporate greed and should be shaped by people, not just profit. Let's raise a glass to The Rainbow Tree and our beautiful queer community here with us and those gone too soon. Through huge public support, a venue in the Joiners Arms' honour will soon become London's first community-run, late-licence LGBTQIA+ pub, coming to a railway arch in the neighbourhood soon! As the landlord David Pollard used to say, 'As soon as this pub closes, the revolution starts!'

These are our spaces, our freedoms, our diamonds. Enjoy them.

6

You Think the Dead We Loved Ever Truly Leave Us?

King's Cross

Everything in life only happens a short distance from King's Cross.

—Arthur Machen

Humans are protected by our ability to love – so teaches the wisdom of Harry Potter. Here you are about to be inspired by the powers of the queer spirit, which stretch far beyond platform 9¾ here at King's Cross station.

Have you ever wondered how powerful the magic of the queer community really is? Have you ever wanted to know how to learn from the dead to fight for the living? Keen to work out how bigotry, transphobia, homophobia and all evils can be banished forever more? Welcome to sweaty all-night raves, pumping tunes and powerful queer activism that all tell a very different story to the shiny King's Cross we know today. Ready 1 … 2 … 3 … abracadabra … here we go!

START: KING'S CROSS STATION

1. Mary Trashton – *King's Cross Conservative Club, 26 Argyle Square*

1. *MARY TRASHTON – KING'S CROSS CONSERVATIVE CLUB*, 26 ARGYLE SQUARE

'Bona to vada your dolly old eke', Mark Ashton (or actually 'Mary Trashton') purrs at you in a blonde beehive wig and full drag behind the Conservative Club bar, surrounded by homophobic men staring into the bottom of their empty pints. This means 'nice to see your pretty old face' in Polari, the gay subcultural language. Polari is a 'patchwork language' made up by stealing the best bits of other languages, cultures or dialects and then sewing all these bits together. One of many treasures in the fiery queer hearth of our alchemically powerful community here in King's Cross.

It's 1984, and across Britain people are taking to the streets and grannies are throwing brick-sized sponges every time prime minister Margaret Thatcher comes on the TV. She's telling the nation that 'there is no such thing as society', but you wouldn't know it by looking at Mark Ashton and Mike Jackson and their friends and comrades in Lesbians and Gays Support the Miners (LGSM). Rosy-cheeked and with a twinkle in their eyes, Mike and Mark are laughing while planning their outfits for when they will hit the town after the end of Mary's shift serving pints to bitter old Conservatives. They have no aspirations to work in the city and drive flashy cars, they didn't want anything to do with the glossy, shiny life that was being sold to them by the establishment. They knew they were under siege – and Polari, camp, gallows humour and vulnerability were all magical and queer ways to exist in response. Laughter, debauchery and activism were the best medicines when actual medical treatments didn't yet exist for their friends beginning to fall ill around them with fevers and rashes, caused by a disease that was not yet known. And the clock was ticking.

It's May Day, the first of May, the celebration of workers' struggles, and a few doors down the red flag is flying high from St Pancras Town Hall. Mike and Mark are raising a glass. Finally, they are in their element and they can put their teenage years of silence behind them. Mike had recently moved down from the north where he was the only gay in his village – and Mark, growing up against the backdrop of the Troubles and Ian Paisley's 'Save Ulster from Sodomy' campaign in Northern Ireland, dreamt of a new life too. Though a branch of the Sexual Liberation Movement was set up in his hometown of Coleraine and Ireland's first conference on sexual freedom had taken place there too, like many other queers Mark decided to move to London. King's Cross became Mike and Mark's stomping ground, just a few stops up on the Northern Line from where a giant 'Vote Labour' sign hung proudly from Mark's flat in the monumental Heygate Estate, Elephant and Castle. As a militant trade unionist and a Marxist, Mark had been blazing a trail in the Communist Party's Youth Movement challenging its inadequate response to centring anti-racism and women's and gay liberation, at the heart of working-class struggles. They saw the struggle of the miners as the same one faced by gay people fighting for their rights, against a government that would not listen. Their guts roared with hunger to catalyse movements that might create the world anew.

Looking back, the heavy atmosphere of Conservative Britain in the 1980s still looms over Mike. As a key activist with LGSM, he built unexpected and vital systems of solidarity with striking miners that have been immortalised in the film *Pride*:

> I still have tears of joy, anger and of course loss. Right at the beginning of the film, when Mark is watching the news and a lorry driver says 'All we've got left is our pride and she'll not be having that', will never leave my heart, but thankfully a strong sense of cultural and community identity began to form, with wit as our weapon of survival, and we weren't afraid to put up a fight.

This is a trait that became potent alchemy throughout their lives. Together they resolved to back the miners with financial support, 'but we agreed "let's do it as lesbians and gays"'.

People's movements against dire inequality were occupying buildings left, right and centre, participants in an impassioned tradition of radicalism and communism. A resurgence of working-class organising was in the air. With steely grit, they continued the struggles that are the cornerstone of our freedoms in London today – from campaigns to end child labour, to defending the right to unionise, and for us all to enjoy the weekend.

By the early 1980s, the Elizabeth Garrett Anderson Hospital, the main hospital in the area, had been occupied by hundreds of people to prevent its closure. Camden Town Hall had been squatted to protest against poor housing, and the Holy Cross Church, just around the corner from Argyle Square, London's premier red-light area, was occupied by hundreds of screaming angry sex workers in protest against police harassment. TV presenter Debby Lee remembers inner city London's mean streets: 'it was a bit like the Wild West because King's Cross was desolate and very dodgy in terms of street crime, prostitution and drug dealing. It was very low-rent, especially in the early years, but for a lot of people the location added to the whole adventure of the night, it was quite daring in a way.'

2. *REVENGE OF THE TEENAGE PERVERTS* – THE BELL, 259 PENTONVILLE ROAD

Imagine punk, new wave and indie rock music fans kicking mischievously about these streets. These tastes were on the musical menu here at Mark and Mike's favourite stomping ground. The Bell was a gay activist pub on Pentonville Road, a centre point for queers wanting to take part in the uprising against Thatcher and

173

the fascist National Front's Britain. The Bell serviced 'the freaks, one of whom was me', chuckles Mike, who often, once the pub doors closed, got up to all kinds of hanky-panky in the nearby Scala cinema and club, with its saucy B-movie all-nighters, later renowned for its polysexual indie night Popstarz. Sometimes on a Saturday night after chuck-out, the Bell crowds continued on a mass walk to the megaclub Trade at Turnmills, in neighbouring Clerkenwell, on a particular route which was affectionately known by the punters as the 'fairy run'. Bell regular and Mark's mate Ashtar Alkhirsan smiles as she tells me:

> I remember the walk to Trade in the dark because it was such a spirited moment with everyone together. Lots of squealing and yelling and I can still see friends, who like so many aren't here anymore, swishing along the streets in their drainpipes and leather jackets.

Lining the walls and stomping on the dancefloor were all manner of revellers from elaborately-quiffed rockabillies to plumed punks, black swathed goths to shorn skinheads, many of them students and unemployed. Bronski Beat's first single in 1984, 'Smalltown Boy' was a massive hit and became a key song of the generation, often played loudly here at the Bell. 'It was alternative, the music was really good! The cabaret, comedy and performances sent a message to the fascists that they are not welcome here. You could dress as you'd like, it was a breath of fresh air' as Ian Johns, another Bell regular, fondly recalls.

One memorable night, the pub landlords charged in swinging a toilet seat around their heads. Some of the positively glowing dykes inside the Bell burst into fits of laughter after giving the bathroom a makeover while making out in there. Mike was probably at the door. He loved being the 'door whore' as it 'was a perfect place for cruising'. One night, however, he was queer-bashed when leaving there. 'Are you fucking queer?', three tall skinheads shouted at him. 'Yes, I am!' Mike shouted back, before he was punched and fell to the ground. His lover took him, with his bleeding nose, back inside the Bell, where the owners came down and said 'it's your own fault for saying you were queer'. The lesbian bouncers pounced and ran out into the night air, chasing the fascists down the street.

Mark Ashton and Mike Jackson helped organise the founding solidarity meetings for the miners' strike here where the alliance between the LGSM and the strikers in South Wales grew. This became a turning point for gay rights by fostering ties with the trade unions. Mike recalls, 'Many of us who became involved in LGSM had grown fed up of having to compromise our sexuality for the sake of comradeship with people'. The Bell community had raised £1500 for LGSM by December 1984, a huge amount given that they were mostly students and unemployed.

One month later, Mark and Mike and their friends gathered at Gay's the Word bookshop around the corner in Marchmont Street and asked 'Whose got a motor? We need two vans, we are going to support our friends, the miners, in person next month in Wales.' Soon after, two Hackney community minibuses, along-side Mike's straight friend Tim's clapped-out Volkswagen camper van, came to the rescue. 'As we were preparing for our trip, Mark wrote the words of the first verse of "Solidarity Forever" on the back of the LGSM banner so it became our anthem', Mike recollects, smiling. *Pride* (the movie) opens with Pete Seeger singing it. Mike recalls:

I'll always remember when we arrived on our first visit when 27 of us walked into the Onllwyn Miners' Welfare Hall in October 1984. We were young, conspicuous and feisty. As we walked in the room everyone went quiet and for a second, it was a tense moment. Then someone started clapping and within seconds everyone in the room applauded our arrival. It was the proudest moment of my life. That's comradeship and it is mighty powerful.

It wouldn't be long before Mark and Mike helped pack out Camden's famous Electric Ballroom up the road for the 'Pits and Perverts' benefit concert in 1984, featuring Bronski Beat, supported by the Neath Dulais and Swansea Valley Miners mining communities that raised around £20,000 during the strike. They partied together, they fought together, because as Mark said, 'It's not enough to always be defending. Sometimes you have to attack to push forward and that is exactly what we are going to do'.

Seismic changes were going on elsewhere too. He didn't know it yet but as the punks, ravers, goths and activists took to the streets, Mark was already HIV positive and maybe had been for a while. As for thousands of others, the fevers were becoming more noticeable.

3. *NEVER GOING UNDERGROUND* – KING'S CROSS STATION

'Do not pity the dead, Harry. Pity the living, and, above all, those who live without love', Dumbledore declares in *Harry Potter and the Deathly Hallows*. Upon waking up here at King's Cross station, Harry's heart is still at Hogwarts, searching for a life beyond bullying and in desperate need for acceptance.

However, the mystical powers of King's Cross run far deeper than Harry Potter's racing heart here on platform 9¾.

King's Cross was renamed from Battle Bridge in the 1830s, when it was a huge dust heap at the end of what is now Gray's Inn Road. At that time, it included a smallpox hospital, mounds of horse bones, and dilapidated cheap housing for the working classes who laboured on the canal, the railways, and the factories and warehouses that grew up around them. 'Bridge' as the now-underground River Fleet runs through the area and was crossed here. 'Battle' because the location was traditionally connected with the climactic combat in which Queen Boudicca was thwarted. Boudicca was a fearless freedom fighter who led a campaign against the occupying Roman forces, culminating in the total destruction of London, then called Londinium, in around 60 CE. She was one fierce queen indeed. Legend has it that Boudicca's final resting place is beneath either platform 9 or platform 10 at King's Cross station.

'Professor, is this all real or is it just happening inside my head?' Harry cries out to Dumbledore, who leaves the platform, turns back to Harry and says 'Of course it's happening inside your head, why should that mean that it's not real?', and minces off in a puff of smoke. They both knew that they were connected by something other than fate, but you don't have time to wait, as there is a train to catch.

It's 20 February 1988 and you can't feel the biting cold because 5000 people are blasting into the station. In studded leather jackets, tight jeans and multicoloured hair, the crowds are chanting 'Lesbians and Gay Men – Out and Proud' and 'We are Never Going Underground!' from a march that began at Embankment Station. Suddenly you feel something at your ankle. Looking down there's a cute black greyhound dog, wearing a sticky pink triangle on her back. 'Pandora's a big activist too, she's already been on five "Stop Clause 28" demos', Atalanta says, while Pandora's tail wags excitedly: 'It's a really big day for us all, having our own special train helps. I think it definitely is, you know, significant,' Atalanta Kernick, from an ass-kicking lesbian Dyke punk crew, smiles up at you.

In ten hours' time, after 20,500 people have taken over the streets of Manchester at the Stop Clause 28/Never Going Underground/Gay Rights Rally, legendary actor Sir Ian McKellen steps up to the podium in Manchester Free Trade Hall:

I am here because I am one of millions of normal homosexuals who are affected by this new law. Clause 28 is in parts designed to keep us in our place, but it didn't work with me, because I, like you, I am now out and about in the streets in Manchester. We must be out in the media, we must be out and about in pubs, clubs and in the classroom talking about homo-sexuality, encouraging our friends and families to think about homosexuality and in fact in that sense promoting homosexu-ality until the whole country realises as we do that this new law, this Clause 28 is itself, to coin a phrase, an unnatural act and should be made illegal.

The listeners erupt into rapturous applause, and the dream for acceptance unravels, like Harry Potter's, in their heads and on the streets. Faced with extraordinary oppression, the crowds rise to the challenge. They didn't know what they were capable of, but knew, like Harry, that they had to harvest their reserves of bravery and try with all their might.

Mike was in the demonstration crowds that day and looks back today grinning:

The crowd went especially wild for the actress Sue Johnston who played Sheila in the soap *Brookside*, a shero and an icon because of her suffering mother/housewife character with values, compassion and decency. The soap was based in Liver-pool and had a big gay following. Sue Johnston couldn't speak for a few minutes due to the crowd adoringly chanting 'Sheila! Sheila! Sheila!' It was High Camp. That demo was the first demo for the LGBT+ community I'd been to where I felt there were significant numbers of non-LGBT+ allies there too and in that respect I think it was a turning point. The LGBT+ com-munity had been enduring the firestorm of AIDS for several years and now the government were assaulting us with Clause 28 and I think the two things just swayed many heterosexuals to thinking that LGBT+ people were part of society, they were including and embracing us. In Manchester they stood side-by-side with us.

As the AIDS pandemic erupted, paving the way for Section 28, the papers left on the bar tabletops at the Conservative Club had headlines that included 'No one is safe from AIDS', with the final word, printed much larger than the rest, measuring a full four inches high in *Life* magazine featured in 1985. Or the *Sun* newspaper's 'Britain threatened by gay virus plague' that was 'Spreading like wildfire', encouraging 'Pub ban on gays in AIDS panic' and continued a racist agenda that the disease originated in Africa. But times were changing fast.

Among the drag queens, disco boys and rebellious dykes in the applauding crowd was Michael Cashman from iconic London soap *EastEnders*, stepping up to the stage. At the time Michael was playing a ground-breaking gay character. He recently shared:

I clearly remember reading about section 28 in January 1988 in the weekly paper *Capital Gay*. June Brown, who played Dot Cotton, helped me get the time off rehearsals. When I told her where I was going, she said: 'OK, Mike, but don't get arrested, dear'.

The tension, excitement and squeals, arising from thousands of valiant people collectively ready to confront this politically opportunistic and deadly policy, helped calm Michael's nerves. 'Section 28 had been brought in on the back of the stigmatisation and discrimination suffered by gay men; in particular those dealing with HIV and AIDS. Some people were facing the most appalling deaths, and this was designed to kick us firmly underground. When I got to the 20,000-strong march, people pushed me towards the front and I've never been so proud.' The electrifying energy at the demonstration continued throughout the evening, with Tom Robinson singing 'Glad to be Gay', Jimmy Somerville doing a rendition of the Communards' 'There's Nothing Holding Me Back' and music from acapella group the Hot Doris Band bolstering the crowds all across Manchester's Albert Square, with the chants of 'Never Going Underground!' reverberating off the stone walls into the night. The effects in Manchester as a 'gay capital' were felt for a long time after.

The Communards performed, inspiring the masses, and it was Mark Ashton who inspired them, as band member Richard Coles recounts:

It was Mark who was responsible for us being called the Communards. He took me and Jimmy to see the wall against which the original Communards — members of the Paris Commune — were executed in 1871 in Père Lachaise cemetery and so we named ourselves after them.

The demo had a snowball effect and Michael was resolute, which was vital because the next day Parliament enforced Section 28. This catalysed one of the deadliest pieces of legislation in modern history that seeped homophobic cruelty into the atmosphere of the time, compounding and encouraging societal bigotry and giving it government sanction. Ian McKellen, Michael Cashman, campaigner Lisa Power and others formed the LGBT rights organisation Stonewall to lobby against Section 28. Lisa Power reflects today, 'Looking back, if we had won the battle of section 28, Stonewall would probably never have been founded. I don't think we would have progressed to equality as far as we have now.'

Pumped up and landing back at King's Cross station, you know that the battleground of good versus evil is under way, but where to begin? No matter how much the King's Cross vicinity tries to clean up its act, the visitors arriving on the station platform at Eurostar can still disappear in a pride-fuelled puff of smoke to immerse themselves in Dumbledore's quest to find that 'where your treasure is there will your heart be also'. Formerly derelict and wild, King's Cross was literally dark, as there wasn't much street lighting, promoting sexually charged, sometimes liberating behaviours. Beginning around 1996, the dramatic regeneration of King's Cross covers up a new muggle-crushing culture of secrecy and control where cultural werewolves watch your every move. When the new order began, the powers that be even considered completely removing the name King's Cross from this place so that people would not be reminded of the battlegrounds it held before. Coal Drops Yard, which once held 15,000 tons of coal for a fuel-hungry city, is now home to cool, bright, shiny and pricy retail stores. Here you can now find every option under the sun of avocado toast with a choice of sourdough, grain, or gluten free bread, but protesting, taking photos or even looking too scruffy can get you arrested.

Looking around the area at the end of the 1980s it seems like the vaults containing the treasures of life may have been shut just when they were needed most because so many people were beginning to get sick. Mark seemed tired now too. Scratching your head, Dumbledore's words come back to you: 'we are only as strong as we are united, as weak as we are divided'. The lessons of building love in community exist here in abundance, in these incredible movements formed in times of unrest. Eat that for your bigoted breakfast, J.K. Rowling.

4. *IN THIS OUR LIVES* – SOMERSTOWN COMMUNITY CENTRE, 150 OSSULSTON STREET

'I worked with a lot of gay men who had HIV. I witnessed a lot of pain, suffering and death.' In his twenties, Dennis L. Carney became a founding member of a housing association specifically set up for people with HIV. In the early 1980s Black gay men were disproportionally affected by HIV as it was even harder for them to seek medical help due to lack of specific services and because the stigma against them was so palpable. So it was here that the first Black Gay Men's Conference was held on 31 October 1987. Black men from across London, as well as Manchester, Leeds, Leicester and Bristol, landed here at this building to attend 'In This Our Lives', a conference that provided space for empowerment. Participants considered a range of issues including Black lesbian and gay history, fears and prejudice within the Black community, spirituality, bisexuality and a range of health concerns.

Being so open and explicit was a radical move for that time, but for organisers it was about being visible in the general community as well as to each other. Dennis explains:

Putting adverts in the Black press was a first. We were determined to get published. At the centre I didn't think we would
even get ten people. By the third meeting, we had over 50 guys
turn up and this was before the internet!

More than just articulating negative experiences, it gave them a
space for shaping their sexual, racial and political identities:

Coming along was a real eye opener for me. It was a real step
forward and it was very reassuring that not only could we
actually lead the way as far as general civil rights were concerned but we could actually take an initiative ourselves as
Black gay men ... that was a real step forward.

When this series of workshops ended, the men in attendance
wanted more spaces to be created. 'That is how Let's Rap was
formed. Let's Rap was the first official Black gay men's discussion group in the country.'

Like many projects, 'In This Our Lives' was catalysed by the
first London Black Lesbian and Gay Centre (BLGC), established
in Peckham in 1985. 'There was a huge amount of internation-
alism and even Pan-Africanism among the Black LGBTQ+
community', Dennis reflects. 'Through the BLGC, we were
involved in organising the International People of Colour Conference in the 80s. It used to be held every other year in a different
country around the world', he adds, and the rest of the world
also came to them. 'I'll never forget the afterparty of the conference. It was fantastic. I would say that it was a watershed moment
for the Black LGBT community. LGBT people from all over the
world – It was like, "Wow!".'

5. *MAKING BLACK WAVES* – CAMDEN LESBIAN
CENTRE, 54–56 PHOENIX ROAD

The teachings of wizardry fomented at 'In This Our Lives' pro-
liferated in parallel around the corner at 54–56 Phoenix Road,
home to the Camden Lesbian Centre and Black Lesbian Group,
the Borough of Camden being the home that King's Cross exists
within. The grand opening on Saturday 31 October 1987 was
'fun for all the pretended family', in defiance of Section 28 antag-
onistic statements that viewed homosexuality as a pretended
family relationship.

The centre hosted many groups including the lesbian disability group GEMMA and Zamimass, a significant Black lesbian
organisation that promoted a Black lesbian and gay section on
the Pride march. Batik classes and lesbian herstory workshops
weaved strength and insight through the community and trips to
the seaside re-charged their spirits to come home and campaign
against Section 28 and continue providing their multifaceted
services for all lesbians.

Alongside the movements were club nights and the group
'envisioned a world where all women, trans included, were free
from evil', because 'none of us are free until we all are', as activist
and DJ Yvonne Taylor reflects, smiling:

We invited all types of women. Whether you were a style
queen or if you wanted to wear mini-skirts or whatever. We
had a representation of all types of lesbians. There were Asian
women there, punks there, feminists there, where elders found

community from chic lesbian parties and international confer-
ences, to HIV safehouses.

They handed out flyers across the city with large lettering stating
'Black Lesbian Struggle is Black, Black Lesbian Struggle is
Lesbian, Black Lesbian Struggle is Working Class, Black Lesbian
Struggle is Women, Black Lesbian Struggle is International. The
experiences that join us are thicker than the water that divides us',
with an illustration of two Black women reaching for one another
across an expanse of water, across from one corner of the earth
to another.

At the time, London was fast-cementing its place as Britain's
most multicultural city, and with that label came backlash from
some who felt displaced, and the centre responded by creating
a distinctive Black lesbian group for diverse women who, in
addition to facing sexual discrimination, also had to overcome the
difficulties brought on by racial and ethnic difference. The centre
soon started generating wide local support: from other squatters
including Bengali families creating housing and protection from
racist attacks, from community groups and from local business
people. As a teen, Veronica McKenzie found herself active in the
weekly sessions and taking minutes for the many meetings:

A big factor in community organising back then was a focus on
raising the collective consciousness around important issues.
People used to run sessions where we would sit and read
important texts to learn more about these topics.

Sitting in circles on the floor, long into the night, the group shared
experiences and offered support with housing, welfare, family

affairs, to self-defence classes over coffee evenings and through poetry workshops. Together they read books like *Zami* by Audre Lorde and *Making Black Waves*, the UK's first Black lesbian anthology, strengthening their resolve to create their own space and carve out their own position in society. Despite the multiple layers of discrimination they celebrated and platformed the term 'Black lesbian' as profoundly intersectional, as being connected to every struggle faced by Black women and not ranking oppressions by importance, and they soon became point of contact for Black lesbians from across the world. The physical centre closed in the 1990s due to funding troubles but the magic continues up the road at the Crossroads Women's Centre in Kentish Town. Crossroads continues to be a community space for a diverse range of women's groups, including the English Collective of Prostitutes and Women Against Rape, Legal Action for Women, Single Mothers' Self-Defence, and disability campaign group WinVisible, co-founded by the trailblazing author and organiser Selma James.

6. *THE FAMOUS FIVE* – BAGLEY'S, GRANARY SQUARE

Movement is vital for healing broken hearts. Today this area is home to the world-famous Central Saint Martins art college and the exciting Queer Britain museum. But in a previous life this was Bagley's territory, with its 3000+ capacity pleasuredome, where at the height of London's 1990s electronic music and nightlife explosion, the political landscape, raves and community activism all fed into each other and connected to put polyfilla in a cracking system premised upon divide and rule. Dyke and activist Atalanta

Kernick remembers, 'I mean, how many more did we have to lose? In the day, we would demonstrate against the unequal age of consent and Section 28 outside the Houses of Parliament.' Ian Johns from the Bell adds, 'We would then spend the rest of the weekend, thousands of us, dancing between the "Famous Five" raves in King's Cross.'

The train tracks, running across the pavements of the Goods Yard complex, dating back to 1852, tell a different story of Battle Bridge Road, a street of run-down tenement blocks and railways stock dropping tonnes of coal directly into horse-drawn carts in the arches below. But here in the summer of 1988 a new world was in motion. Rave culture was on the rise with giant warehouses full of happy, sweaty people dancing to acid house until the morning.

Put on my favourite teenage tune 'Let Me Be Your Fantasy' and join me here with Mike letting loose on the dancefloor. Bagley's was an inexhaustible source of magic, hosting some of the 'Famous Five' raves: Love Muscle, G-A-Y, Sherbet, Fruit Machine and Fist. Bagley's was part of a golden triangle of clubbing in N1 and set forth 'Summer Rites', the open-air LGBT Festival that took place here between 1991 and 2007. The area became a unifying hub where clubbers would gather after the West End had closed for the night, no matter what music or scene they were usually into. The music was acid house; the drug was ecstasy.

'The queue to get in is enormous but you can hear this bassline, it's throbbing and it's like the walls are shaking', Natalie Wade says in the *Kings X Clubland* documentary:

You get in and there's this enormous room in front of you, it's so loud and it's heaving with bodies and light and movement.

For a moment you feel like you've walked into a cult, as everyone understands what's going on but you ... It's one of the most memorable sensory experiences I've ever had in my life.

1980s nightlife was amplified by renegade promoters like Dirtbox and The Lift kickstarting London's warehouse party scene, and for them even the dilapidated buildings behind King's Cross station suddenly had potential. By the time Bagley's closed, on New Year's Eve 2008, the superbly talented photographer Dave Swindells remembers, it had played host to 25 years of naughty-but-nice nightlife – illegal warehouse parties, gay superclubs, full-on fetish nights, roller discos, cutting-edge fashion shows, underground techno, UK Garage raves, and secret bashes for the likes of Prince, Depeche Mode and the Rolling Stones. In the surrounding abandoned warehouses, artists went wild. Meanwhile, the most radical performance art collective in Britain were squatting a disused coach station off the Battle Bridge Road. Joe Rush and the Mutoid Waste Company were busy creating a trippy, post-apocalyptic 'adventure playground for adults' with massive mutant metal sculptures that were inspired by punk, anti-Thatcher rebellion, Mad Max and Judge Dredd ... Their parties rocked to post-punk, dub reggae and psychedelia until acid house came along and 'blew everything wide open' – the kind of party I scrambled over walls to get into the summer of '88.

The revelry carried on all the way to the morning tubes, parties convening in the last carriage, continuing as they travelled throughout London.

Among the lights and the raves an essential collective healing process was taking place. Ian Johns continues:

We would work twelve hours on the phone lines at Switch-board, answering hundreds of calls from people scared shitless about AIDS in the face of government inaction and a public culture of silence. When we finally put the phones down for the night, we would get our glad rags on and head out to the 'Famous Five' raves and could go around from warehouse to warehouse with maybe 1000 people or more in each one. It was absolutely fantastic. My mind's there somewhere in the bottom of the pit underneath a new block of flats.

A community facing death, they were building a community full of loving kindness and shaping their own futures, at a time when they didn't know if they would survive.

7. *MORNING GLORY* – CENTRAL STATION, 37 WHARFDALE ROAD

After leaving the thumping sounds of Bagley's, and maybe a cruise down the canal as the sun rises, you could make your way to the perfect place for a post rave 'morning glory' pint. The Central Station, established in 1992 continues to be a heartbeat for the LGBTQIA+ community. When it began it hosted a weekly club night called a 'Glory Hole' with the opening of its dark room in 1993. Glory holes are holes usually in toilet walls for people to enjoy anonymous oral sex. I love the pride in celebrating holes in toilet walls as a resourceful oral sex method, which have probably existed for a great deal of joyful time.

However, the joys of public displays of queer affection came at a cost. Just two days after opening Central Station, as an explicitly

LGBTQIA+ venue, National Front skinheads who had previously frequented the pub as the former Prince Albert smashed windows and threw CS gas canisters in and tried to attack people. 'The whole time though I thought, this is the end, this is it. People are going to just fear the place', co-owner Duncan Irvine remembers, nerves shaking.

These fascists denied themselves their own magic by attacking queer love, the ultimate source of humanity and crept around here in the middle of the night. During the 1980s and 1990s racist movements like the National Front were emboldened by a nation trying to cling onto the lost glory of the British Empire that was in decline. Without spaces to explore the patterns in society which create good and evil, it's easy to step into the shoes of the oppressor. Even some gay people were prevalent in racist groups that were flourishing across London and one night a group of gay skinheads turned up here and began making Nazi salutes. Nicky Crane was at that time a good-looking, swastika-tattooed six-foot-two poster child for the movement, and was built like a brick shithouse. He described himself as 'Britain's hardest skinhead,' and to call yourself that you have to really be Britain's hardest skinhead. Crane was a leader of Combat 18, a fascist group, the numerals converting to AH for Adolf Hitler. He led skinhead gangs marching in military formation down high streets, clutching iron bars, knives, staves, pickaxe handles and clubs.

It wasn't so easy to unpick the different armies in London's cultural battleground. Since the 1960's, skinheads had borrowed the fashion of Caribbean immigrants and shared their love of ska and reggae music. Confusingly, gay men then often resembled fascist skinheads. In an era when all gay men were widely assumed to be camp and effeminate, the look was a hyper-masculine cloak that 'you were less likely to get picked on if you looked like a queer-basher', recounts Murray Healy, author of *Gay Skins: Class, Masculinity and Queer Appropriation*.

However, the sense of community within Central Station was strong, and performers like music-hall-inspired pantomime dame 'Dockyard Doris', well known for her impression of the Queen Mother, helped them all pull through. Over the years Central Station has been a hub of community life. 'Honestly, half the people who come in here seem to say, "I'm sure I used to go clubbing around here"', reflects Duncan. The venue has raised tens of thousands of pounds for HIV charities through Pink Angels fundraisers, and has provided foundational support for Stonewall FC, the first LGBTQIA+ football club, King's Cross Steelers and Grace's CC, the world's first LGBTQIA+ rugby and cricket clubs. Back when it was still the Prince Albert, it also supported a number of key LGBTQIA+ campaigns to organise, including to continue the Lesbian and Gays Support the Miners (LGSM) mission, organising for unconditional support for the miners.

After the jam-packed 60-strong LGSM meetings, there was fun to be had. Mike smiles and remembers a friend, another activist called Mark:

When coming up on eccies [ecstasy] Mark used to tear down the stairs to the dance floor. Once he was wearing a kilt and Mark's cock ring fell off due to pilly-willy [when you can't get an erection] and I heard the whole pub turn around and roar with laughter as they saw it rolling around the floor.

As regulars continued to fall sick and die, the community's focus shifted to those sick and dying from AIDs-related illnesses. It was an emotional space, for support, grief and hosting funerals too. 'I think that was the moment I thought 'wow, this is a real community we have here', reflects Noble.

How many more queer treasures did we have to lose?

8. *YOU ARE ENOUGH* – LONDON FRIEND, 86 CALEDONIAN ROAD

Have you ever found yourself in the pouring rain or the morning sunshine, sitting on the side of a road or canal that runs through the meandering buildings like here in King's Cross, alone and upset? The magical alchemical potency that runs through the veins of Dumbledore's queer army are strong. The life-affirming energy felt from queer pubs, clubs, communes, community centres and raves are powerful too. However, sometimes they just ain't enough. But remember one thing: 'you are enough'.

Step away from the bright disco lights, seismic cultural changes and tense political moments, and take a moment to look in the mirror and ask, amongst it all, 'am I OK?' Listen to the lyrics of Alan Wakeman's 'Everyone Involved – A Gay Song', the first recording by a British act to explicitly address the LGBTQ+ community in a positive way in 1972:

Listen to me sister, and every brother too
This song contains a message and it might apply to you
There is a little bit of gay in everyone today
So why not let it out? That's what we say

Gay is natural, gay is good, gay is wonderful
Gay people should all come together and fight for our rights
Listen to me people, no matter what you do
The thing that really counts in life is
To yourself be true.

'Everyone Involved' became a soundtrack to Gay Pride in Britain that began in Trafalgar Square the same year, and to the work of the London Friend organisation too.

London Friend was founded in Islington's Upper Street in the same year that song was recorded. Pioneered by gems in our community, for over 50 years London Friend has provided a counselling service helping people to navigate London and find footing and control over our lives in a wise, friendly and completely non-judgemental way. It is the UK's oldest lesbian, gay, bisexual and trans charity, established in 1972. It started up as an offshoot of the Campaign for Homosexual Equality (CHE), the first British gay activist group. Since then, London Friend continues to deliver support through helplines, counselling sessions, social meetings, a specialist service Antidote offering support around drugs and alcohol use for LGBTQIA+ people and much more.

Often we feel our magical powers as queers losing their shine, and that's understandable and ok. It is here that we can pull out our inner treasure chest, take out the feather duster and polish, and learn how to renew ourselves.

9. *MY PROUDEST MOMENT* – SWITCHBOARD, 5 CALEDONIAN ROAD

'Welcome to Switchboard, Mike, let me show you the ropes.' Mark Ashton, wearing pink socks, open-toe sandals and high cut-off denims smiled at Mike as he interviewed him to be a volunteer at 'Gay Switchboard' in April 1983, where their friendship began.

Gay Switchboard is now Switchboard LGBT+ Helpline and based around the corner at Penton Street. But 5 Caledonian Road is where the organisation's life initially flourished, now the UK's largest LGBTQIA+ helpline, as Mike shares:

> We connected and giggled straight away and that was the start of our friendship. But we were beginning to see a world in rapid transition. The phones would ring all night from people in need of validation, help and also to find out what 'ents' (entertainment) was going on. Stories were just so phenomenal. For the volunteers the help went both ways and while they were supporting others they were getting nurtured too.

Beginning life in a packed basement underneath Housmans Bookshop, Switchboard answered their very first phone call in March 1974. The volunteers out a small advert in the fortnightly Gay News newspaper, for the brand-new LGBTQ information and support helpline expecting about six or seven calls on their first day. By 1975, Switchboard was open 24 hours a day, seven days a week and running an accommodation service for finding gay-friendly house-shares. Callers requested advice on practically everything: from legal rights to events to meet others around town.

Callers, lonely and isolated, were greeted by other gay people sometimes with 'sweetie' or 'darling' soothing their souls. Nick Partridge, a volunteer, recalls:

I remember calls that were silent to begin with, and you'd stay on the line and say 'I'm still here'. The release when people began to talk – it would maybe be the first time that somebody had spoken to anyone else about the struggles they were having with their sexuality. Almost immediately, they felt so much better.

The titans answering the phones were cultivating love not just for the callers but all across London, providing a roadmap out of the centuries old intertwined homophobic and healthcare crises. Dudley Cave was a former prisoner of war, who was forced to help build the bridge over the River Kwai and who laid out the pink triangle wreath at the Cenotaph to remember queer victims of war. Julian Hows blazed a trail as one of the first GLF activists, starting Gay Pride in 1972, and Boo Armstrong, possibly the youngest volunteer, started the Camden women's health centre around the corner. Some Switchboard volunteers have been there since they were teenagers, and are still engaged now in their 60s and 70s.

Switchboard's volunteers have responded in the past to people angry about Section 28 and devastated after the Admiral Duncan nail bombing in Soho in 1999, and today take calls from more and more trans folks struggling to deal with ignorance from doctors and the transphobic system, coming up against barrier after barrier. Regular questions included 'Where can I meet other lesbians?', 'If I am out at a protest, how do I deal with arrest?', or questions whispered from a phone box in the corner of a club by men who'd forgotten the 'Handkerchief Code', a colour-coded system used to indicate preferred sexual fetishes, and wanted to identify the preference of whoever they had just picked up. Today, in partnership with GALOP, who work to support those affected by LGBTQIA+ hate crime, Switchboard advises activists on their legal rights including to 'NOT answer any police questions and NOT make or sign any written statements' as they continue building movements for queer power on the streets. The helpline still attracts a number of dreaded 'wank calls' (callers arousing themselves when ringing the hotline) – and volunteers have tried and tested responses to these. 'With a wank call, you absolutely bring out the long Latin words, the unsexy biological terms, and they just hang up', Switchboard's co-chair Tash Walker recalls giggling. Genius.

Steven Power remembers ringing Switchboard:

I was a working-class lad from a Dagenham council estate whose needs were glossed over in sex education classes as a passing phase, isolated and confused. I plucked up the courage to call Switchboard from a phone box. Excited and apprehensive I dialled and a man named Phillip Cox answered and offered some advice about London LGBT venues. But once he knew our ages, he gave us the opportunity to attend a meeting at London Gay Teenage Group's new premises in Holloway Road. Despite my nerves, London Gay Teenage Group (LGTG) gave me the confidence to be openly gay. I am proud to have been at the start of a movement that led to many of the freedoms young LGBT people have today.

In 1986, when the government's 'Don't Die of Ignorance' billboards were erected and the pamphlets about HIV and AIDS were delivered to every door and the 'AIDS tombstones' were seen in TV adverts that were beamed across the nation's screens, the phone lines went wild. 'The phone would ring as soon as you put it down', remembers Lisa Power, who began volunteering in 1979. 'If you needed to stop after a call to go to the loo, you had to leave the phone off the hook'.

Ignorance was rife and often led to bizarre beliefs. 'This is a time where people thought you could catch HIV from touching someone', explains Tash. 'I will always remember the little old lady who was worried that her cat might bite a gay man who had AIDS, and he might give it to the cat', adds Lisa.

Switchboard became a field hospital of love and support for the public battlefield at the height of the AIDS crisis. Everywhere people were dying in the trenches, including within Switchboard's four walls where the deadly illness hit the community hard and everyone was working around the clock. 'You think the dead we loved ever truly leave us?' Dumbledore teaches, but where was the philosopher's stone when they needed it?

On a cold February afternoon in 1989, red balloons bounced in the sky over the office wall after volunteers joined AIDS Coalition to Unleash Power (ACT UP), in the wake of a largely neglected public health crisis. They aimed to raise awareness of the HIV/AIDS epidemic and to pressure governments into taking action. Switchboard volunteers supported the ACT UP protest outside Pentonville Prison. The masses held 'Prison Condom Ban = More AIDS' placards, and sent hundreds of helium-filled condom balloons over her majesty's prison walls to the inmates beyond as inmates were denied condoms, activism that paved the way for official prison policy in 2014 stating that prisoners should be able to access condoms. Inside, back on the phones, as thousands were dealing with terrible symptoms like fevers, chills and rashes turned into mouth ulcers, skin lesions and diarrhoea, hundreds of lesbians were calling and signing up to donate blood.

Switchboard volunteers knew that the quest for queer love and support was fragile, and much was at stake. While always alert to attacks by forces of homophobic hate and evil, the Switchboard volunteers began to witness remarkable change. Former neo-Nazi Nicky Crane had revealed his homosexuality and began to own it in the public eye. For years he had been living a double life, even serving as a steward at the London gay pride march in 1986, and was a regular at London gay clubs such as Heaven, Bolts and the Bell pub, and as a doorman at an S&M club. The internalised homophobia had become too much for him to bear and he eventually came out as gay, live on TV. 'Nazi Nick is a Puff', the *Daily Mail* declared. While, in the end, he did work his queer magic to set himself free, he didn't have long to make amends before he died of AIDS in 1993, joining the masses of people that Switchboard supported before antiretroviral (ARVs) in combination therapy became available in 1996.

'We were supporting people who were dying, and people whose family members were dying', Tash says. 'Switchboard lost many people to AIDS. Our volunteers were grieving as they helped others to grieve.' Nick Partridge, who volunteered at Switchboard in the mid-eighties, remembers:

Until the arrival of effective therapy in 1996, probably one trustee of [Terrence Higgins Trust] would die each year. That made the whole experience very intense, but we were very determined. We were battling on all fronts, with extraordinarily brave feats of both activism and personal courage in the face of a terminal illness.

Together the volunteers worked night and day until finally there was light at the end of the tunnel. 'I'll never forget being in the office at Switchboard when the fax came from San Francisco that Antiretrovirals in combination therapy were working', remembers Ian Johns, who was a director of Switchboard at that time. 'My proudest moment', he declares.

Switchboard inspired millions, but who inspired them?

10. *RUN YOUR OWN LIFE* – HOUSMANS BOOKSHOP/ GLF OFFICE, 5 CALEDONIAN ROAD

'There needs to be somewhere central for people all over the world to drop into when they find themselves in this big wicked city', a Gay Liberation Front (GLF) office collective call-out stated.

It's 1971 and the GLF have just appeared on the infamous Jimmy Savile's *Speakeasy* TV show, alongside the Campaign for Homosexual Equality (CHE). For the next twelve hours, the phone lines at the GLF office based here at Housmans didn't stop ringing and became a base for queers travelling to the city from across the world. Andrew Lumsden, GLF activist and the founder of *Gay News*, reflects of the times:

The process of liberation is a long and painful one which never finishes; there are people all over the country who are in various stages of the process. They need pamphlets, badges, information, contact, speakers, assurance and a voice to fill fantasies while they wank off into a public telephone booth. Laugh not, brother, for there you go …

Ever since, Housmans, the radical booksellers at the bottom of Caledonian Road, has been an epicentre of movements seeking love and justice for all. It is owned by Peace News Trustees, a non-profit which also oversees the publication *Peace News*. The windows are full of posters: the Anarchist Festival, Justice for Grenfell, the Karl Marx Walking Tour, and you can still buy a t-shirt from the 1984 'Pits and Perverts' LGSM fundraising event. Current residents are War Resisters International, Network for Peace, Forces Watch, which scrutinises military recruitment, and anti-sweatshop outfit No Sweat.

It was here, in the basement, the GLF office catalysed a global movement, full of strife, victories, giggles and life in all its abundance. Andrew continues:

GLF was a dandelion which grew, flowered and then degenerated into a fluffy but insubstantial head full of seeds which were then blown by several gusts into new areas of the meadow. It is easy to then understand the way in which it is connected to a whole host of major lesbian and gay initiatives of the 1970s, 1980s and even 1990s. Seeds blew everywhere and then returned to the earth. GLF was a school for revolutionary activists. We voted against membership in a meeting in 1970. We discussed 'do we want membership?' and everyone responded 'No!' It was a 'dis-organisation'. People got involved and developed a sense of self-confidence and pride and then were able to go on and do things they'd never dreamed were possible. Nobody came into GLF and remained the same, everybody was changed by their involvement.

The GLF office collective represented two poles in the gay activist scene that were increasingly at odds with each other: those within the GLF who felt they were doing the 'gruntwork' and were ignored or unappreciated and others who felt they were too allied to what they called 'straight gays', aspiring for respectable equality in a broken homophobic system. The Queens didn't want 'equality' and acceptance, they wanted to tear the whole structure down and were out to provoke and experiment with new forms of living, starkly illustrating different views of how you change the world. In September 1973 some of the 'RadFem' Queens from the GLF Bethnal Green commune took direct action, staging a raid on the office in Housmans, attempting to seize as much GLF material as they could. Not long after this the GLF office collective announced its divorce from London GLF.

After *Gay News* launched in June 1972, Andrew recounts, 'we were inundated with calls – everything from suicidal to wanting to know where the nearest cottage was. So *Gay News* organised gay groups together and said we need a switchboard like they do in America.' A few years later Switchboard utilised the existing network of individuals and groups who had been part of, or been touched by, the forever ongoing sexual revolution begun by the GLF who challenged attitudes towards gays of the medical orthodoxy in the 1970s, which proved vital when the HIV crisis began in the 1980s.

Movements flowered from this root across the UK into the Brixton Faeries, Gay Men's Press from the GLF Media Group,

Icebreakers helpline from the Counter-Psychiatry Group, out of the GLF communes came world-renowned theatre troupe Bloolips that was connected to GLF Street Theatre, as well as campaigning groups Stonewall and OutRage!, and internationally across revolutionary queer movements, FAHR Paris and Mario Mieli's *FUORI!* in Italy too.

In 2020, during building renovations when layers of plaster were stripped from the basement wall, underneath were revealed heartfelt gay liberation graffiti stating 'Homosexuals unite', 'Run your own life' and 'Gay is good so don't be scared to tell anybody'.

Timeless advice.

11. *FAR MORE THAN A BOOKSHOP* – GAY'S THE WORD, 66 MARCHMONT STREET

Let us reunite now with Mike and Mark to celebrate our powerful queer and magical journey here in King's Cross. But Mark Ashton, or Mary Trashton in her blonde beehive wig and full drag, isn't around anymore, no longer downing a pint after a shift at the Conversative Club.

Mark was murdered in 1987 by the government of the punters he served at the bar. Diagnosed with AIDS, Mark was admitted to Guy's Hospital on 30 January 1987 and died twelve days later of pneumocystis pneumonia. He was 26 years old. Dumbledore's queer army lost a brilliant freedom-seeking soldier that day, slain in Margaret Thatcher's war against the poor and oppressed.

Mark's friend Ashtar Alkhirsan tells me today:

It's totally unacceptable that people are forgotten. It's totally unacceptable how people were treated in their life for being lesbian and gay and then to be treated so inhumanely when they were sick and then to be forgotten! Mark came out with his sexuality and I came out as a witness to what was going on, and that changed my life really.

But for now there is no danger that they will be forgotten. Today, Ashtar is working away on the UK AIDS Film Project that exists to 'remember the dead and fight for the living', based out of Acorn House around the corner on 314–320 Gray's Inn Road. The building is also home to the Food Chain, which provides nutritional support to people living with HIV in London, and a few streets away, the Institute of Race Relations at 2–6 Leeke Street researches issues including the rise of racial violence and extreme-right parties, and empowers the most vulnerable in society. Around the other corner at 116 Judd Street is the Helios Centre, providing holistic HIV+ healthcare – to whom I owe my life to after I was diagnosed – which has contributed to a massive fall in HIV+ diagnoses, for most, but not all, communities in London Town. Step into a side street a little bit further on, with a multi-coloured rainbow-zebra crossing ten minutes away, and here lies the philosopher's stone.

Surviving government raids, homophobic attacks and extortionate rent prices, let's celebrate where Mike and Mark's journey began. Gay's the Word bookshop is the shining gem that dedicates every millisecond to remember the dead and fight for the living. Look above the door and raise a glass to Mark's plaque, forever placing LGBTQIA+ rights at the heart of the global trade union movement. In Mike's garden opposite Central Station, under a twinkling disco ball there is also a plaque from Hôtel-Lamoignon in Paris, the Mark Ashton Garden, named after him to honour his role in placing LGBTQIA+ rights in the workers movement, that has also now become an AIDS memorial. Mike smiles knowingly today and turns to me:

Gay's the Word is far more than just a bookshop, the place has changed hundreds of thousands of LGBTQIA+ lives. The minute you go in there by definition you come out. It is a safe place that nurtures people. You know, Dan, life in central London is better now. It is much easier to be openly queer even though we see a resurgence of hate crime. It's hard to conceive how we can ever be put back into the closet anymore. It's too late, the bottles have broken and the genies are out – and that's fantastic.

Can we ever forget legends like Mark Ashton? As Dumbledore knows, 'to have been loved so deeply, even though the person who loved us is gone, will give us some protection forever'.

WHERE'S THE PUB? CENTRAL STATION,
37 WHARFDALE ROAD

Mince back over to Central Station where friendly faces will always welcome you and raise a glass to our fabulous community in King's Cross. Currently celebrating their 30th anniversary with the 'Making an Exhibition of Ourselves', which includes photos, press cuttings, letters, memories and oral histories from the last three decades, your queer-soul-batteries will be sure to be re-charged too.

7

All Power to the People!
Ladbroke Grove

Each and every one of us has a creative spark that helps us question life around us and pushes us out of bed in the morning. Whether you have connected with your creative toolkit or not, do you realise just how transformative creativity can be?

Notting Hill is known across the world for the tunes, laughter and costumes at Notting Hill Carnival that inspires millions of people every year. What's less well known is that the carnival was born out of isolation, fear and struggle. How did this happen? What happened in between? How have queer lives shaped the cultural landscape? And how can we learn from this phenomenal neighbourhood to help us face the world today?

START: LADBROKE GROVE STATION

1. Creativity in Place of War – *Ladbroke Grove Station*
2. Universal Black Improvement Organisation – *Westbourne Park Road*
3. Princess Diana and the Handshake – *Lighthouse, 111–117 Lancaster Road*
4. Only a Catastrophic Event – *Grenfell Tower*
5. Gardens in Our Hearts – *Electric Cinema, 191 Portobello Road*

1. *CREATIVITY IN PLACE OF WAR* – LADBROKE GROVE STATION

Skip out of Ladbroke Grove station, breathe in the cool breeze and feel the striking sunshine tantalising your skin. It's 1963 and a young group of teenagers are tucking into their deli-cious-smelling lunch. Where did they get that, you wonder? 'Why, the Mangrove of course!', they tell you. Laughter, revelry and a sense of dedication permeate the air, and you hear a satisfy-ing, deep, almost banjo-like tinkling faintly in the distance. Turn around and up the street a small band of musicians playing steel drums energise a one-hundred strong crowd of local residents. At the helm stands Claudia Jones, a tall, elegant woman wearing a

210

satin gown, fur stole and chain smoking through a long cigarette holder. She is directing everyone to march onwards.

On 31 August 1963, Claudia wrote about this day in her diary. At a time when movements for civil freedoms were erupting across the world, Dr Martin Luther King Jr wasn't the only one who had a dream. Claudia organised this procession with her Committee of Afro-Asian Caribbean Organisations in solidarity with King's March on Washington, where he made his famous 'I have a dream' speech. Marching forward from Ladbroke Grove station to the US embassy in Grosvenor Square, Claudia and her comrades demanded an end to racial segregation, fighting persecution with each step. Claudia was born in Trinidad and Tobago and as a child migrated with her family to the US. Her freedom-seeking fiery soul led her to become a trailblazing communist activist, feminist and fighter for Black liberation. In 1955, during the political persecution of communists in the US, she was deported. Her exile, however, failed to crush her spirit. Upon arriving in the UK, she immediately joined the Communist Party of Great Britain and would remain a member for the rest of her life.

In the early 1960s, Ladbroke Grove was full of street life led by the beat of calypso and steel drum musicians. Similarly to Railton Road in Brixton and St Paul's in Bristol, 'Grove' was also a warzone. The battle lines were drawn with institutionally racist police brutality on one side and organised people power on the other, as they still are drawn today. The authorities did not want oppressed people opening shops, building businesses, cultural spaces or daring to educate themselves, because that might mean they were here to stay. Claudia believed that 'people without a voice are lambs to the slaughter' and she started a quest to turn everything on its head. She had learnt that the British Empire was the most tactical and lethal of colonisers and understood their tactics of trying to suppress Black consciousness and force people to assimilate into the status quo. She was unwilling to be a 'subject' in the British Empire. When local resident Kelso Cochrane was murdered by white fascists, this was the final straw for Claudia. At that same time, the appetite and ingredients for Notting Hill Carnival, inspired by the annual Lenten tradition of 'playing mas' (masquerade) in the Eastern Caribbean, were already emerging. Sizzling in the cooking pot of revolutionary life, this key recipe included a secret – that in the face of systemic violence, creativity and celebration can end war.

Three years after that 1963 march, a small steel band arrived around the corner at Portobello Green, accompanied by a crowd of regulars from the leather-clad gay Coleherne pub in Earl's Court. Community worker Rhaune Laslett invited jazz legend Russell Henderson and his three-piece steel band to play at the first Notting Hill fayre. After a set, Russell suggested that everyone should embark on a march through the streets. The procession, joined by the public, was repeated the following day and became the first manifestation of the Notting Hill Carnival – an international event now attended by more than one million revellers annually.

But wait – look down the street outside the station and you haven't spotted Hugh Grant and Julia Roberts smooching in a doorway yet? 'Where are they?', you might ponder. Well, if you came to find out, you're holding the wrong book. The film *Notting Hill* tells one tiny part of the area's story, but please watch

Kidulthood or the *Grove Roots* documentary instead. Here, we celebrate titans who brought love to the masses, like Nina Simone, Frank Crichlow, Bette Bourne and Nettie Pollard, and movements for Black, Queer, Trans and Women's liberation. Against a social background of consistent racism and cultural erasure, they have taught us all to refuse to be small.

The true story of Notting Hill is one of Black culture, Black entrepreneurship and Black love – both queer and heterosexual – that has given rise to a host of organised, militant and empowered activities. An area so rich through its transformations, it is fundamental to the make-up of the UK. Rewind back before Conservative politicians and film stars colonised it, in the late 1960s and early 1970s Notting Hill was England's parallel to Haight-Ashbury in San Francisco or Greenwich Village in New York. It was a hotbed of revolutionary ideas. 'It was cheap, it was Black, it was run-down and it was too scary for lots of nice white folk to want to be in', as fellow street-life enthusiast and author Hari Kunzru will teach you in his tour, dubbed the 'Not Hugh Grant's Notting Hill'. Known for its waves of migration, tight social bonds across race and class lines, and standing up to simmering white fascism – what is lesser known are the examples of intersectional solidarity, queer courage and activism that have blossomed across the community.

You only need to look at a flyer that, if you were standing in here in 1972, might have landed in your hand. Looking up you'd have seen warmly greeting you a gaggle of determined sassy radical queens taking a break from dancing in their communal squats in the neighbourhood to recruit you. In full drag, by the way. These Queens ain't messing about. They declare:

To the people of Notting Hill: At last, during the Notting Hill People's Carnival, we felt what it was like to be part of a community. We danced, sang and got high together, and it felt good. Did you notice if the man or woman standing next to you was Black or Gay or Greek, and if you did, did it make any difference? No. During the Carnival, you probably went to a pub for a drink. We, as Gays, couldn't go into at least three pubs in our community. We have been banned because we're gay, openly gay. Let's keep our 'People's Carnival' spirit alive. Help us by boycotting these three pubs until they lift their ban. Who knows, soon you may need our help as we now ask for yours. Love, ALL POWER TO THE PEOPLE! Gay Liberation Front (GLF)

What is this Gay Liberation Front and how can I find out more about them? Well, hold your horses! Vital cognitive shifts happen on every street corner here in Ladbroke Grove and the neighbouring Notting Hill. You will discover those living in the burgeoning queer communes, a flourishing Trans community, life in the theatres, pissed-off police and coalition-building between Black and queer communities who once locked po-faced authoritarian councillors in a church hall. These lessons are all for the taking, but first let's explore some of the inspiration behind the GLF's change-making toolkit.

2. UNIVERSAL BLACK IMPROVEMENT ORGANISATION – WESTBOURNE PARK ROAD

All along Westbourne Park Road in the 1970s, a growing number of young Black people with long dreadlocks were reclaiming their heritage. Young Rastas sat on doorsteps whistling the lyrics of Bob Marley's greatest anthem 'One Love' and calling on humanity to 'get together and feel all right'. Rastafarianism is far from being just about dreads. Bob Marley was a convert to Rastafari and its ceremonial chant, the Nyabinghi, the rhythms of which influenced reggae, ska and rocksteady's unmistakable beats. The music and the religion were woven together. Reggae came out of the slums of Jamaica in the 1960s and within a decade, it reached a global audience. It still permeates this area's sound-scape to this day. Contemporary reggae artist Etana subscribes to many of Rastafari's core teachings, which she describes as 'love, togetherness, oneness, unity, unconditional love, fighting for the rights of the people, for the poor, the sick, the elderly, the needy'. Simultaneously absorbing influences from reggae, Rastafari and global Black liberation movements, 'Raggamuffin' became the term for these self-actualised young people, intent on instilling cultural, spiritual and political empowerment and self-suffi-ciency, with a deep sense of pride.

Developed through 'reasoning' discussions in people's houses and the neighbourhood at large, young Black people were encour-aged to attend 'supplementary schools'. Fundamental to Rastafari is the belief that Black people are not free until Africa is free. This idea would never be expressed in the dominant white-cen-tric school system, but the concept of 'Overstanding' or having 'the big picture' flourished in supplementary schools. Say the word 'overstanding' out loud right now. Can you feel how the sound and shape of it brings positive vibrations of aliveness and dignity? Such a contrast to the insufficient picture of society that the British 'educational' curriculum touts. The root of the word education is *educere*, which literally means 'to lead forth'. These streets are paved with examples of catalysing transformation.

The deeply entrenched nature of segregation in the UK at the time, required the development of community consciousness both in community-led education like the supplementary schools, and on a far wider scale. The principles of international solidarity rejected racist and orientalist depictions of Black, Arab and other peoples from the Global South. The GLF, since its formation at the London School of Economics (LSE) in 1970, was directly inspired by the civil rights movement in America, jumping into action after the Stonewall Uprisings and Black Panther Huey Newton's famous speech in New York City in 1970. There Newton urged the building of solidarity among oppressed people's struggles. Dialogue between the Black Liberation Front (BLF) and GLF developed from there. Solidarity with labour struggles was also key: in 1976, regular GLF delegations to the nearby Grunwick factory expressed solidarity with picketers against the police, who were protecting the factory owner's interests instead of workers' rights. Many LGBTQIA+ activists travelled there in support, exemplifying how the GLF helped smash the misrepresentation of queer struggles as 'isolated'.

Bigoted hate crime has such a long history. The 1968 Olympics – when Tommie Smith and John Carlos each raised a black-gloved fist – had birthed a new era of Black consciousness across the world. This act inspired the foundation of the 'Universal Black Improvement Organisation' (UBIO). They were intent on challenging the 'school to prison pipeline'. This would require consciousness raising and action to intervene against arrests and detention, borstals and being sucked into the prison system.

Founded by Pinto Fox, one of the first Rastafarians in Britain, the UBIO paved the way for Black-led programmes and youth centres such as the Metro Club against a backdrop of ongoing racist police assault via the 1976 'Sus Laws'. These laws gave the police the power to stop, search and arrest anyone they considered to be acting suspiciously, and disproportionately impacted young Black people. As Stafford Scott, co-curator of the powerful exhibition 'War Inna Babylon: The Community's Struggle for Truths and Rights', writes:

> Young Black people reported that police beat them up after barging into their homes, and then charged them with assault. Black children were arrested for stealing sweets, and teachers called police to school playgrounds ... In Magistrates' Courts, young people protested their innocence, but they were convicted regardless; the police needed neither a victim nor any physical evidence to justify their allegations.

Ismahil Blagrove, author of the brilliant *The Frontline – A Story of Struggle, Resistance and Black Identity in Notting Hill*, highlights how the attacks were so rife, that the community *Grassroots* newsletter called the police truncheon a 'youth club'. *Grassroots* was inspired by the Kwanzaa principles of 'unity, self-determination, collective responsibility, co-operative economics, purpose, creativity and faith'. In defiance, the 'UBIO became like a training ground for Black Consciousness. Black films were being shown and activists were coming in and educating the youths'.

The movement for Black consciousness was informed by music, teachings and culture and continues to be instrumental in

supporting young Black people to take ownership of their neighbourhoods. The beating drums and calypso rhythms of regular
carnival-building preparations were bringing Claudia's dreams
into effect.

UBIO's purpose was bringing 'One Love' front and centre,
but that takes time. In the 1990s, bigotry came to the fore in the
reggae scene. Stars like Buju Banton and Beenie Man performed
and popularised songs that were blatantly homophobic. Notorious lyrics in Jamaican patois included 'Boom bye-bye, Inna batty
bwoy head, Rude bwoy no promote no nasty man, Dem haffi
dead'. This translates as 'Boom, bye-bye, in a faggot's head, the
tough young guys don't accept fags, they have to die'.

'It is not One Love in Jamaica', Shaquille Abi Abi, a homeless
19-year-old Jamaican transvestite, said to the press in 2017.
While Jamaica threw off colonial rule in 1962, it retained the
British prohibition on sodomy. Today, it's still punishable by ten
years in prison with hard labour. Any gay person reporting a hate
crime to police risks arrest.

Present day artists like Etana believe they're taking reggae
back to its roots. Many in the reggae scene are now at the
forefront of the fight against homophobia. Mr Lewis, head of
Jamaican LGBTQIA+ group J-Flag agrees: 'We're optimistic.
We know that social change takes time and we know we're in
it for the long haul [and] you have more and more people that's
been feeling more comfortable and coming out.' The new wave
of phenomenal Jamaican reggae artists taking the world by storm
are changing the course of musical and queer herstory. 'I am into
women and I've been making reggae music', Lila Ike announced
in 2021, and Koffee's song 'Toast' is a celebrated anthem in
lesbian communities.

Over in East London, since 2018 thousands have turned up every summer at Faggamuffin Bloc Party. Its mission, Virginia Wilson, co-founder and Director shares, 'to increase the visibility of QTBIPOC (Queer Trans Black Indigenous and People of Colour) Pride at carnival', through 'a reclaiming of a tradition of resistance and liberation through celebration by and for queer people of colour ... a celebration at which echoes of those tribal beats, inherited via the Caribbean, will reverberate in a new context: a celebration of freedom that is precious to us as Black and Brown people and as queer people'. Faggamuffin Bloc Party celebrates and champions LGBTQIA+ people from African and Caribbean heritage within the context of Carnival.

In 2022, a statue of the arch-coloniser British Admiral Lord Horatio Nelson was removed from the Barbadian capital Bridgetown's main square, just two months after announcing plans to replace Britain's Queen Elizabeth II as its head of state and move on from its colonial past. This includes overturning homophobic legislation that was catalysed by the British Empire's 1533 Buggery Act that was exported throughout the world. Barbados is calling for revised healthcare too, as in every country where homosexuality is illegal, HIV and AIDS proliferate because people fail to access support for fear of disclosing their sexuality. Change is coming.

Great news, then, that recently Botswana and Trinidad and Tobago successfully overturned these laws too. In 2018, Trinidad-born LGBTQI+ activist Jason Jones, who lives in the UK, took the Trinidadian Government to court to challenge the constitutionality of Sections 13 and 16 of the Sexual Offences Act, which criminalised same-sex activity between consenting adults.

Jason argued that the two sections of the Act violated his right to privacy, liberty and freedom of expression. On 12 April 2018 he won the landmark legal challenge in the high court, when Justice Devindra Rampersad ruled that these sections were 'unconstitutional, illegal, null, void, invalid and are of no effect'. Today, Phyll Opoku-Gyimah, widely known as Lady Phyll, Executive Director of Kaleidoscope Trust, a UK-based charity working to uphold the human rights of LGBTQIA+ people across the world, and co-founder and Executive Director of UK Black Pride, Europe's largest pride celebration for LGBTQIA+ people of colour, reminds us, 'As a community of diverse and dynamic LGBTQIA+ people, we have to be aware and stay alert; we have to organise in solidarity with our siblings around the world, and we have to understand the role we can play in ensuring a free world for everyone'.

Now it might be time for Trafalgar Square's Nelson's Column, erected about 30 years after the one in Barbados, to go too. The fading nervous smiles of prince William and princess Catherine when they visited the Caribbean on a royal tour in 2022 and were met with a strong republican sentiment, shows us how much has changed since UBIO began.

3. *PRINCESS DIANA AND THE HANDSHAKE* – LIGHTHOUSE, 111–117 LANCASTER ROAD

Princess Diana wasn't like the other royals. She ceremonially opened the country's first AIDS ward at Middlesex Hospital, and also the Landmark AIDS Centre in Brixton, where AIDS most directly impacted marginalised people – people of colour, queers, women, migrants. At a time when police dealing with

AIDS patients still wore rubber gloves, Diana refused to keep silent. She helped change how the world saw HIV and AIDS with one simple yet touching gesture. Diana gave Landmark Centre director Jonathan Grimshaw, who was living with HIV, a firm handshake before going inside the centre for a private tour. You are now standing outside the former London Lighthouse, which until 2015 was a drop-in centre and residential unit for people living with HIV and AIDS. A beacon of light against isolation and grief, the centre was supported by private funders as well as Princess Diana. She visited regularly, bringing global attention, regularly shaking hands with dying patients, showing to the world that HIV couldn't be transmitted by touch. Just as Notting Hill carnival turned racial hatred into a force for life, the Lighthouse turned AIDS into an opportunity for collective healing.

While the government created TV adverts of tombstones crashing to the ground, catalysing fear among the nation, the Lighthouse stepped up with standards of care, research and treatment that made people's lives worth living. In 1989, candles adorned the brick walls; families, lovers and friends mourning the deaths of their loved ones, gone too soon. Clusters of people prepared to weave their way from here to the prime minister's home at number 10 Downing Street. It was here that brave queer activists from the radical, direct action LGBTQIA+ civil rights movement OutRage! organised queer political funerals and candlelit vigils to celebrate the gone, but not forgotten. Knock on the front door today and ask at the reception of what is now the Museum of Brands if you can go to the back and visit the memorial garden. Dotted among the lush green flora are tributes to patients who didn't survive and to the centre's volunteers. The community of West London was hit especially hard by the number of

AIDS deaths and the subsequent closure of LGBTQIA+ venues. This absence is still felt today.

4. *ONLY A CATASTROPHIC EVENT* – GRENFELL TOWER

Leave the garden and walk back round to the road. Looming over you stands the burnt-out Grenfell Tower, a totemic example of systematic inequality that stands here in the Royal Borough of Kensington and Chelsea, where the richest lords live alongside the most marginalised. On 14 June 2017, the 24-storey Grenfell Tower block of flats went up in flames. Seventy-two people were killed in the fire, victims of the cladding company who cut corners for profit and a government who failed to protect them, including two who later died in hospital. Seventy others were injured and 223 people escaped. Theresa May, the prime minister at the time, did not even meet with survivors or residents of the blazing tower.

The collusion of politicians, regulators and corporations in permitting building practices they knew were unsafe and could lead to mass death is one of the major scandals of our time. The failure of successive governments to address the issue of fire safety in buildings exposes a culture of impunity that has had deadly consequences. As Grenfell Tower resident Edward Daffarn posted on social media in November 2016, the year before the disaster, 'Only a "catastrophic event" would bring about change'.

A year later, streams of green balloons would be rising above your head. Edward survived but 72 others died that fateful night. Working-class, queer and migrant families were among the devastated. For months following the fire, a weekly community-led silent vigil demanded government accountability. A few decades earlier, before the government criminalised squatting, the community might have taken it into their own hands to find new homes for the survivors. Now, millionaires' homes stand empty.

Grenfell is a stark reality where everyone has an impassioned opinion and no one is neutral. If only it was 'one' catastrophic event. Decades after Claudia Jones began organising in this area against the warzone she witnessed, the alarm bells of injustice continue ringing louder than ever. How has this been allowed to happen?

For the people of Ladbroke Grove, it's the same story time and again.

In 1981, the community rose up and joined the 'Black People's Day of Action' in response to the New Cross Fire that killed thirteen teenagers, and was suspected to be an arson attack motivated by racism. Co-ordinated by the New Cross Massacre Action Committee, 20,000 people marched from New Cross to Hyde Park, crying out for justice. It was the largest demonstration of Black people in the UK up until that time, its many participants shocked by the indifference of the white community and a cover-up by the police. At the time, prime minister Margaret Thatcher showed no concern and the Queen said nothing after the fire, emboldening racists with the signal that they are welcome to attack and get away with it. During the height of spiralling HIV and AIDS deaths in the 1980s and 1990s, activists mobilised against the deafening silence of government inaction, and after Grenfell Tower burned, we have seen here in these streets another example of community resilience. The tears flowed, the answers never came and so the quest for justice continues. Another Lighthouse of Love against the privatisation of grief where systems of brutality flick Black, Queer and all marginalised lives onto the scrapheap of the money-market economy. The construction company Rydon Group, who were responsible for the refurbishment before the fire, have seen a 50 per cent rise in profits since Grenfell burned to the ground. In the year after, company profits rose to £19 million and the salary of the highest-paid director rose 8 per cent from £424,000 to £459,000. At the time, the rebuilding cost was estimated at £500 million. This is a small amount compared to the £15 billion profit that the connected building firms as part of the UK wide cladding industry, have made ever since. Yet the local community are still protesting, demanding light in the darkness. Holding a resilience in their collective soul, a skill learnt from the past.

5. *GARDENS IN OUR HEARTS* – ELECTRIC CINEMA, 191 PORTOBELLO ROAD

Shopping here in the bustling Portobello Market in the early 1970s, you might have been in for a treat. Coming down from the gay communes to do their weekly shopping, the members of the GLF were here to refill their drag wardrobes, darlings. Searching for fur coats, hats, wigs, handbags and ceramics, there was never a dull moment. 'Cheer up darling, you can't have a sausage for your breakfast every morning' shouted a market trader with a knowing wink, followed by "Ere, got some nice bananas for you and your friends'. Other traders might be shouting 'Market! Watch yer backs!' And the Queens would chortle back, smiling, 'Don't bother darling. We like meat with our potatoes!'

Here, outside the Electric Cinema on 3 February 1991, the queer community congregated to make their presence felt. OutRage! was celebrating activist and artist Derek Jarman at a special screening of his film *The Garden*. Surrounded by OutRage! members wearing 'Queers with Attitude' t-shirts and brandishing placards stating 'Stop crucifying queers', a few 'Sisters of Perpetual Indulgence' dressed as morally righteous nuns enthusiastically embraced the crowd. The cinema was heaving, the energy was electrifying.

Derek Jarman died in 1994 as a result of an AIDS related condition, gone too soon like thousands who perished at the hands of government inaction. To nurture our tenaciousness in the face of such adversity we need gardens in all our communities and in all our hearts to let a new world blossom and grow. *The Garden*, produced using a tiny Super 8 camera, was created against the background of AIDS activism and the anti-nuclear power movement. It was inspired by Jarman's garden at Prospect Cottage in Kent, a healing space that prompts visitors to ask essential questions of our society and its future: questions about environmental pollution and disease, collectivity and resilience. Just another example of extraordinary people on the streets of Notting Hill putting their heads above the parapet to make the most of our short time on this beautiful, divided planet.

6. *A PEOPLE'S ART IS THE GENESIS OF THEIR FREEDOM* – CORNER OF TAVISTOCK ROAD AND PORTOBELLO ROAD

The battle of love against hate flourishes in practically every house here. Look up to the plaque here in honour of Claudia

Jones, where the idea for a carnival was born. Organised by the *Nubian Jak Community Trust*, along Tavistock Road there are no fewer than six plaques paying tribute to musicians, activists and visionaries including Rhaune Laslett-O'Brien, Frank Gilbert Crichlow, Leslie Palmer and Russell Henderson, all trailblazers for 'One Love'.

A writer of poetry and a lover of people, Claudia would spend day and night here editing the *West Indian Gazette*. She founded the paper in 1958 as a tool to fight for equal opportunities for Black people. Between 1948 and 1970, immigration to Britain dramatically increased as nearly half a million people moved from the Caribbean to Britain, responding to a government invitation to address post-Second World War labour shortages. In the 1950s, white working-class teddy boys displayed open hostility towards Black families. Subsequently, racial tensions exploded across St Ann's neighbourhood in the City of Nottingham, which then spread across the UK. Oswald Mosley, leader of the British Union of Fascists and who lived around the corner at 47 Kensington Park Road, was manipulating and inflaming disaffected white residents to keep Britain white, straight, patriarchal and deeply patriotic. Mosley orated atop of the lions in Trafalgar Square with responses from his audience including 'No Blacks, No Dogs, No Irish', and shop fronts across London that displayed racist signs that read, 'If they're black – send them back'. This was a social banishment the queer community could empathise with well.

Over the August bank holiday weekend of 1958, a reverberation of the Nazi Kristallnacht 20 years previously, a local fascist mob indulged in a carnival of hate. Shattering windows and throwing whatever they could – mutating milk bottles, dustbin lids and car tyres into missiles, armour and roadblocks. The attacks continued every night until 5 September. Unwilling to stand by amidst the smoke and rubble, Claudia knew the community would need to change tack from street-fighting alone. She organised a Caribbean Carnival in response, the precursor of the Notting Hill Carnival, which was first held on 30 January 1959 in St Pancras Town Hall and was epitomised by the slogan, 'A people's art is the genesis of their freedom'. On 17 May 1959, Kelso Cochrane, a 32-year-old Antiguan carpenter living in West London, was walking home from hospital after sustaining a work injury. As he passed along Southam Street, where the iconic Trellick Tower now stands, he suddenly heard racial slurs being shouted, and was surrounded and stabbed to death by a gang of white men. But, rather than starting another riot, the killing turned the tide against the fascists. United in their resolve to stay put, the community came together at Kelso's funeral in a proto-Carnival procession, to forge a new Black British Afro-Caribbean identity catalysing a culture of music in place of war. Thanks again to the Nubian Jak Community Trust, another blue plaque was put up to mark the scene of the crime and Kelso's death is marked annually by the community on Southam Street.

To this day, there have been no arrests in connection with Kelso Cochrane's murder. In 2002, files were released that revealed that senior police officers at the time had assured the then home secretary, Rab Butler, that there was 'little or no racial motivation behind the disturbance', contradicting even individual police officers' reports.

Fast forward to 2018 and the Windrush generation are threatened with deportation from a country they were initially invited to. The Windrush generation were the smartly dressed pioneers who arrived on the ship MV *Empire Windrush* to the UK between 1948 and 1971 from Caribbean countries full of hope for new wealth, adventures and life. Instead they were welcomed with overt racism, 'Keep Britain White' graffiti on street walls and a 'colour bar' segregating community life, all instilling subconscious messaging to 'know your place'.

The Nationality and Borders Act in 2022, an outrageously hateful piece of legislation, is the latest consolidation of the 'hostile environment' strategy to deter, detain and send migrants packing on treacherous journeys. This includes Queer people who are being sent to their potential deaths due to homophobia in their countries of origin, the result of seeds planted where the British Empire began.

Can the past ever truly be the past? Will justice prevail? Yes, if Claudia Jones and those she has inspired have anything to do with it. Today, the community is strong, vibrant and integrated, and, thankfully, tells a different story.

7. *BY ANY MEANS NECESSARY* – THE METRO CLUB, ST LUKE'S ROAD

It wasn't easy to be out in the 1960s, even though freedom-seeking movements were emerging across the world. Several thousand years of bigotry does not disappear in one generation. We are standing here outside the former Metro Club, a popular Black community centre frequented by the community's youths and often raided by the police. It was also a haven for reggae and soul legends, with Bob Marley, Nina Simone and Johnny

Clarke being just a few icons performing on the stage floor. Here in 1964, after celebrating the *West Indian Gazette* with his friend Claudia Jones, Malcolm X delivered fiery speeches. Malcolm X was a tireless and selfless champion for Black people and bringing together pan-African, pan-Arab and pan-Islamic networks across the world. His words cultivated an equilibrium of community consciousness, love, agency and equal standing against the backdrop of supremacist authority. It was a spiritual idea of complete transformation.

Prior to his political revolutionary life, Malcolm X was a street hustler. His illicit sexual activity at the time has been well-documented and debated, even by himself in his autobiography. Travelling to Britain eager to explore and publicise the social and political barriers faced by Black people living here, Malcolm X cemented transatlantic political relationships under the banner of his Organisation of Afro-American Unity. An electric speaker, razor-sharp politician and master networker, the crowds at the Metro would have been ecstatic. Like Claudia, Malcolm X was ahead of his time, and in many ways they both still are. Understanding the connective tissues of social transformation he engaged with women's movements, which was not so common at the time. Malcolm X inspired the formation of the American Black Panther Party two years later in 1966 in Oakland, California, which led to the British Black Panthers formation here in Notting Hill in 1968. Agitating under the flag of the same logo as their American counterparts – the leaping Panther – they took on racial inequality in housing, welfare, education and the criminal justice system and, in many cases, they won.

8. *I WANT YOUR SEX* – SARM STUDIOS, 8–10 BASING STREET

Welcome to the former SARM Studios, the creative mecca of free-dom-seeking artists who recorded here, including Bob Marley and Peter Tosh. Now luxury flats, the tenants might not realise the salaciously lustful history of another artist who worked his magic here. It was here that the grande dame of defying state oppression recorded a masterpiece. This is where George Michael sang 'I Want Your Sex' and recorded the bulk of his album *Faith*. Relish his lyrics – 'I swear I won't tease you, Won't tell you no lies, I don't need no bible, Just look in my eyes ...' – and take a moment to soak in the grand multicoloured buildings on the street.

With a well-publicised history of cruising for sex in public places, George Michael was arrested by an undercover policeman in a Beverly Hills men's room in 1998 and again ten years later here in London. He turned the arrest into the celebratory song 'Outside', with one of the most self-aware, hilarious and sassy music videos in history, featuring a public restroom that turns into a disco. Dressed as a cop, he sings about the joys of having sex outside. After his arrest he opened up to the Guardian news-paper about his love of cruising, saying, 'the handful of times a year it's bloody warm enough, I'll do it'. No mistake. No guilt. No mincing the truth. Just being outspoken, clear as day, about his desires and how he enjoyed them. This helped millions to re-evaluate and transform how they saw and embraced sexuality.

At a time when the London Lighthouse was heaving with people living with HIV crushed by the homophobic moral panic enforced by the Conservative government, this was nothing short of a miracle. Yes, he was adored and respected globally for his outstanding contribution to creative musicianship, but his legacy must not be cleaned up, George wouldn't have wanted that. Indeed, he would have resented it, in fact. Contemplate what he told the media in 2005:

> You only have to turn on the television to see the whole of British society being comforted by gay men who are so clearly gay and so obviously sexually unthreatening. Gay people in the media are doing what makes straight people comfortable, and automatically my response to that is to say, 'I'm a dirty filthy fucker and if you can't deal with it, you can't deal with it'.

George, that gorgeous faerie communist, went above and beyond sexual freedom too. Formerly a member of the Young Communist League, George raised funds for labour rights during the miners' strike with his band Wham!, volunteered in a local food bank supporting thousands impacted by welfare cuts, and spoke out against imperialist war and greed. Authentic, sex-positive and unapologetic, he even left a credit at the end of 'Outside', filmed in the style of a Swedish porn movie, to the police officer Marcelo Rodríguez who entrapped him, and respelt it to say 'Marcello Uffenwankūm' in an act of sweet revenge. Iconic.

9. *TO BE YOUNG, GIFTED AND BLACK* – THE MANGROVE RESTAURANT, 8 ALL SAINTS ROAD

If George Michael was the ultimate sinner coming at the tail end of centuries of sexual repression, Nina Simone was the high priestess of soul-fire and fury, sharpening the public's imagination with every lyric, every note. Five years after the race riots in

Credit: Richard Braine/PYMCA/Rex/Shutterstock

Harlem, New York's Frontline (1964) and a year after Dr Martin Luther King Jr was assassinated (1968), a shaken but ever-fierce Nina said 'Are you ready, black people? Are you ready to do what is necessary? Are you ready to smash white things, to burn buildings, are you ready? Are you ready to build black things?' in 1969 at the Harlem Cultural Festival to the crowd at her performance. How resonant her words still are in Notting Hill today.

Nina Simone, singer, pianist and civil rights activist, was bisexual, and when she was in town, she enjoyed going to the Mangrove restaurant. Stepping into All Saints Road in the early seventies, surrounded by restaurants, shebeens and gambling houses, Nina's soul was hungry and so was her belly. What better place to go than Frank Crichlow's Mangrove? Its interior walls were decorated with Black carvings and African paintings, and it was here that owner Frank would greet most customers with

'Good day Tom Strokes'. Of course Frank, the unintended 'god-father of the Black community', knew his customers' names – this generic pseudonym was a way to protect people's identity away from police surveillance. Tyrants like PC Frank Pulley would storm in while the community ate, pushing aside tables and putting fingers into customers food, trying to terrorise them into submission.

Rejecting the musical, sexual and social conventions expected of African-American and female artists of her time, Nina was determined in her fight for freedom. Still today, her furious, lonely and darkly playful lyrics have led the LGBTQIA+ community to connect with her as outsiders in a world set against them. As she continued her unrelenting mission for freedom, she stated:

It was very exhilarating to be part of that [civil rights] movement at the time, because I needed IT. I could sing to help my people and that became the mainstay of my life. Not classical piano, not classical music, not even popular music but civil rights music.

A towering, regal figure, her showomanship blended searing racial critique, tender lovingness and apocalyptic warnings. Aligning songs like 'To Be Young, Gifted and Black' with the Black Power movement, she composed protest torch-song staples. Her 'Mississippi Goddam', responding to the assassination of the civil rights leader Medgar Evers and the murder of four African-American girls in a church bombing in Alabama in 1964, fiercely exemplifies the unflinching pursuit of musical and political freedom that has given her an enduring appeal for contemporary activists.

An occasional drinker and cigar smoker, Frank Crichlow was very health conscious, keeping strong to better deal with police raids. Making the Mangrove the base for the British Black Panther movement, it wouldn't be long before Frank was arrested, becoming an iconic symbol of resistance. In 1970, the community fought back against repeated raids and marched to the police station in protest, portrayed in the brilliant Steve McQueen's *Uprising* documentary series.

After the arrest of nine community leaders, they were tried in court and became known as the 'Mangrove Nine'. Charged with incitement to riot, standing by Frank's side the other defendants were Barbara Beese, Rupert Boyce, Rhodan Gordon, Darcus Howe, Anthony Innis, Altheia Jones-LeCointe, Rothwell Kentish and Godfrey Millett.

Alongside many allied movements, the Gay Liberation Front (GLF) were in regular attendance at court solidarity demonstrations, which in turn led to many of the Black community activists supporting the GLF. 'One of the very first GLF marches', activist Ted Brown recalls cheerfully, 'was held in Notting Hill Gate, and supported by people from the Mangrove'. In 1971 the Mangrove Nine's case became a cause célèbre that lasted two months at the Old Bailey. All the defendants eventually were cleared of the most serious charges with five of the defendants being completely acquitted. The case set a legal precedent for creating the first judicial acknowledgement of 'evidence of racial hatred' in the Metropolitan police force. Formative in the fight for race equality, relations with the police along All Saints Road remained tense, finally exploding in 1976 when riots broke out at the Notting Hill Carnival leaving 160 people hospitalised. In 1987, there was another series of police raids on the Mangrove. The subsequent closure of the squats and the installation of surveillance cameras marked the start of Notting Hill's gentrification. Today, the chic and sleek Ruby & Sequoi restaurant stands in Mangrove's place.

Nothing scares the police more than oppressed people organising together, demanding their freedom. Thankfully spaces like the Mangrove existed. The Caribbean restaurant became a hub of organising activity, connection and a sanctuary for community healing. Inside the restaurant, calypso music played while outside James Brown's 'Say it Loud, I'm Black and I'm Proud', Marvin Gaye's 'What's Going On' and Nina's 'To Be Young, Gifted and Black' blasted out of the street's sound systems. After recording at SARM Studios, Bob Marley and the Wailers would drop in to the Mangrove to replenish over steaming black-eyed peas and delicious vegetable stew, and the Supremes and Jimi Hendrix would pop in when in town too. Another bisexual icon, Sammy Davis Jr, loved it here as well. Completely open about his sexuality and reflecting on the eclectic people he got to hang out with, he'd say, 'Hell, man, I'm living my life the way I want to. No restraints, no hang-ups. It's my time and I'm gonna do it the way I want to.'

'How can you be an artist and not reflect the times?' Nina Simone once asked. All around, cultural life was developing in defiance of state oppression. It was the street of the first Black business in the neighbourhood and community-led housing initiatives were blossoming, a far cry from the millionaire rows of today's housing crisis. Every Saturday night after returning from sparse and sacred Black clubs like the Q Club in Central London, jubilant friends would return to dance at house parties. High-energy ska, and the fluid movement of dub and reggae collaborations within and across racial lines, captured the imagination. The well-known song 'My Boy Lollipop' by Millie Small was just the tip of the iceberg. Ever since, musicians like M People, Aswad, Sons of Jah and the Specials are just some of those who have lifted the community's spirit. Queer relationships blossomed over the restaurant tables and sound systems but a more explicit tentative alliance with the Gay Liberation Front was blossoming too. Resident musicians such as Russell Henderson and his band would travel to neighbouring Earl's Court, playing lunchtime jazz sets at the Coleherne, where drag entertainers performed in the afternoon. The bar had been segregated in the 1950s, one part for the straight crowd and one for the gay community at a time when homosexuality was illegal. Throughout this period music, as ever, was the force for love and connection.

10. *HOW DARE YOU PRESUME I'M HETEROSEXUAL?* – ALL SAINTS CHURCH, CLYDESDALE ROAD

The centre of glorious Christian campness here at All Saints church hall in the 1970s witnessed a homosexual cultural conversion when in 1971 the church became the meeting point for activists from the GLF. It welcomed 'Hippies, activists, students', recalls Michael James, who brought along the urns from his Portobello Road cafe to provide tea at the meetings. 'When I got involved with the GLF it was a light coming on; as if the whole of my life had been leading to that moment. It cut me free from my last vestiges of guilt.' Resolved in the commitment to overturn segregation, the community took over the church.

When GLF moved their meetings here from the London School of Economics (LSE) and Middle Earth (the basement of a former nightclub in Covent Garden), Notting Hill police warned pub landlords in the area not to serve anyone wearing a GLF or women's liberation badge. So the GLF and their allies in the community planned to fight back.

Often living in poverty in squats as far off as Brixton, GLF activists travelled here to meet hundreds of other radical dykes and queens. The regular GLF gatherings were about organising actions but also about 'awareness raising'. These were an expression of freedom that would derive from the real interests and struggles of ordinary people. Topics included 'Coming out in the workplace', 'The breakdown of the traditional family' and 'Building international solidarity', among many others, but 'all from a very personal angle where you trusted others in the group to keep everything within the group', GLF activist Nettie recalls. New understandings, boldness, acts of kindness, friendships, and lots of sexual relationships flourished as well as debates, disputes and fractions within the movement too. Newsletters, magazines and badges with brilliant slogans such as 'How dare you presume I'm heterosexual' and 'we are the people our parents warned us about' disseminated the GLF energy into the wider community.

Dykes travelled from the women's commune around the corner in Faraday Road. One of the birthplaces of modern feminism, the building belonged to absentee landlords and had gone without renovation since it was built. 'The house had come without hot water, and at one point, someone fell through the floorboards – situations that the communal occupants resolved and repaired themselves', Julia L remembers, giggling. The women settled, transformed and pursued social visions of queer living and transcending gender binaries at the beginning of the

1970s. 'If there was anybody weird in the neighbourhood', be they 'gay, transsexual, whatever, they were down at our house', Julia L continues, proudly. Experimenting in living during the day, through these years, the Women's commune activists went on to set up women's discos all over London at night. Activist Cloud Downey remembers: 'It was all very intense and spiritual and sexual. Then every Saturday we'd go to the Crown and Woolpack disco in Islington, drink as much as we could as fast as we could. It was the first real gay women's pub disco.' Trans liberation was also coming to the fore. Cloud looks back: 'We were into gender confusion and sexuality, not into passing as women, but we felt we had a duty to welcome transvestites and transsexuals into GLF, so some of them went to the women's group'.

At the time, GLF women's activists were firing on all cylinders: joining the 'Free Angela Davis' protests outside the US embassy in Grosvenor Square, demanding the legendary Black Panther, communist and activist be released alongside all political prisoners; and organising protests in support of Angie Weir, champion of women's and gay liberation movements. Angie was held on remand, and eventually acquitted, for her actions with the Angry Brigade, a vigilante group of young people holding the government accountable for their war crimes; demonstrating outside Holloway women's prison against incarceration and for a world beyond prisons at large; building solidarity for May Hobbs and the Night Cleaners' strike demanding fair wages, decent working conditions and unionisation; joining the 1972 miners' strike and being pummelled by police horses in Whitehall and where a GLF lesbian chastised male trade unionists who were shouting 'Heath's a poof'; protesting on Downing Street about

Bloody Sunday on 30 January 1972, when British soldiers shot unarmed civil rights demonstrators in Northern Ireland; creating the second lesbian issue of the GLF newsletter *Come Together*; participating in the 'Gay Days' in parks celebrating being out in public and spray-painting 'Sod the Cock Brokers' on the London Stock Exchange, letting London know where the battlelines for freedom were drawn.

Pressure was rising in the community here too. At the time, the local authority was not keen on working-class people squatting homes because there was profit to be made from the crumbling housing stock. Gentrification accelerated and by 1973, 40 per cent of properties had been changed from low to high rent accommodation and All Saints church hall was even scheduled for demolition. This would leave the whole of North Kensington without a decent public meeting place. The market traders were increasingly aggrieved because the council wanted to do away with the fruit and vegetable market (they still do), as it supposedly makes the area dirty. So on 15 May, 300–400 residents, including GLF activists, friends from the Mangrove restaurant and local squatting activists, market traders and small shopkeepers descended here for a public meeting with councillors against these proposals. They had created a raft of demands for social housing and community provision including the unused Baptist Tabernacle Church next door to be purchased as a community centre, with provisions for the elderly, children's playgroups and as a free school.

As the clock ticked late into the evening, it was becoming apparent that the councillors would not sign up to the demands. So the doors of the hall were locked and barricaded overnight until some agreement was forthcoming. Nearly 200 residents remained and snuck out to bring back food, homemade wine for the masses and drums, flutes and a wide array of musical instruments to entertain for the long night ahead. They ate and danced together and small groups formed to discuss how the neighbourhood could meet everyone's needs instead. Even if the councillors tried to escape they would be met on the other side of the door by fierce dykes in Doc Martens boots and radical queens draped in kaftan scarves. As the morning light entered the church's stained-glass windows, the police were gathering outside, and the councillors were released. Now hungry for breakfast, the community was nourished by the knowledge that fate isn't absolute. That people power can win.

11. *LSD EVERY SATURDAY NIGHT* – GAY LIBERATION FRONT COMMUNE, 7A COLVILLE HOUSES

Join the GLF for breakfast here at 7A Colville Houses. Weaving down the staircase wrapped in a red feather boa, Julian Hows is here to show you a good time, personifying the 'Queendom' of Notting Hill at the time. In 1970, homosexuality was still criminalised in Scotland and Northern Ireland, public displays of same-sex relationships remained illegal, and the age of consent for gay men stood at 21 in contrast to 16 for heterosexuals. The GLF had just formed and the first step for activists was to proclaim your sexuality – and to come out.

Squatting an empty building was not illegal; the criminal offence was breaking and entering, so it was necessary to find some other way of getting in. Julian recalls from 1971:

It was at the end of Colville Houses, a cul-de-sac, and it was like the Secret Garden because there was this long fence with ivy growing over. Underneath all the ivy was a gate and if you pushed it then you walked in.

The timing couldn't have been better. Aged fifteen, he decided to join GLF, finding a sense of empowerment. 'I'd run away from school – well, I was thrown out for being a corrupting influence on the younger pupils.'

GLF realised that homophobia stemmed from gender norms, from sexism and patriarchy. Radical Queens, then, became pivotal. Among the group's preferred activities was a form of subversive, genderfuck drag. For nine months in this former film studio, members of the GLF commune enacted a political protest, couched in humour and performance, 'sharing all possessions and all money and taking LSD every Saturday night', beams Julian. While other pressure groups campaigned for legal reform, the GLF fought for hearts and minds.

One night Julian had an idea. 'Let's have a Roman orgy!' Julian announced to the bemused gang, as off he minced to get grapes and cardboard from the shops to make pantheon-esque pillars. Sexual tension ricocheted off the commune's walls and GLF activists Nettie Pollard and Andrew Lumsden loved visiting this naughty paradise. Nettie remembers, 'Every time I visited I was immediately handed a joint.' Andrew reminisces:

It was like stepping off the planet. You went into a no-day-light zone where there were places to sleep strewn all over the floor, posters to do with pop groups, endless sounds always in and you were always offered dope or acid. The welcome was lovely. It was unstructured to a degree that was terrifying if you had led any kind of structured life. Somebody might be walking around without their clothes on, somebody else spending hours and hours putting makeup on and getting ready. Somebody might be making love on one or another mattress, all in this twilight. Twilight gives the wrong impression, I remember colours. There were blue and golds, yellow, and all under artificial light.

Stepping out of the communes and into the streets, alliances were built. The Lesbians from GLF handled all communications between other organisations, in particular women's liberation and their allies. The queens 'were asked to support the women on trial for causing mayhem at the 1970 Miss World Contest at the Royal Albert Hall'. Bombing it 'with flour', a winking irony to the scandals following the Angry Brigade, one of the signs read: 'Homosexuals Support Women's Liberation'. Following in the footsteps of Claudia Jones, they even picketed the American Embassy as the Vietnam War intensified, standing alongside trade unionist and anti-war movements. As Michael James remembers:

Everything was timed and we were told we would be paired with the Boilermakers Union on the steps of the embassy. They were lovely, warm and welcoming. On the appointed day it was nails done, eyelashes on, whatever makeup and whatever frock we decided to wear. We didn't usually wear evening gowns to serious political demonstrations, we wore nice smart dresses.

The Schools Action Union, a British students' union for school-children active in the early 1970s, came in support too. Once on a march in Notting Hill Gate, a young boy, about twelve or thirteen years old, said to Nettie, 'I'm not gay myself, but what you are doing is important'. Public displays of affection continued through joining local demonstrations, patrolling trains and offering bewildered passengers refreshments and conversation, educating about gay liberation.

'I've got to do some street theatre!' commune member Bette Bourne announced one day. Bette adored the theatrics of life at the time and picked up twelve copies of Lysistrata, an ancient and salacious feminist anti-war Greek comedy which denied all men any sex until they negotiated peace, from a local bookshop to have a collective reading. Everyone took on the parts in caricature movie style roles, Marilyn Monroe impressions causing ripples of laughter, queer commune life buzzing joyfully by.

12. *THE UGLY DUCKLING* – THE TABERNACLE THEATRE, 34–35 POWIS SQUARE

The Tabernacle Theatre has a colourful theatrical and revolutionary history and continues to be the heartbeat of art in the community.

It's August 1978, and tapping their heels on the wooden stage floor behind the wings here, and checking that their wigs were equally balanced, the mischievous GLF radical queens had been looking forward to this day, their show premier. It was time to step out from the gay communes and activist gatherings, and take their theatrics to a bigger audience. Bette Bourne started the legendary radical drag performance troupe Bloolips with a show called *Just Myself* with John Church and Diva Dan at Hampstead

Credit: Bishopsgate Institute

Town Hall. The next show for this pioneering and sensational group came here to the Tabernacle, with *The Ugly Duckling*. The cast included Lavinia Co-op, Bette Bourne, Stuart Feather, JonJon (who wrote the show), Diva Dan, Paul Theobald, Miguel, Little Mickey and Dick Cox. Trailblazing performers including Precious Pearl and Ivan Cartwright who joined shows soon after. Bloolips was inspired by the 1920s golden era of Broadway, of vaudeville and satire as well as the Hot Peaches of New York, whom Bette joined for a season before creating the Bloolips. They taught Bette that it was possible to create theatre shows without any money – an essential lesson at the time. Bloolips hijacked the earnestness of 1970s gay theatre with shows like *Lust in Space* and *The Ugly Duckling*, and songs including 'Let's Scream Our Tits Off'. 'Out of plastic laundry baskets, broken lampshades, and tat from second-hand shops, sometimes using mops as wigs', they changed theatre forever, re-lives Bloolips legend Lavinia Co-op.

While queer performers are quite rightly the top acts at many of London's key cultural venues today, the experience back then wasn't all rosy. As the first out gay group to rehearse and perform at the Tabernacle, many of the staff were astonished. A difficult and double-sided relationship developed. Precious Pearl remembers the time, 'on one occasion the local kids involved with the Tabernacle, finding out we were gay, destroyed our rehearsal piano by chiselling off the ivories from the piano keys to make sure we could not rehearse. At a management meeting I attended with Bette bringing up a number of issues we had with performing there, one of the management committee, who we took to be a friend, said 'We have always tolerated you Bette'. At which point Bette exploded, as only he can do: 'Tolerated? I don't need your "toleration" thank you very much.'

Despite the difficulties, Bloolips turned the Tabernacle into a wild celebration of campness and queerness littered with anthems, and as AIDS began to hit the LGBTQIA+ community hard, continued in their resolve to entertain and inspire the masses, which they did with good success in America and Europe and in London and the Edinburgh Festival into the heart of the 1990s. Precious Pearl continues, 'My feeling was that the only reason they 'tolerated' us at all was because Bette had the sheer balls to insist we were taken seriously – for as gay people we know, comedy is the most serious thing in the world'.

Today, Bette Bourne is a grand dame in his eighties. As an actor, drag queen and activist, he continued performing across the world for decades. Recalling the long struggle that led to Gay Liberation and the acceptance of queer theatre into the mainstream is 'completely alarming, absolutely fit-making. Especially to the young queens, the youngsters', says Bourne affectionately. The Tabernacle has continued its legacy of platforming art, theatre and dance as a tool for freedom including legends such as Mark Elie. In 1986 he started a ballet school here which now collaborates with the world's leading dance companies: Rambert Ballet, Lisbon's Ballet Gulbenkian and the sensational Dance Theatre of Harlem.

Cast your eyes across the leafy Powis Square that leads to the entrance of the Tabernacle. In the run-up to its opening as a community arts space in 1970, this area was the world's smallest country – 'the Free and Independent Republic of Frestonia!', based around nearby Freston Road. Surrounded by decaying mansions, peeling and sooty, the walls were covered in graffiti calling for the community to defy authority.

During the summer of 1967, a group of activists gathered one night when as few people were around as possible, with all the tools necessary to get through the ten-foot-high fence. They called themselves Notting Hill People's Association and, threatened with eviction, they were intent on storming the private gardens between Powis Square and Colville Gardens, opening them up for public use. Sweaty, triumphant and landing over the other side of the fence, they opened their lunch boxes to fairy cupcakes and cocktail sausages, and proceeded to picnic on the lawn and set up a short-lived camp. In their new self-proclaimed state, they unilaterally declared independence from Britain and sent a telegram to the UN asking for membership and a peacekeeping force, should the Greater London Council decide to invade. They even printed a coat of arms, issued stamps and passports. A strict immigration policy of radical queens and revolutionaries only, that's how to turn a visa office into a Donna Summer concert.

The area was awash with squats, alternative advice centres and underground press, and was the first port of call if you needed somewhere to live or a vegan meal. After the House of Dreads for homeless Black youth was set up at 13 Colville Square, the Black Liberation Front set up Ujima Housing in Powis Square – community-led housing for low-income families, while the Gay Liberation Front were reclaiming buildings for queer people. Release, the drugs information service and underground magazines *Oz*, *Friendz* and the Black activist magazine *Hustler* were all born on these streets. Also on the square was the headquarters of the Angry Brigade, who were accused of carrying out 25 attacks on government buildings, embassies, corporations and the homes of ministers between 1967 and 1971. They were an anti-fascist movement against the British invasion of Northern Ireland, the Vietnam war, the government's industrial-relations policies and sexism. They believed the violence caused by their protests was incomparable to the violence faced by the communities they fought alongside.

Avant-garde phrases like 'armed love' and 'fighting for peace' would permeate through the atmosphere. Stand by the brightly coloured slides and swings harking back to the atmosphere of the times and ask yourself, can the lessons from the whole of this vibrant Square inform us with the toolkit we need to reorganise society today? At the end of 2022, 34 out of 56 Commonwealth nations formed out of the former British Empire still criminalise homosexuality. We can't stop mobilising. Can the wealth of art, theatre, music and activism formed in these streets fire us up with the passion to continue, until everyone is free? Yes, it can.

13. *LURE ME TO RAPTURE* – CHEPSTOW PUB, 38 CHEPSTOW PLACE

Stroll onwards, past burnt-out empty buildings next to expensive boutiques and a stream of 'Justice for Grenfell' graffiti lining the neighbourhood walls. The tug of war of bottom-up love and top-down power in Notting Hill will never die. En route is My Beautiful Laundrette. If your frock has become dirty along the tour, make the most of this laundrette, a tribute to the landmark LGBTQIA+ film of that name, featuring a utopian inter-racial relationship. Onwards to 38 Chepstow Place, where the hugely popular Chepstow pub had a drag cabaret act upstairs and downstairs became the helm of the underground gay and women's liberation community, who plotted a feminist revolution around the pub tables here.

Throughout herstory, lesbians have been at worst invisibilised and at best seen as an add-on to the gay man's story. Tired of being sidelined in the public realm, Gay Liberation Front (GLF) women were definitely not going to stand for it in their personal lives too.

Most of the GLF Women's Group lesbians were already activists within the Women's Liberation Movement (WLM) and so gay women's liberation was catalysed upon leaving the mixed organisation. Frankie Green shares:

Lesbians were pathologised, as were gay men. There was some overlap of both experiences, but we did not have the legal prohibition which criminalised and imprisoned them. Films such as *The Killing of Sister George* presented the tragic outcome of lesbianism as suicide or in 'The Fox' as death from a falling phallic tree. These provided nothing positive, other than creating a desire to go the Gateways, the lesbian club in Chelsea. There were no books, plays, music, no hint of the great flowering of lesbian, gay and feminist culture that was to come.

Twelve women from a diverse, cross-class community met here in early 1972 to respond to the need for a publication representing their lives. A trailblazing activist and unapologetic roaring dyke, Jackie Forster was the founding editor. She wrote in the magazine's first issue:

> The intrepid dyke makes herself vulnerable just by being visible in a not always gay-friendly world. She invents herself visually, socially and sexually. Lesbians have always been a sexual avant-garde, redefining their own notions and challenging societies clichéd ideas of feminism.

The group included Nettie Pollard, who remembers battling against stigma from all directions, from the homophobia within the heteronormative framework of the Women's Liberation Movement (WLM) and misogyny within the GLF. They persevered and named the magazine *Sappho* after the Greek icon and lesbian poet whom describes her passionate love of women in these tantalising words: 'Melt her mood to mine with amorous touches, Till her low assent and her sigh's abandon. Lure me to rapture.' Indeed the word 'lesbian' derives from the name of the island of Lesbos, where Sappho was born.

The magazine spread fast throughout Britain to 'educate society about the true facts of lesbianism, support lesbians and women's causes'. As well as holding vibrant public meetings with guest speakers monthly for many years, the magazine included thoughtful, astute articles about lesbian love, political status and women's liberation and the fight for lesbians to become mothers. Nettie contributed a piece on Icebreakers, the gay help service with revolutionary aims to end oppression within the psychiatric establishment. This all helped pave the way for *Gay News* to erupt into the world soon after, the first LGBTQIA+ publication since partial decriminalisation in 1967 that was first sold at Pride. Within a few years 'the right to a self-defined sexuality' came to be a preface added to the WLM list of demands, as well as the call for 'an end to discrimination against lesbians' – a huge paradigm shift for lesbian culture in Britain.

WHERE'S THE PUB? – THE CHAMPION, 1 WELLINGTON TERRACE

Emboldened by the seismic cultural shifts, pioneering people and actions that have peppered these streets, Nettie and her girl-friend Gaby Charing had a plan that would permanently crack through the divisions once and for all. You are standing outside the Champion, London's answer to the Uprisings at the Stone-wall Inn in New York where in 1969 the GLF journey began before its official formation in London the following year. Get yourself a well-earned refresher and soak in the scenery because 50 years ago this pub certainly wasn't as calm.

I hope you are still clutching the flyer you were handed back at Ladbroke Grove station, because here is the evidence of a movement that changed the world forever, boycotting pubs that banned homosexuals, people in drag or anyone wearing a gay or women's liberation badge. Pull it out and read:

PISSED OFF – WE'RE PISSED OFF BEING OVER-CHARGED, HERDED TOGETHER IN A SMALL NUMBER OF OVERCROWDED GAY GHETTO PUBS AND COFFEE BARS WHICH EXPLOIT GAYS AND GIVE LITTLE IN RETURN • WE'RE PISSED OFF being beaten, and hustled and pushed around on the streets for simply being ourselves, gay. SO, WE'RE DOING SOMETHING ABOUT IT – THAT'S WHY WE'RE TOGETHER – And that's why, next Wednesday, we're going to some Notting Hill pubs that the police and landlords have barred us from WE'RE GOING TO DEMAND FROM LANDLORDS AND POLICE EQUAL RIGHTS FOR ALL OUR HOMO-SEXUAL BROTHERS AND SISTERS

Nettie and Gaby weren't here just having a drink. Gaby rang London Broadcasting Company (LBC) radio station stating that there were hundreds of homosexuals in drag on their way to the pub. In reality there were only about ten of them, but Gaby believed that this announcement over the radio would bring them there – and it did. 'Hundreds of furious homosexuals!' soon blasted across the airwaves. On 16th September 1972, within moments the occupation began, 'We decided to sit down on the floor and let the police drag us out. I remember Gaby, who was dressed in purple loons and a tank top, saying in a rather posh voice, 'Tell me, officer, am I in drag?' Nettie recounts wearing her favourite purple velvet jeans, a smile growing across her face. Chanting 'Gay is Good!' It wasn't long, GLF activist Andrew Lumsden chimes in, 'before [she was] being carried out, put in a van and taken to Notting Hill police station'.

Throughout these years of 'sit-in' protests, it was at Marylebone Magistrates Court where 'Drag queens were charged with a number of offences including one of obstructing the footpath, two of obstructing the police and two of threatening behaviour'. The GLF commune residents made the most of it. Julian Hows would blow bubbles from the public gallery and in the defence box the outfits captivated the crowd. Richard Chappel in an ankle-length black satin dress with matching pill-box hat and net veil; Douglas MacDougall in a pink polka-dot dress and green glitter eyeshadow; and Bette Bourne in a startling red patterned velvet dress. They all pleaded not guilty, but were eventually charged with £15 fines. At a later reappearance in court, the judge sternly told Bette, 'Take off that hat – you're a man'. And Bette, slowly, with a glint in her eye quipped back, 'I can't take off my hat – it goes with the shoes'.

Next time I leave the pub in Notting Hill with my queer friends and allies, without being ousted and radiating a sense of possibility, as I mince back to Ladbroke Grove station through these streets, I will pause and take a moment. With the sun of queerness on my back, I'm going to remember Bette's legendary words and smile at the incredible, hard-fought creative spirit we have all inherited, a world in place of a war.

8

Mini-Minces

Short Queer Power Stops

NORTH

1. Like a Comet in the Sky – *Highbury Fields, Highbury Crescent, N5 1AR*
2. Club Asia – *Paradise Club, 1–5 Parkfield Street, Islington, N1 0PS*
3. Back to Black – *Abney Park Cemetery, 215 Stoke Newington High Sreet, N16 0LH*

SOUTH

4. No Borders, No Nations, End Deportations – *Peckham Library, 122 Peckham Hill Street, SE15 5JR*
5. Doing the Washing Up – *Royal Vauxhall Tavern, 372 Kennington Lane, London SE11 5HY*
6. How UK Black Pride Began – *Goding Street Bus Stop, Vauxhall, SE11 5AW*
7. Poo Power – *23 Station Road, South Norwood, Croydon, SE25 5AH*

EAST

8. Home Away from Home – *Bishopsgate Institute, 230 Bishopsgate, EC2M 4QH*

9. Queer Night Pride – *The Glory, 281 Kingsland Road, E2 8AS*

10. Platform for Eternal Fierceness – *Hackney Downs Park, Downs Park Road, E5 8NP*

11. Back Up! Back Up! – *Hackney Town Hall, Mare Street, E8 1EA*

12. Revenge of the Teenage Perverts – *Ridley Road Market, E8 2NP*

13. East London Strippers Collective – *The White Horse, 64 Shoreditch High Street, E1 6JJ*

WEST

14. Pinkwashing Protesting – *Israeli and Russian Embassies, 6/7 Kensington Palace Gardens, W8 4QP*

15. Leather Queens – *The Coleherne, 271 Old Brompton Road, SW5 9JA*

16. Sweet, Juicy Revenge – *Sainsburys, 118–120 Brompton Road, SW3 1JJ*

CENTRAL

17. Gay is Good! – *Harley Street, W1G 6AQ*

18. Ten Amyl Nitrate Capsules – *Le Duce, 25 D'Arblay Street, W1F 8DZ*

19. Cult of the Clitoris – *Palace Theatre, 113 Shaftesbury Avenue, W1D 5AY*

20. Chirruping – *Bow Street Magistrates Court, 4 Bow Street, WC2E 7AT*

21. The Notorious Urinal – *Corner of Wellington Street and Strand, WC2E 7DN*
22. Reach Out and Touch – *Hyde Park, W2 2UH*
23. Abseiling for Freedom – *Big Ben, Westminster, SW1A 0AA*
24. Nuns on the Run – *Methodist Central Hall, Storey's Gate, SW1H 9NH*

North

1. *LIKE A COMET IN THE SKY* – HIGHBURY FIELDS, HIGHBURY CRESCENT, N5 1AR

On the first small cottage on the West Side at the beginning of the Fields, you will find a plaque that commemorates the first ever open, public demonstration for LGBTQIA+ rights in British history against unjust laws and police misconduct, which took place in Highbury Fields, a popular cruising spot at the time.

Two days before the demonstration, Louis Eakes, then chair of the Young Liberals, was caught in a sting operation, and although Louis maintained he was merely looking for a light for his cigarette, he was arrested. The policemen were acting as agent provocateurs and he was subsequently found guilty of 'importuning for an immoral purpose'. At the time, merely smiling, winking or flirting with another man could result in an arrest for importuning. When word made it to the Gay Liberation Front (GLF), the lack of evidence, combined with the immense volume and prevalence of arrests, compelled the group to mobilise. In 1967, homosexuality had been decriminalised for men over the age of 21 for consenting acts in private, and the GLF wanted homosexual love to be public.

On 27 November 1970, between 50 and 150 GLF activists gathered outside London's Highbury and Islington station before marching arm-in-arm, leading a torchlight procession and rally to Highbury Fields. In the words of GLF newspaper *Come Together*, GLF members were 'seething with anger at this [arrest], the latest among hundreds of crimes committed against gay people by the police and the establishment every year'. While the entrapment by 'pretty policemen' of Eakes and others was an issue which immediately impacted men, a number of lesbian and trans women also joined the demonstration, as long-standing GLF campaigner Nettie Pollard recalled, 'in defiance and solidarity'.

'It was a very exhilarating moment for homosexuals in Britain, to actually be banded together in public for the first time', remembers Aubrey Walter. As the adrenaline wore off when they retired to the nearby Cock Tavern for a celebratory drink, Stuart Feather, GLF activist and author of *Blowing the Lid: Gay Liberation, Sexual Revolution and Radical Queens*, began to realise the significance of what they'd achieved: 'I always thought of [GLF] as a stellar event ... it was like a comet passed over this country, if you like, and it came, and it was suddenly there, it appeared in the sky, and after a while it disappeared.'

2. *CLUB ASIA* – PARADISE CLUB, 1–5 PARKFIELD STREET, ISLINGTON, N1 0PS

The Paradise Club was the venue for Asia, the UK's first queer 'world music' club, founded by Don Tyler and Andy

Piccos, on Thursday nights in 1988. Paradise was a huge 700-capacity venue and very luxurious too. It is now the O$_2$ Islington Academy. It was a turbulent era during the Thatcher years, a time of 'pretty police', Section 28 protests, and a very active, overtly racist National Front. At Asia, the global music DJs were DJ Ritu and David McAlmont, spinning bhangra, Latin and African sounds. Upstairs at Asia was the techno floor featuring Bell DJs Peter Thomas and the Sleaze Sisters. By 1992, the Block club night had taken over the upstairs on Friday through to Monday nights, with a leather, rubber, uniform, denim dress code. Lesbian London listed a Women Only Pool Night upstairs at Paradise in 1994. Popstarz was launched by club promoter and DJ Simon Hobart here in 1995, an attempt to provide an antidote to the mainstream gay scene, with the emphasis on 'boozing not cruising'. It became a huge success, becoming the UK's biggest indie club night, gay or straight, before moving to the West End. DJ Ritu went on to create Club Kali at The Dome in Tufnell Park – the UK's first queer Bollywood club – which also had an eclectic range of culture-connecting music from Madonna to Asha Bhosle, as well as Arabic and African genres. 27 years later, Club Kali has fostered a huge global LGBTQIA+ community and was recently awarded a Pink Plaque from Islington Council. The club celebrates diversity, but most of all, music through queer expression, and has been the launchpad for generations of performers and the home of the glamourous Chutney Queens – drag queens and trans folk dressing in elaborate and ornate sarees and jewellery.

3. *BACK TO BLACK* – ABNEY PARK CEMETERY, 215 STOKE NEWINGTON HIGH STREET, N16 0LH

There's something particularly queer about graveyards. Maybe it's because queers share a deep recognition that life is short and that death is the most dramatic thing we can do. In fact queer icon Amy Winehouse filmed the promo video for 'Back to Black' here. Her legendary talents will continue to survive long past her untimely death. Her rejection of mainstream norms and her razor-sharp wit will make her a friend of the gays and the queers forever more. Abney Park cemetery also includes the graves of queer music hall icons like actor, singer, and burlesque and pantomime performer Nellie Power (stage name of Ellen Maria Lingham, 1854–87). And you'll find the grave of George Leybourne (1842–84), who in his short years eclipsed other singers of his time in fame and riches. He was better known by his stage name Champagne Charlie and by his trademark long Newmarket coat, immaculate evening dress suit and white gloves.

Cemeteries are often top cruising spots (this one in particular) too. If you do fancy cruising here, why not get yourself a hankie to stick in your back pocket? The hankie code has long been a colour-oriented signifier to connect with fellow queers. Featuring hundreds of combinations of differently coloured handkerchiefs in either side of the back pockets, it facilitates the sharing of preferences for oral, anal, and bondage and discipline, dominance and submission, sadism and masochism (BDSM), and much more. My favourites are the wearing of a leopard-print hankie in your right back pocket to show you find tattoos sexy, or a silver lamé hankie in your left back pocket to show that you are a 'celebrity star fucker'.

South

4. NO BORDERS, NO NATIONS, END DEPORTATIONS –
PECKHAM LIBRARY, 122 PECKHAM HILL STREET,
SE15 5JR

On 20 February 2016, hundreds gathered here for the first annual Peckham Pride, a politically charged pro-migrant, pro-LGBTQIA+ march and celebration. Peckham – an inner-city area of London with a large migrant population, particularly from Nigeria and Ghana – has been the site of regular aggressive raids by the UK Border Agency. Often the targets of the raids are LGBTQIA+ asylum seekers being dragged away from their homes. Less than one hundred miles away in the Bedfordshire countryside sits the Yarl's Wood detention centre where many are sent to. Shopkeepers came out and gave speeches about the raids that were happening so regularly that it was now time to fight back. Organised by activist groups Lesbians and Gays Support the Migrants (LGSM), Movement for Justice by any Means Necessary and South East London Sisters Uncut, the marchers chanted 'No Borders, No Nations, End Deportations' in unison. The day unfolded with art, spoken word, DJs, performances and talks. Highlights included a performance by Glamrou from drag supergroup Denim and queer club nights, Mari Cumbia and Queefy Cabaret. Ida-Sofie Picard said, 'LGBT rights depend very much on migrant rights. We're much stronger united.' Purpose built on an unassuming industrial estate, the centre is populated by those facing deportation. Predominately housing women, Yarl's Wood has never been far from controversy, and accusations of sexual assault and abuse hang over the centre.

5. *DOING THE WASHING UP* – ROYAL VAUXHALL TAVERN, 372 KENNINGTON LANE, LONDON SE11 5HY

A former Victorian music hall, the Royal Vauxhall Tavern (RVT) is not only iconic for being South London's oldest surviving gay venue, back to when it was an epicentre for drag life since the 1940s. In 2014 the community rallied together to fight it being closed down by property developers. Campaign group RVT Future formed and acted fast, rallying support for the RVT to become registered as an Asset of Community Value (2014) and Grade II Listed Building (2015), because of its importance to the LGBTQIA+ community – both firsts for an LGBTQIA+ venue. Unashamedly working class and unapologetically irreverent towards the authoritarian regimes that try to repress us, it provides a space for performers from the local neighbourhood and around the world to express our queer soul-fire! Projects include 'Duckie!', 'Club Wotever' and 'Queers Against the Cuts'. A major inspiration of mine is David Hoyle who regularly performs here, a brilliant crusader constantly speaking truth to power, defiantly maintaining queer performance art both as anarchic and cathartic.

At the height of the AIDS epidemic in 1987, police were carrying out aggressive raids on LGBTQIA+ venues in 'space suits' (early versions of boiler suits protecting against hazardous materials) and rubber gloves for fear of contracting the virus. The harassment often had the pretext of a concern for public order rather than sexual offences. Pubs, clubs and other venues were threatened with closure, and people feared losing their livelihoods. At the time, stellar performer Paul O'Grady had an eight-year residency here as the inimitable Lily Savage, his catty drag persona with sky-high boots and even higher blonde hair. Lily was on stage on the evening of 24 January 1987, when 35 policemen raided the venue and carted customers into waiting vans outside. This was the club's second raid that winter, based on the flimsy excuse of 'customers being drunk on licensed premises', though few saw it as anything but an attempt to intimidate the LGBTQIA+ community. 'I was doing the late show and within seconds the place was heaving with coppers, all wearing rubber gloves. I remember saying something like, 'Well well, it looks like we've got help with the washing up', remembers Lily Savage of that night. Legend.

Long live the RVT.

6. *HOW UK BLACK PRIDE BEGAN* – GODING STREET BUS STOP, VAUXHALL, SE11 5AW

This bus stop outside 'Bootylicious' nightclub birthed the biggest and most vital pride movement in modern herstory. In 2004 a coach full of Black lesbian and bisexual women left this bus stop for Southend-on-Sea for a face-to-face Black Lesbians United Kingdom (BLUK) event. This trip, organised by Phyll Opoku-Gyimah, widely known as Lady Phyll, proved so popular that they returned the following year to celebrate LGBTQIA+ pride in a space that felt open to people of all ethnicities. In 2005 Lady Phyll co-founded UK Black Pride, Europe's largest pride celebration for LGBTQIA+ people of colour, Black in its political sense including the 'African and Asian diaspora'. 'It was amazing', Lady Phyll says of UK Black Pride's founding get-together. 'It was a moment I will never forget. Just to be in a space where you've got so many people with a shared commonality. We understood each other's struggle, and felt empowered.'

Today Lady Phyll is also Executive Director of the 'Kaleido-scope Trust' a UK-based charity working to uphold the human rights of the global LGBTQIA+ community and overturn laws that criminalise LGBTQIA+ people. Forty-one countries in the commonwealth still criminalise homosexuality, so Lady Phyll is on hand to remind us:

As a community of diverse and dynamic LGBTQIA+ people, we have to be aware and stay alert; we have to organise in sol-idarity with our siblings around the world, and we have to understand the role we can play in ensuring a free world for everyone.

In 2016 Lady Phyll turned down the Member of the Most Excel-lent Order of the British Empire (MBE) that she'd been offered by the Queen and her advisers in government. Phyll refused to accept an award linked to 'colonialism and its toxic and enduring legacy in the commonwealth, where – among many other injustices – LGBTQIA+ people are still being persecuted, tortured and even killed because of sodomy laws'. Why? Because Phyll's whole life has been about promoting Queer Black Pride with integrity and to nourishing the intersectional bonds of people power that connect us all. 'I knew when we went to Southend that we were going to have a great time', says Lady Phyll, 'but when I think about how it's grown, sometimes I pinch myself, or cry, or both.'

7. *POO POWER* – 23 STATION ROAD, SOUTH NORWOOD, CROYDON, SE25 5AH

On Worlds AIDS Day 2014, at 5 a.m., a merry band of activists from the London chapter of AIDS Coalition to Unleash Power (ACT UP) dragged half a tonne of horse manure to the Croydon North and Lambeth office of anti-immigration, anti-European Union political party UKIP (UK Independence Party) here at 23 Station Road, South Norwood. Two months before, Nigel Farage, leader of UKIP, reportedly said that HIV positive migrants should not be allowed to enter the United Kingdom. And the previous week, Farage's former deputy leader had made outrageous comments blaming gays for HIV, saying we lead 'short, miserable lives'.

Decorating the manure with a giant red world AIDS Day ribbon, the activists also hung a banner on the garage door reading 'What goes around comes around', along with 'Solidarity on World Aids Day', '#ukipstinks' and '#actuplondon'. ACT UP activist Gary Hunter said:

We've had enough of UKIP's misinformation and offensive attacks on minorities. We wanted to show Farage that people living with HIV aren't going to take his B.S. any longer – so we've returned it. The vile crap that UKIP keeps spreading stigmatises and ostracises people living with HIV, gay people and immigrants. We thought this steaming pile of muck was a great representation of what we, as HIV-positive people, think of UKIP's agenda.

Two weeks later the headlines in the *Croydon Guardian* announced that the landlord had evicted Winston McKenzie, the UKIP branch chairman, after the action. One headline stated, 'Things are a bit shit for UKIP's Winston McKenzie.' I laughed so hard that morning I spilled my tea.

East

8. *HOME AWAY FROM HOME* – BISHOPSGATE INSTITUTE, 230 BISHOPSGATE, EC2M 4QH

Open to the public since 1895, this is my 'home away from home': the biggest campaigning and counter-culture archive in Britain. I researched *Queer Footprints* here, supported by the nicest LGBTQIA+ enthusiasts and fellow herstory geeks you could ever hope to meet. Hilariously wedged between banks and hedge fund offices in the city's square mile, this glorious building tells a different story. Civil rights, trade union, and suffragette banners line the walls, and inside the Special Collections and Archives you will find one of the most extensive collections on LGBTQIA+ history, politics and culture in the UK, from the late nineteenth century onward.

The collections encompass LGBTQIA+ history politics and culture, with archives from Stonewall, Switchboard, GMFA/ The Gay Men's Health Charity, OutRage!, material relating to the Terrence Higgins Trust, Schools Out, UK Leather and Fetish Archives, *Achilles Heel* and *QX* magazines, The Gay Liberation Front (GLF), Rebel Dykes, East London Strippers Collective, and the emerging anti-colonial Queer Revolution. The library also holds 20,000 LGBTQIA+ titles, from academic works, biographies, fiction and poetry to pulp fiction, along with over 2000 journal titles from around the world. The LGBTQIA+ Pamphlet Collection contains around 2500 items including programmes for festivals and events, as well as extensive ephemera such as club flyers, t-shirts, banners and badges.

Also, the toilets are great for cruising.

9. *QUEER NIGHT PRIDE* – THE GLORY, KINGSLAND ROAD, E2 8AS

In 2020, Queer Night Pride demonstrations took over the street in London as well as in Bristol, in response to a massive rise in hate crimes. Speakers included representatives from Traveller Pride, the Transprisoner Alliance, UK Black Pride, Gay Liberation Front, Make Poland Queer Again and Queer China UK, and drag queen Naya, who organised a protest in Liverpool in solidarity with Josh Ormrod, who was attacked. The demo took place between East London's finest queer spaces. It started outside the Glory, marched to Dalston Superstore and ended with an after-party at Vogue Fabrics.

One speaker at the demo was Sarah Jane Baker, formerly Britain's longest-serving trans prisoner, who now coordinates Transprisoner Alliance in support of trans people behind bars. Sarah beamed to the crowd as she addressed them:

Night Pride is a protest. Not a demand for equality. We are not shadows of the past, hiding behind curtains of shame and fear. We are not a dream of a future that can never be realised. We are here, now, and with love, support and sheer determination, we can create a safer and more equal society where none of us have to live in fear. With love to you all.

Next to the mic was Tyler Hatwell, who founded Traveller Pride up the road at the Mildmay Community Centre in Dalston. Traveller Pride are a UK-based collective made up of LGBTQIA+ Travellers working to provide support, representation and a platform for LGBTQIA+ Travellers, who are empowering their community in response to ever increasing hostility within the current government's Police, Crime and Sentencing Act:

Even when hate crime doesn't happen to you, knowing that someone was victimised due to an immutable characteristic which you also have sends chills through you. Whole communities feel the reverberations of a hate crime, and the message that we're unsafe gets bolstered. Events like this, visibly and proudly challenging that feeling of isolation, therefore become vital.

10. *PLATFORM FOR ETERNAL FIERCENESS* – THE YARD
IN QUEEN'S YARD HACKNEY WICK, E9 5EN

Since 2018 Pride of Arabia had many of their pioneering parties here. With the exhilarating mission set as 'platform for eternal fierceness', Pride of Arabia is a feminist, queer, anti-capitalist social support network and platform offering space (physical and digital) for engaging in politics of care, resource sharing and knowledge production. They centre LGBTQIA+, SWANAs, migrants and people of colour (POCs) who are navigating their identities and finding community through mutual interdependence and owning their narratives:

> SWANA is a decolonial word for the South West Asian/North African (SWANA) region in place of Middle Eastern, Near Eastern, Arab World or Islamic World that have colonial, Eurocentric, and Orientalist origins and are created to conflate, contain and dehumanise our people. We use SWANA to speak to the diversity of our communities and to forward the most vulnerable in our liberation.

The surrounding area has historically been a site of challenges to fascism and tyranny too. In nearby Hackney Downs in December 1875, several thousand people assembled to take part in the destruction of fences newly built around enclosures on what had traditionally been regarded as common land. In September 1991, in response to white-nationalist hate attacks, Anti-Fascist Action sponsored Unity Carnival on Hackney Downs, and 10,000 people joined the biggest anti-fascist event in more than a decade. 'We have organised today's event to draw attention to the growing number of racist attacks especially in East London. The fact that some sections of the community virtually live under siege is unacceptable and we hope you are prepared to do more than just come to this symbolic show of unity,' stated the organisers.

11. *BACK UP! BACK UP!* – HACKNEY TOWN HALL, MARE STREET, E8 1EA

For most of the 2010s and continuing today, trailblazing, intersectional, queer feminist direct action group Sisters Uncut have led the charge and captured the public imagination in tackling the scandal of domestic violence and targeting the government policies that make it harder to respond to the challenge.

In 2016 you would have seen purple smoke blasting into the air as Sisters Uncut activists unleashed a mass of flares from the balcony chanting 'Social housing is a right, is a right, is a right. Social housing is a right, not a privilege.' They were here to celebrate a significant win in the borough after occupying an empty council property for nine weeks in protest against huge cuts to support services tackling domestic violence. After two rounds of negotiations with the Hackney Mayor Phillip Glanville he said he was committed to making all of the currently empty units at the Marian Court estate – the site of the activists' occupation – fit for habitation and filled by Christmas, while agreeing to fill all empty units in Hackney by September of the next year.

Previously Sisters Uncut dyed the Trafalgar Square fountains red and occupied the red carpet at the *Suffragettes* movie premier with 'They cut, we bleed' painted on their trouser legs. This slogan sums up their analysis of the impact of austerity on domestic violence services. In another action they organised a 'funeral march' that began at Soho Square, with a giant purple and green 'Domestic Violence Services' funeral wreath as a tip of their hats to the Suffragettes who used the same colours to build, and win, freedoms for women one hundred years earlier.

A fierce sense of solidarity and determination comes through in their chants of 'Back up, back up! We want freedom, freedom! All these sexist, racist cuts, we don't need 'em need 'em.' The sisters won their demands as they squatted a local flat, turning it into a temporary women's refuge and support centre. As a result 50 homes set for demolition were refurbished for families in need, council-run women-only hostels have been given extra training about domestic violence and many more survivors have been placed in self-contained flats or in Council-run accommodation.

12. *REVENGE OF THE TEENAGE PERVERTS –* RIDLEY ROAD MARKET, E8 2NP

In 1983, some of the regular DJs from the Bell pub in Pentonville Road included the Sleaze Sisters – Trill Burton and Pom Martin. Together with Rose Collis, Lorraine Trenchard, Nicola Field and Jimmy Somerville, to name only a few, were part of the Lesbian and Gay Youth Video Project (LGYVP), members of which interviewed Femi Otitoju, Isaac Julien and others in the brilliant scratch video *Framed Youth – Revenge of the Teenage Perverts*, winner of the BFI Grierson Award.

One fresh winter morning, the film captures Rose, Nicola and other LGYVP women members doing vox pops in Ridley Road market in Hackney in February 1983. They were asking the bustling crowds, 'Can you tell me what a lesbian is please?', 'What would you say if your daughter was a lesbian?' and 'What would you say if I was a lesbian?' The responses were varied, horrific and hilarious. One young woman responded, 'Why are you concerned about lesbians? By any chance is there a lesbian around here?' Rose didn't hold back: 'Yeah, me. Would it surprise you to know that all the women here are lesbians?' she said proudly. Another woman took a moment and said that if her daughter was a lesbian, 'I'd stand by her, definitely. It doesn't matter what she turns out like, I'm still her mother and I'd try to help her as much as possible'.

13. *EAST LONDON STRIPPERS COLLECTIVE* – THE WHITE HORSE, 64 SHOREDITCH HIGH STREET, E1 6JJ

It's impossible to write about queer history without acknowledging the history of sex work, and the presence of queer sex workers in activism. Many sex workers have been 'queering' traditional social norms and disrupting the fabric of social respectability since the dawn of time. So, in the summer of 2016 a battle for the soul of Shoreditch raged outside the White Horse pub – a family-run, independent strip pub – as a coalition of activist-strippers launched 'RIP Shoreditch', a funeral procession through the East End. As they marched through the streets, they held a coffin with a stripper's pole in it alongside other mementos: a pair of high heels and a thick-glass collection jug, used traditionally by strippers in East London to collect tips from punters before going onstage. This action followed the shutdown of key LGBTQIA+ venues in the area – Chariots sauna, the Joiners Arms and the George and Dragon, plus numerous music venues. The East London Strippers Collective (ELSC) are all working strippers who fight for decent working conditions in the industry, and challenge the stigma around their work. 'Some might think that it's a good idea to clear an area of 'vice', says Edie Lamort from ELSC:

But it's part of the history and traditional culture of the area. Independent businesses are just not tolerated [anymore]. Shakespeare set up his first theatre in Curtain Road away from the rules and regulations of the city so people could have a bit of mischief. That's what Shoreditch has always been.

ELSC are part of a wide coalition of sex worker advocacy organisations who, alongside the Sex Worker Advocacy and Resistance Movement, English Collective of Prostitutes, and trade union 'United Sex Workers', have demonstrated against the criminalisation of sex work that would shut down online consumer spaces that are a lifeline for workers. The campaign to save the White Horse failed, but ELSC are intent on setting up their own strip club and continue advocating for decent working conditions. In the meantime, Harpies, the very first strip club in Europe to feature and celebrate queer and trans performers, opened its doors in 2019 at Metropolis Gentleman's Club in London, up the road in Cambridge Heath. 'Fun and pleasure is everything to me as a performer', says drag artist Chiyo Gomes, a long-time resident of Harpies – the brainchild of prolific Trans activist and founder of London Trans Pride, Lucia Blayke. Since then, Amsterdam has followed suit with the opening of LGBTQIA+ strip club Va Va Voom.

West

14. *PINKWASHING PROTESTING* – ISRAELI AND RUSSIAN EMBASSIES, 6/7 KENSINGTON PALACE GARDENS, W8 4QP

This street is packed with the London headquarters of countries who violate international human rights, including LGBTQIA+ rights.

It is bookended by criminals. At the Notting Hill end there is the Russian Embassy. Since December 2017, Chechen authorities have been rounding up people based on their actual or perceived sexuality. LGBTQIA+ people have been illegally detained, tortured and executed. Multiple organisations and media outlets have verified the horrors happening in Chechnya, in the Northern Caucasus region of the Russian state. The Russian LGBT Network is helping to evacuate people from Chechnya. They are sheltering them in safe houses, providing them food, clothing and psychological support.

At the Kensington end is the Israeli Embassy. Israel is a leading practitioner of what critics have dubbed 'pinkwashing', or the highlighting of gay-friendly attitudes in order to detract attention from their otherwise appalling human rights record. Thankfully groups like London Palestine Action exist. They are a network of people in London taking creative action against Israeli apartheid. Over the years the group and many others have organised demonstrations here, saying loudly and proudly 'NO to Israel's pinkwashing, YES to BDS!' BDS stands for 'boycott, divestment and sanctions', the most effective strategy by which the global community can hold Israel to account for its crimes, similar to the boycott effectively used against Apartheid in South Africa.

You can get involved with groups like the Kaleidoscope Trust or All Out, who support and empower people from all countries affected by homophobic criminalisation.

15. *LEATHER QUEENS* – THE COLEHERNE, 271 OLD BROMPTON ROAD, SW5 9JA

During the 1970s and 1980s, punters would struggle to get to the bar here at the Coleherne – the poster-child of seductive gay culture in London Town. (The former Coleherne is now a gas-tro-pub called the Pembroke.) Scores of men in leathers lining the walls, some even turning up with motorbike crash helmets (even if they came by bus) just to complete the look. Gays started attending in the 1950s, but it was in the 1970s that the pub offi-cially turned itself into a leather bar with blackened windows and acquired worldwide fame. So much so that the Coleherne is featured in Armistead Maupin's book *Babycakes*, part of the Tales of the City series. Famous regulars were Freddie Mercury, Rudolf Nureyev and Kenny Everett. Within these walls a real atmosphere of queer desire and deep bonds were made among those who faced a harsh world beyond. The venue and punters also helped expose a number of police entrapment operations. It had a number of less salubrious regulars too, as it was the stalking ground of three serial killers, including Colin Ireland, known as 'the Gay Slayer', who murdered five people and died in HM Wakefield Prison in 2012.

After the pub doors closed, the lust still lingering in the air, the fun often continued in the alleyways afterwards.

16. *SWEET, JUICY REVENGE* – SAINSBURYS, 118–120 BROMPTON ROAD, SW3 1JJ

At the time of writing there is a Sainsbury's supermarket at 118–120 Brompton Road. I hear they sell some juicy tomatoes. Also at the time of writing, there are hundreds of thousands of people across the UK who still have to deal with the psychologi-cal consequences of being totally demonised in society. A whole generation, including myself, who are trying to recover from one of the UK's most lethal homophobic legislation in recent history. Section 28 – known at the time as Clause 28 – banned the promotion of homosexuality by local authorities and public institutions from 1988 to 2003, creating a culture of intolerance, homophobia and fear among the British public. Research carried out by NatCen in 1987 shows that at this time 75 per cent of the British public believed that 'homosexuality was always or mostly wrong'.

Have you found some nice ripe tomatoes? Goody good. Because around the corner from this Sainsburys is Belgrave Square. In the square is a certain £8 million home of Brian Souter, the founder of the Stagecoach bus company, who donated £1 million to the Keep the Clause campaign, its largest supporter.

I'll let you, dear readers, work out the rest.

Central

17. *GAY IS GOOD!* – HARLEY STREET, W1G 6AQ

Bob Mellors was a student at the London School of Economics (LSE) and a founding activist of the Gay Liberation Front (GLF). A pioneer of non-binary identity, Bob was part of the GLF counter-psychiatry group. Late one night in May 1971, they came here to Harley Street, the epicentre of private healthcare institutions for over 200 years. The GLF activists spray-painted slogans including 'People Not Psychiatry' and 'Gay Is Good' on the street's walls and doorsteps, to confront the use of aversion therapy, which involved the administration of electric shocks or nausea-inducing drugs coinciding with the patient being shown homoerotic images. Creative and resourceful as ever, the following day GLF activists attached mattress springs to colanders, put them on their heads and marched down the street, feigning involuntary spasms from electric shocks with fake blood running from their mouths. Doctors came out to the street to watch the demonstration unfold as flyers were handed out, which read: 'We accuse or slander those psychiatrists who call homosexuals immature or sick. Homosexuality is not an illness. It is not arrested development. It does not require treatment.' Paul Theobald remembers that day: 'We had to take a few drinks before we could get up the nerve to do it, but it was worth it, it made a real difference to see it there the next day.'

The levels of street surveillance we have now would make these spray-painting tactics harder (but not impossible), but today the GLF and allied LGBTQIA+ movements are part of a wide coalition calling for an independent inquiry into aversion therapy. Demands include compensation for those physically and psychologically affected, the establishment of specialised NHS counselling for victims of aversion therapy, and for the Department of Health to issue guidelines against the use of all transphobic and homophobic therapies.

18. *TEN AMYL NITRATE CAPSULES* – LE DUCE, 25 D'ARBLAY STREET, W1F 8DZ

Opened in 1964, Le Duce was a small basement bar where queer mods, dressed in Carnaby Street finery, danced to Motown and Bluebeat. Jimmy Ruffin's Motown classic 'What Becomes of the Brokenhearted?' was a Le Duce favourite. Most of the queer bars of the 1950s and 60s didn't serve alcohol, so people became inventive and found recreational uses for Preludin, a slimming drug which delivered a nice buzz for quite a few hours, or a tin of ten amyl nitrate capsules, intended to treat angina. You snapped or 'popped' the capsule into a hankie and inhaled. Poppers weren't widely available in bottles until the late 1970s.

Manager Peter Burton remembers the heavy use of purple hearts and black bombers – that is, everyone was off their heads on speed:

A transvestite called Samantha was a regular and got high from sniffing her wig-cleaning fluid. It was where the hip hung out and bright trousers and shirts swept away a grey past. Even Levi's jeans were new – all those lads sitting in tepid baths to shrink-wrap their arses and a little sandpaper around the crotch to show off a packet; they shouldn't be too tight, or your partner couldn't get his hand down the back and dance with his fingers stroking your arse when no-one was looking. There was no DJ, just a jukebox and a seating area screened off by a massive fish tank. Police raids were frequent and whenever they arrived clubbers chucked their pills into the tank.

The fish bills must have been astronomical!

19. *CULT OF THE CLITORIS* – PALACE THEATRE, 113 SHAFTESBURY AVENUE, W1D 5AY

Maud Allen published a sex manual for women in 1900, and created 'The Dance of the Seven Veils' in 1906 from Oscar Wilde's *Salome*, subsequently performed here at the Palace Theatre, with women making up 75 per cent of the audience. Maud also took MP Noel Pemberton Billing to court for threatening legal action against 'gays destroying the moral fibre of this country' and declaring Maud their 'lesbian accomplice'.

Billing had created the Vigilante Society, whose aim was the 'object of promoting purity in public life'. Maud's legal battle outraged Billing, and his Society's paper denounced on 16 February 1918 the 'Cult of the Clitoris [that] exists in this country who would gather together to witness a lewd performance for amusement during wartime on the Sabbath'.

We have a lot to thank her for. Defiant, Maud Allen paved the way for sex-positivity by asserting the right to a public life free from homophobia and patriarchy – from which we can learn a lot as we confront rampant institutionalised transphobia in Britain today.

20. *CHIRRUPING* – BOW STREET MAGISTRATES COURT, 4 BOW STREET, WC2E 7AT

In 1870, gender non-conforming pioneers graced these courts. Ernest Boulton and Frederick Park were arrested for 'conspiring and inciting persons to commit an unnatural offence'. They had been arrested while wearing women's clothes at the Strand Theatre, and were better known as Fanny and Stella. Their trial took place here. In court Fanny wore a cherry pink evening dress trimmed with lace, and Stella was dressed in dark green satin with a matching shawl. The jury learned that they had recently been thrown out of the Alhambra Theatre in Leicester Square for making 'chirruping' sounds to attract male attention. The London public found Fanny and Stella hugely entertaining. They were loudly applauded whenever they left court, and their testimony in the courtroom was greeted with uproarious laughter. A botched medical examination, and the confused evidence of the police as to what Fanny and Stella were actually meant to have done, resulted in a verdict of not guilty, whereupon Stella fainted. Today Bow Street Magistrates Court is to become a 'boutique hotel', Westminster Council having turned down a request that it become a police museum.

21. *THE NOTORIOUS URINAL* – CORNER OF WELLINGTON STREET AND STRAND

You've perhaps heard of the 'Notorious B.I.G.'. Here lies the site of the 'Notorious U.R.I.N.A.L.'

This was a heavily policed cruising spot on the Strand in the early 20th Century and was frequented by Oscar Wilde, Joe Orton and Sir John Gielgud. Situated within the Adelphi Estate, it was built on sloping ground between the Strand and the Thames, a network of narrow alleys and passageways both above and below ground. In Matt Houlbrook's phenomenal work *Queer London: Perils and Pleasures in the Sexual Metropolis, 1918–1957*, he quotes a police inspector of that period when noting that 'by the 1920s it was [...] a well-established "resort of the persons of the sodomites class"' since 'the locality is badly lighted' and housed 'several notorious urinals'. Men of all social classes resisted the attacks on 'good order' and 'decency' and met here. Today it is a glitzy cocktail bar and cabaret club, called Cellar Door, with unisex toilets with fully see-through doors (until you lock them). If these walls could talk …

22. *REACH OUT AND TOUCH* – HYDE PARK, W2 2UH

What's this red balloon landing at your feet?

It's 15 September 1991. Look up and hundreds of red balloons are glistening in the sun. Listen closely and a voice touches your soul. Wait a second ... that's Whitney Houston!

As head of HIV services in the London Borough of Brent, Vernal Scott was saying precious last goodbyes as more friends died, and he was determined to do something. He came up with the idea of a national vigil that would show the human face of the crisis. 'Reach Out and Touch', a UK HIV/AIDS vigil and procession with flowers in Hyde Park was founded to soothe the nation's broken spirit and offer a tonic to the communities hardest hit by HIV and AIDS. Vernal needed £20,000 to make it happen and here's how he did it:

> I asked many celebrities to help me out and they were all very supportive, but only one came up with the cash. Step in Mr George Michael, my absolute hero, but asked to keep his name secret. As a result most of the press at the time speculated that Whitney Houston, my surprise guest on the day, had funded the event. And so on Sunday 15 September 1991, the 6000-person strong Reach Out and Touch vigil assembled in London's Hyde Park and proceeded to Trafalgar Square. We inserted the flowers we were carrying into nets and hoisted them up to create a giant floral wall. We laid the remaining blooms out like a giant carpet. And, of course, there were speeches as well as a gospel choir. George was very pleased with how it turned out and even sent me an autographed copy

of his then CD, *Listen Without Prejudice*, signed with a kiss. I treasure it to this day.

The Fitzrovia Chapel, near Goodge Street, is all that remains of the former Middlesex Hospital, which housed some of the few dedicated AIDS wards that existed in London. It is now reopened as a place of quiet contemplation for the community. Take some time there to 'remember the dead and fight for the living'.

23. *ABSEILING FOR FREEDOM* – BIG BEN, WESTMINSTER, SW1A 0AA

In 1988 a group of trailblazing friends and activists were intent on stopping the lethal Section 28 law, that would 'ban the promotion of homosexuality' in local authorities and in Britain's schools. The prime minister Margaret Thatcher had whipped up a frenzy in the British public with her statement: 'Children who need to be taught to respect traditional moral values are being taught that they have an inalienable right to be gay … All of those children are being cheated of a sound start in life. Yes, cheated.'

The night before the bill was passed, the activists were in one of their flats in Clapham discussing possible ways to resist Section 28. They'd been on marches, signed petitions and started support groups. 'We had done lots of actions, lots of blockades and breaking into places. But this was different', recounts Sally Francis:

The day before, one of my friends went into the main chamber of the House of Lords wondering what we could do there. She had the idea of swinging from the microphones hanging from the ceiling. We thought they were probably not strong enough. In the end, we bought a washing line in Clapham market and knotted it up on the bus on the way up – it was pretty low-tech stuff.

So on 24 May 1988, the activists abseiled over the guest gallery on washing lines tied together, descending into the House of Lords after peers voted in favour of the bill. Sally remembers:

I smuggled the rope in under my donkey jacket and didn't set off any alarms. We waited till the vote went for the clause. If they had voted against it, we weren't going to do it. But they voted for it, so that's what we did. When the vote finished, we were all looking at each other, and then we did it!

The security panicked and politicians leapt to their feet. The legends were 'marched across the large lobby outside the entrance to the House', shouting 'Stop the Clause!!!', and taken up to a room that 'seemed very close to Big Ben', where they were held for several hours:

The police were very friendly to us, and kept opening the door to tell us that we were on the 6 o'clock news, then the 7 o'clock news, etc. When we were released from detention the others were waiting for us outside the houses of parliament, alongside some press, requesting interviews. We all agreed to go to a pub off the bottom of Whitehall, and talk about the action.

Thatcher's die-hard fan, David Cameron, voted against the repeal of Section 28, but was eventually forced to apologise in 2012, when he was prime minister – a hollow 'fauxpology' which counted for little while he was slashing budgets for LGBTQIA+ welfare resources. The results of Section 28 left a whole generation of students without any understanding of queer issues, while teachers failed to stop homophobic bullying in schools, fearing for the security of their jobs if they did. Though discussion around LGBTQIA+ inclusive relationships and sex education has improved, important and necessary topics are still rarely covered. A 2017 Stonewall report found that 40 per cent of current UK pupils have never been taught about homosexuality – the figures are even higher for bisexual or trans identities – and 90 per cent have had no teaching whatsoever on safe sex for same-sex couples. Trans people still have neither identity rights nor legal protection, and risks of suicide, anxiety and depression in our community are still twice as high as for homosexuals. 'Yes, cheated', indeed. No further questions 'your honour'.

'Nothing's going to make up for that damage' says Dani Singer, LGBTQIA+ activist and Queer Tours of London guide.

24. *NUNS ON THE RUN* – METHODIST CENTRAL HALL, STOREY'S GATE, SW1H 9NH

'Enter the hall in small groups. Ones or twos. Act unobtrusively. Dress conservatively. Act cool. Make no sign of protest until it is your turn.' These words were written on a note by activist John Chesterman, handed out at a Gay Liberation Front (GLF) organising meeting.

It was 1971 and the fundamentalist Christian group, the Festival of Light, were launching a campaign for church-based morality to dominate British life. They were intent on 'cleaning up Britain'. Backed by figures such as Mary Whitehouse, Cliff Richard, Malcolm Muggeridge and Lord Longford, the Festival of Light held an opening meeting here in Westminster, lobbying for an end to 'moral evils' including openly gay lifestyles and the 'evils of pornography'. They aimed to recriminalise homosexuality and abortion. John Chesterman explains:

'Networking' as a word didn't really exist then, but it's what we did over the Festival of Light. We started to put word out through the underground press. I persuaded Janet (another activist) to volunteer for the Festival, in their main office, so we had access to all the literature and even the mailing list. We sent out fake mailings on it. For the big final rally, we sent out false parking plans for the coaches, which gave people real hassle.

The big day arrived: on 9 September 1971 Parliament Square was filling up with coaches loaded with Christian evangelists arriving from across the country. The activists placed themselves strategically all over the hall, all in disguise. Stuart Feather was there and recounts in his memoir, *Blowing the Lid: Gay Liberation, Sexual Revolution and Radical Queens*, 'as the evening wears on, it becomes obvious there's going to be some aggravation, British-style':

As the meeting settled once more, nuns in blue habits and white wimples filed out of their pews to stand in line abreast across the central aisle, before moving solemnly to the front of the hall. The pious sisters turned to face the congregation, lifted up their skirts and Can-Can danced their way down the aisle [and mice were released to scurry around]. There was pandemonium. People were utterly staggered. They couldn't believe their eyes; nuns going mad, exhibiting themselves in public ... 'Let there be light!'; the Minister welcomed them and as soon as these words left his mouth, 'Bang!' and the lights went out, plunging the entire hall into darkness.

The *Guardian* headline proclaimed 'Darkness in our Light'. The Festival of Light collapsed a month later and never recovered. The morally crusading nuns and their mousey accomplices were victorious. Today, as homophobic and transphobic fundamentalists continue to trot out their bigotry, we can see that the nuns won the battle but not the war, and we still have work to do. Squeak Squeak.

Resources for Further Reading and Action

TEN-POINT PLAN TO REACH TOTAL QUEER UTOPIA

1. Abolish the police and the prison system
2. Decriminalise sex work
3. Decriminalise drugs
4. Create housing co-operatives
5. Enable free access to healthcare at point of service
6. Build a world beyond capitalism
7. Break down all borders
8. Life-long free education for all
9. End privatisation of all resources
10. Reproductive freedom for all

MOVEMENTS AND SPACES

Aids Coalition to Unleash Power (ACT UP) London
The Cocoa Butter Club
Faggamuffin Bloc party
Friends of the Joiners Arms
Gay Liberation Front
Green and Black Cross
Hungama
Lesbians and Gays Support the Migrants
London Bi Pandas
London Trans Pride

The Love Tank
Make Poland Queer Again
Opening Doors
Pride of Arabia
Pxssy Palace
Queer Tours of London – A Mince Through Time
Radical Faeries
Remember Olive Morris Collective
Royal Vauxhall Tavern
Schools Out
'This is My Culture' George Michael Party
Traveller Pride
UK Black Pride
UK Lesbian and Gay Immigration Group (UKLGIG

COMMUNITY CENTRES AND BOOKSHOPS

Brixton Advice Centre
Crossroads Women's Centre
Freedom Bookshop
Gay's the Word Bookshop
George Padmore Institute
Glass House / Common Press
Housmans Bookshop
London LGBT+ Community Centre
The Outside Project
Queer Britain
Queercircle

RESOURCES

HEALTHCARE AND SUPPORT

HIV I-Base
56 Dean Street
Albert Kennedy trust
Blackout UK
Cliniq
cliniQ (inclusive trans sexual health and wellbeing)
The Crossroads Women's Centre
ELOP
GALOP
Gender Identity Clinic
Gender Identity Development Service
Gendered Intelligence
Helios Centre
London Friends
Mermaids
Mildmay Mission Hospital
Mortimer Market/Bloomsbury Clinic
Mosaic LGBT+ Young Person's Trust
National AIDS Trust
Positive East
Positively UK
PREPster
Safe Only
SH! Women's Erotic Emporium
Stonewall
Stonewall Housing
Sweatbox
Terrence Higgins Trust

ARCHIVES

Bishopsgate Institute
Black and Gay Back in the Day
Black Cultural Archives
British Library
LGBT Community Archives at London Metropolitan Archives
LSE Hall-Carpenter Archives including Sheba Feminist Press and The Women's Film
Marx Library
National Archives
Rebel Dykes history Project
Ruckus! Black Lesbian, Gay, Bisexual and Trans (BLGBT) Cultural Archive
Television and Video Network (WFTVN)

BOOKS – LONDON FOCUSED

Abolishing the Police – Koshka Duff and Cat Sims
Abolition Revolution – Aviah Day and Shanice McBean
Amiable Warriors – Peter Scott-Presland
Black Resistance to British Policing: Racism, Resistance and Social Change – Adam Elliott-Cooper
Blowing the Lid: Gay Liberation, Sexual Revolution and Radical Queens – Stuart Feather
Courage to Be: Organised Gay Youth in England 1967–1990 – Clifford Williams
Cruising Utopia: The Then and There of Queer Futurity – José Esteban Muñoz

RESOURCES

Diary of a Drag Queen – Crystal Rasmussen

London and the Culture of Homosexuality, 1885–1914 – Matt Cook

Mr Loverman – Bernadine Evaristo

No Bath but Plenty of Bubbles: An Oral History of the Gay Liberation Front, 1970–73 – Lisa Power

None of the Above – Travis Alabanza

OutRage! – Ian Lucas

Queer London – Alim Kheraj

Queer London – Matt Houlbrook

Queer: A Graphic History – Meg-John Barker

Rebel Footprints – David Rosenberg

Release the Beast – Bimini Bom Boulash

The Dilly: A History of the Piccadilly Rent Boy Scene – Jeremy Reed

The Ethical Stripper – Stacey Clare

The Frontline: A Story of Struggle, Resistance and Black Identity in Notting Hill – Ishmahil Blagrove Jr

The Squatters' Handbook – Advisory Service for Squatters

The Transgender Issue: An Argument for Justice – Shon Faye

There Ain't No Black in the Union Jack – Paul Gilroy

Transgender behind Prison Walls – Sarah Jane Baker

BOOKS – WIDER INSPIRATION

All About Love – bell hooks

Are Prisons Obsolete? – Angela Davis

Black Skin White Masks – Frantz Fanon

Gentrification of the Mind: Witness to a Lost Imagination – Sarah Schulman

Pedagogy of the Oppressed – Paulo Freire

Pleasure Activism – Adrienne Marie Brown

Teaching To Transgress: Education as the Practice of Freedom – bell hooks

The Politics of Dispossession: The Struggle for Palestinian Self-Determination 1969–1994 – Edward Said

We Can Do Better Than This: 35 Voices on the Future of LGBTQ+ Rights – Amelia Abraham

Zami – Audre Lorde

FILMS AND DOCUMENTARIES

Are You Proud?

Brixton Fairies: Made Possible By Squatting – Laundrette Films

Framed Youth: Revenge of the Teenage Perverts

Grove Roots

It's A Sin

Kidulthood

My Beautiful Laundrette

Pride

Rebel Dykes

United in Anger: A History of ACT UP

Accessibility Guide

At the time of writing the majority of London tube stations do not have wheelchair-level access. Below is a short guide for the routes, but you may prefer to use a journey planner at www.tfl. gov.uk. As you are walking historical routes some of the pavements may be cobbled and uneven.

NEAREST WHEELCHAIR ACCESSIBLE STATIONS WITH PLATFORM ACCESS

Chapter 1. Soho – Tottenham Court Road – step free from street to train for the Northern and Elizabeth Lines, but from street to platform only for the Central Line

Chapter 2. Brixton – Brixton

Chapter 3. Trafalgar Square – Tottenham Court Road or Green Park

Chapter 4. Piccadilly Circus – Tottenham Court Road

Chapter 5. Bethnal Green – Shoreditch High Street (Overground) and Liverpool Street – only accessible street to platform (not to train) for the Northern Line and Overground

Chapter 6. King's Cross – King's Cross

Chapter 7. Ladbroke Grove – the nearest station with step-free access is Paddington

Resources
Disability Rights UK Radar Key Scheme: https://shop. disabilityrightsuk.org/products/radar-key

Plan an accessible journey: https://tfl.gov.uk/transport-accessibility/plan-an-accessible-journey

OUTbound is TfL's LGBT+ staff network group. The group is committed to championing a safe and inclusive work environment so LGBT+ colleagues can be authentic, celebrate who they are and have equality of opportunity

TfL Diversity and inclusion: https://tfl.gov.uk/corporate/about-tfl/corporate-and-social-responsibility/equality-and-inclusion

ACCESSIBLE TOILETS

Chapter 1. Soho – Tottenham Court Road underground station – accessible and gender neutral

Chapter 2. Brixton – Tesco Express Stockwell, 131–143 Clapham Road, SW9 0HR

Chapter 3. Trafalgar Square – Tottenham Court Road underground station – accessible and gender neutral

Chapter 4. Piccadilly Circus – Tottenham Court Road underground station – accessible and gender neutral

Chapter 5. Bethnal Green – Richmix Cinema, 35–47 Bethnal Green Rd, London E1 6LA

Chapter 6. King's Cross – King's Cross Station, Upper Mezzanine

Chapter 7. Ladbroke Grove – Lonsdale Road/Portobello Road

Resources

Gender-Neutral Toilet Finder – https://app-movement. com/d/77. This app will help people locate gender neutral toilets, rate them for their accessibility and other features. You can add locations of where you spot them and add pictures. This is designed to help trans people feel more comfortable when out and about. This app is the brainchild of a trans* youth group in Newcastle upon Tyne.

Toilet Map – www.toiletmap.org.uk. It is possible to filter the search to find gender neutral and accessible toilets.

Refuge Restrooms – www.refugerestrooms.org. Refuge Restrooms is a web application that seeks to provide safe restroom access for transgender, intersex and gender-nonconforming individuals. Users can search for restrooms by proximity to a search location, add new restroom listings, as well as comment and rate existing listings.

A Bit More about Me

The summer of 2023 marks my 18th 'HIVersary' – a moment to reflect and celebrate learning to live and love again since being diagnosed HIV+. Back in 2005 I didn't have a scooby-do what to think or do, until a gorgeous lover took me in his arms and told me to learn about a movement called ACT UP – (Aids Coalition to Unleash Power). I read about them and watched films about them, and their founding principle struck me right in the centre of my heart. ACT UP were 'United in Anger and committed to direct action to end the AIDS crisis, along with the broader inequalities and injustices that perpetuate it'. Who are these people and where can I find them? Soon enough, this movement literally saved my life.

Without them I wouldn't have vital emotional support, practical information and have been welcomed into a family of mutual aid and of course have access to life-saving medication. In fact without ACT UP I wouldn't have become a healthcare and LGBTQIA+ activist and I wouldn't be writing this now.

Before I learned about ACT UP, I actually thought that it was the government who resolved the AIDS crisis. How wrong I was! Real change and real support came from us! It was the hundreds of people at the 'die-in' protests in Trafalgar Square, it was brave friends abseiling in protest into Parliament, it was the radical refusal of nurses working on AIDS wards to leave the dying alone, it was dykes donating blood, it was Queens on support phone lines throughout the night, it was clandestine meetings in the back of bookshops, it was booksellers resisting police raids, it was Whitney Houston singing at AIDS rallies in Hyde Park and so much more – all are covered in this book.

Since learning about ACT UP, I've been hooked on people power and listening to the voices underneath the pavement pushing us to march onwards, hand in hand, heads held high. I knew I had to find out more about how extraordinary people, like all humans, like you reading this book, can change the world.

Acknowledgements

Huge huge thanks to David Shulman and all at Pluto Press for enabling all this, all the support and for continuing to produce radical literature in an industry set against it. Thank you a million to the Society of Authors for your grant and all you do to support working-class writers that helps generate access for as wide a field of writers as possible. To Mark Glasgow, my long-term combabe and collaborator for the gorgeous illustrations, you are such a spark of queer joy.

If you are interested in queer herstory, activism and/or writing please get in touch on @danglassmincer or alright@ theglassishalffull.co.uk as there are many plans afoot to support a new generation to keep the flames of freedom alight.

While London is my love, Berlin has been my sanctuary while writing *Queer Footprints*. As a Queer Jew whose grandparents were all Nazi Holocaust survivors, the pink triangle that commemorates the lives of our queer ancestors who perished in the concentration camps have guided me in this process. The pink cover of *Queer Footprints* makes my heart beat even harder to keep their legacy alive in the spirit of 'never again, for anyone'. Thank you to my biological family for these vital lessons.

Whilst these words on the page were written by me, I was purely a filter for the hundreds of visionaries, artists, scholars, lovers and friends who have provided sense-making and support throughout this process. You have believed in me, which means so much. Thank you James Baldwin! I read your writing tips every morning for the last two years! '...Last but not least, Lady Phyll and Josh Rivers and all at UK Black Pride, Busy Being Black and

ACKNOWLEDGEMENTS

Kaleidoscope Trust for your tireless and illuminating vision and commitment and of course all my comrades at ACT UP, Friends of the Joiners Arms, Queer Tours of London – A Mince through Time and the Gay Liberation Front (GLF), who have been the best, most committed and inspiring cheerleaders, which comes as no surprise from legends like you. The process was transformational and utterly ridiculous and I feel hugely lucky to honour the ancestors.

And to you my darlin Queer Family and our allies, I love you so so much. I am one blessed bender to have you in my life.

May Mackeith, Jessica Cox, Ben Dilieto, Pierre-Yves Dalka, Marc Thompson, Ruth Edmonds, Tilly Gifford, Ragi Gifford, Hannah Downie, Turiel Downie, Patrick Braithwaite, Cathy McCormack, Amy Downing, Emma James, Juliana Napier, Anna Rudd, Giedre Miksyte, Lip Wieckowski, Joseph Wilson, Nina Scott, Kevin Mccormick, Belal Awad, Alice Rodgers, Jakob Rosenberg, Ricarda Bochat, Sergey Khazov-Cassia, Taz Herlihy, Kasia Sadaj, Howe Furber, Dawn Hoskins, Nell Gulliver, Ian Weichardt, Alexandra Molano Avilan, Dirg Aab-Richards, Ted Brown, Nettie Pollard, Stuart Feather, Andrew Lumsden, John Lloyd, Marc Thompson, Silvia Petretti, Angelina Namiba, Atalanta Kernick, Siobhan Fahey, Julian Hows, Ian Townson, Jonathan Blake, Ian Bodenham, Ian Johns, Jenna Samji, Alim Kheraj, Isabel Young, Alex Craddock, Marwan Kaabour, Davy Marzella, Jason Jones, Jeremy Goldstein, Sapphire McIntosh, Eric Thompson, Mike Jackson, Ashtar Alkhirsan, Dani Singer, Ashley Joiner, Sam Wood, Dan de la Motte, Dinah Potthoff, Casey Mae Baum, Jenna Samji, Matt Bonner, Michelle Tylicki, Isis Amlak, Ishmahil Blagrove Jr, Toby Laurent Benson, Robbie Gillett, Tom Barber, Tom Marshman, Ajamu X, Stef Dickers, Rachel Smith, Uli Lenart, Jim Macsweeney, Lisa Power, Rupert Whitaker, Michael

Cashman, Carla Towney, Sally Stone, Josh Hepple, Stafford Scott, Jack Ash, Andrés Saenz de Sicilia, Jon Ward, Magda Oldziejewska, Rob Logan, Bisila Noha, Sam Jones, Will Dunleavy, Eoin McCaul, James Tait, Emma Madden, Koos Couvee, Adam Sach, Ejel Khan, Mazharul Islam, Tashnuva Fardousi, Qiuyan Chen, Jamie Chi, Lyndsay Burtonshaw, Sam Walton, Christian Gordine, Duncan Passmore, Becky Buchanan, Arabella Hope, Sean Robinson, Mark Whiting, Cloud Downey, Miqhael Kannemeyer, Mike Kear, Jide Rowland Macaulay, Zia Almos Joshua, Andria Mordaunt, John Mordaunt, Simon Watney, Shir Freibach, Stella, Tam Vibert, Mzz Kimberely, James Bartlett, David Stuart, Peter Tatchell, Yvonne Taylor, David Rosenberg, Ian Lucas, Stewart Who?, Terry Stewart, Paul Bommer, Jamie Di Spirito, Evan Swisher, Edmund Farmer, Daniel Brennan, Simon Collins, Obie Lindberg, Geoff Hardy, Michael James, Mary McIntosh, Angela Mason, Elizabeth Wilson, Tara Hudson, Luca Modesti, Sarah Schulman, Michelle Ross, Amy Roberts, Peter Cragg, David Pollard, Mark Ashton, Veronica McKenzie, Lavinia Co-Op, Bette Bourne, Paul Shaw, Susie Draper, Geoff Hardy, Brenda Goodchild, Michelle Ross, Phil Wilmot, Tyler Hatwell, Miriam Rose, Joe Ryle, Howie Taylor, Billy Holzberg, Aderonke Apata, Stacey Clare, Ritu Khurana, Holly Buckle, Sarah Nicol, Nell Andrew, Katlego Kao Kolanyane-Kesupile, Mica Coca, Ntombi Nyathi, Maria Lahumatina, Olimpia Burchiellaro, Damien Arness-Dalton, Peter Scott-Presland, Astro aka Alex Fear, Daniel Pini Neis, Michael Christov, Ross Fletcher, Julian Capolei, Victoria Noe, Corinne Williams, Danny Alderslowe, Mark Robb, Jo Brydon, Souleyman Messalti, Pat de Brún, Kaz Kane, Sally Moussawi, Camilli Bhogal-Todd, Marie Mcleod and especially to you Sam Arbor sweetheart – the kettle's on and my feet are getting cold.

Sources

The following are the sources consulted in writing this book. These are listed according to their appearance in the text. Every effort has been made to credit all sources but if there are any errors or omissions, we will be pleased to rectify them in future printings. In most cases, quotations from the author's own correspondence and interviews are credited at the appropriate place in the text.

INTRODUCTION

'Property Developer Funds Pop-Up Gay Bar as Condition of Planning Permission', *Guardian*, 2021, https://tinyurl.com/43pznvp6 (last accessed August 2022)

Queer Tours of London – A Mince through Time, home page at https://queertoursoflondon.com

Dan Glass, *United Queerdom: From the Legends of the Gay Liberation Front (GLF) to the Queers of Tomorrow*, Bloomsbury Publishing, 2020

'OUTbound is TfL's Lesbian, Gay, Bisexual and Trans (LGBT+) Staff Network Group', https://tinyurl.com/mrvd4s5b (last accessed August 2022)

bell hooks, *All About Love: New Visions*, Harper, 2000

Angel Kyodo Williams, Lama Rod Owens and Jasmine Syedullah, *Radical Dharma: Talking Race, Love, and Liberation Paperback*, North Atlantic Books, 2016

'Etymological Meaning of Education', https://tinyurl.com/2p96j682 (last accessed August 2022)

Paolo Freire, *Pedagogy of the Oppressed*, 30th anniversary edition, Continuum, 2000

Amara Ochefu, 'The History of Intersectionality and the Black Feminists Behind it', 2021, https://tinyurl.com/22y8jaj2 (last accessed August 2022)

Fannie Lou Hamer, *To Tell It Like It Is: The Speeches of Fannie Lou Hamer*, University Press of Mississippi, 2010

Martin Luther King Jr., *Letter from the Birmingham Jail*, HarperOne, 1994

Maya Angelou, Shaker, *Why Don't You Sing?*, Random House, 1983

Vox, 'The Rise of Anti-trans "Radical" Feminists – Explained', https://tinyurl.com/nuwk2ypw (last accessed September 2021)

David France, *How to Survive a Plague*, Pan Macmillan, 2017

Chris Godfrey, 'Section 28 Protestors 30 Years on: "We Were Arrested and Put in a Cell Up by Big Ben"', Guardian, 7 March 2018, https://tinyurl.com/yvyak7dk (last accessed August 2022)

El Hunt, 'Call the Switchboard – The Story behind the UK's Biggest LGBTQ+ Helpline', 2019, https://tinyurl.com/2p3hsu68 (last accessed August 2022)

Vernal Scott, 'George Michael Was My Secret HIV Fundraising Hero', 2016, https://tinyurl.com/t3j9cvpr (last accessed August 2022)

'London Remembers – Aiming to Capture All Memorials in London', https://tinyurl.com/yck8f683 (last accessed August 2022)

bell hooks, 'A Love Letter to the Personification of Love', 2022, https://tinyurl.com/4s5fhhsd (last accessed August 2022)

1. *HOMOSEXUALS COME OUT!* – SOHO

'The Number Ones: Diana Ross' "Ain't No Mountain High Enough"', https://tinyurl.com/jskefa29 (last accessed August 2022)

Bishopsgate Institute Archive, 'Come Together: Gay Liberation Front', https://tinyurl.com/3x8ay3k6 (last accessed August 2022)

Matt Houlbrook, *Queer London – Perils and Pleasures in the Sexual Metropolis, 1918–1957*, University of Chicago Press, 2005

Jill Gardiner, *From the Closet to the Screen: Women at the Gateways Club 1945–85*, Pandora Press, 2003

John J. Wilcox, Jr., 'Archives at the William Way LGBT Community Center – Gay Flames', 1970 – https://tinyurl.com/n2zspu7v (last accessed August 2022)

Attitude Pride Awards, 'World's First Pride in London in 1972 Remembered by Gay Liberation Front Veterans', https://tinyurl.com/25zpfs33 (last accessed August 2022)

SOURCES

LSE Library, 'Gays Against Fascism – Gay Pride March' 1974, www.flickr.com/photos/lselibrary/7486040932 (last accessed August 2022)

José Esteban Muñoz, *Cruising Utopia: The Then and There of Queer Futurity*, Combined Academic Publishers, 2009

Dustin Bradley Goltz, *Queer Temporalities in Gay Male Representation: Tragedy, Normativity, and Futurity*, Routledge, 2010

'If You're a Disabled, Gay Twentysomething, Grindr Is a Godsend', *Guardian*, 2016, https://tinyurl.com/4s478uhh

TalkTime Edinburgh, providing free counselling for disabled teenagers, regardless of sexual orientation, www.talktimescotland.co.uk/ (last accessed August 2022)

'Social Model of Disability', https://tinyurl.com/2p822unz (last accessed August 2022)

James I. Charlton, 'Nothing About Us Without Us – Disability Oppression and Empowerment', University of California Press, 2000

'Soho Stories: Celebrating Six Decades of Sex, Drugs and Rock'n'Roll', https://tinyurl.com/yc75j7w7, (last accessed September 2021)

'What Happened to the Great London Nightclubs?', https://tinyurl.com/3nj6wye5, (last accessed September 2021)

'Soho and the Fall of the Dirty Squad', https://tinyurl.com/75syeemd (last accessed September 2021)

Yunfang Ma, 'It's All Gone Madame Jojo's', https://tinyurl.com/bdfep8ey (last accessed September 2021)

Dazed Digital, 'London Music Institution Madame Jojo's Shuts Down', 24 November 2014, https://tinyurl.com/287ppy4k (last accessed September 2021)

Andrew Lumsden, 'Alan Wakeman Obituary', *Guardian*, 20 August 2015, theguardian.com/world/2015/aug/20/alan-wakeman-obituary, 2015 (last accessed September 2021)

Alan Wakeman, *Fragments of Joy and Sorrow: Memoirs of a Reluctant Revolutionary*, Gemini Press, 2015

'Quentin Crisp reflects on trans identity in exclusive final autobiography excerpt', The Pink News, 2017, https://tinyurl.com/3vs63f2u (last accessed December 2022)

Quentin Crisp, *The Naked Civil Servant*, Jonathan Cape, 1968

Nigel Kelly, *Quentin Crisp: The Profession of Being – A Biography*, McFarland, 2018

Dan de la Motte, Queer Tours of London – A Mince Through Time – A Very Queer West End, 24.11.2018

Learning about the passage of time and persons in Darren Coffield's (2020) 'Tales from the Colony Room: London's Lost Bohemia' Steve Bamblett Blog, 2021, https://tinyurl.com/3xfu5bvm (last accessed December 2022)

Chris Godfrey, 'These LGBT Clubbers Say They Feel Shut Out of the Scene Because They Are Disabled – "I'd Love to Shag in Your Toilet, if Only I Could Get in"', Buzzfeed, 2017, https://tinyurl.com/2p8aw5y (last accessed September 2021)

Queer Tours of London, 'For Immediate Release 14.7.17 – LGBT+ Disability Rights Protest at London's Inaccessible Spaces', https://tinyurl.com/bdz829y5 (last accessed September 2021)

Ian Lucas, *OutRage! An Oral History* (Cassell Press, 1998)

'A Policeman's Lot …', *The Observer*, 24 March 2002, https://tinyurl.com/4cs3yzmp (last accessed September 2021)

'London Nail Bomber Must Serve at Least 50 Years', *Guardian*, 2007, https://tinyurl.com/3ephhwz5 (last accessed September 2021)

BBC, 'London Nail Bombings Remembered 20 Years on', 30 April 2019 – https://tinyurl.com/yb3xdate (last accessed September 2021)

'What's the Real Story Behind the Nail Bomber in Netflix's Newest True-Crime Documentary?', *Esquire Magazine*, 26 May 2021 – https://tinyurl.com/3awcwhx5 (last accessed September 2021)

'Drag King by Sister George', https://sistergeorge.bandcamp.com/album/drag-king

'How We Made: Tom Robinson and Nick Mobbs on Glad to Be Gay', *Guardian*, 2013, https://tinyurl.com/2p8vfca5 (last accessed September 2021)

Ian Lucas, *OutRage! An Oral History*, Cassell Press, 1998

'Figures Reveal a "Shocking" Rise in Homophobic Hate Crimes', *The Independent*, 2015, https://tinyurl.com/2p8mfjkv (last accessed September 2021)

SOURCES

'From "Go Home" Vans to Windrush Scandal: A Timeline of UK's Hostile Environment', *Guardian*, 25 May 2022, https://tinyurl.com/5fra84yu (last accessed August 2022)

BBC, 'Orlando Nightclub Shooting: How the Attack Unfolded',2016, https://tinyurl.com/yc5bkbvb (last accessed August 2022)

CBC News, 'London Gay Choir Sings Tribute to Orlando Shooting Victims', 2016, https://tinyurl.com/5an3jn6t (last accessed August 2022)

Matt Broomfield, 'We Watched Activists Ad-hack London to Commemorate LGBT History – Sexual Avengers', *Huck Magazine*, 2017, https://tinyurl.com/7nh5m9na (last accessed August 2022)

'Be Dull and Fucking Boring – Muriel Belcher Colony Room Club', 2016, https://tinyurl.com/yckvbze6 (last accessed August 2022)

Dean Street website, www.dean.st/about-us (last accessed August 2022)

AIDSMap, 'How a London Clinic Reduced New HIV Infections by 90% and Why More European Cities Can Do the Same', 2017, https://tinyurl.com/35hxza44 (last accessed August 2022)

Aidsmap, 'UK Rolls Out Vaccines for Gay and Bisexual Men at High Risk for Monkeypox', 2022, https://tinyurl.com/bdhbx23p (last accessed August 2022)

Filtermag, 'David Stuart: An Inspirational Leader in Chemsex Harm Reduction',2022,https://filtermag.org/david-stuart-chemsex-leader (last accessed August 2022)

Prepster, 'Educating and Agitating for PrEP in England and Beyond', https://prepster.info/ (last accessed August 2022)

'AIDS Activists Go Bare to Target Austerity', *Guardian*, 2016, https://tinyurl.com/muxfshhz (last accessed September 2021)

Deco London, 'The Gargoyle Club, Soho, 2017', https://tinyurl.com/5ce3hmhm (last accessed August 2022)

Ladies Who London, 'Soho – Tallulah Bankhead, Sex, Scandal and Salaciousness on Stage', https://tinyurl.com/mr4yfb9u (last accessed August 2022)

Daily Beast, 'Tallulah Bankhead: Gay, Drunk and Liberated in an Era of Excess Art', https://tinyurl.com/m9kjajf3 (last accessed August 2022)

Factinate, 'Glam Facts About Tallulah Bankhead', https://tinyurl.com/3hc7vn55 (last accessed August 2022)

Jason Okundaye and Marc Thompson, 'This Is Radical Love – the History of Black Queer Britain in Pictures', *Guardian*, 22 March 2021, https://tinyurl.com/26us7p7f (last accessed August 2022)

'"We Tried to Carve Out Our Own Spaces": How the Black LGBTQ+ Community of the 1980s and 1990s Is Being Honoured Online', *GQ Magazine*, 2021, https://tinyurl.com/39yxv7hy (last accessed August 2022)

Jason Okundaye, 'We kept getting people saying: excuse me, you don't look gay' – how Black people fought for a space at Pride', Guardian, 30 June 2021, https://tinyurl.com/62hsvzv8 (last accessed December 2022)

Marc Thompson and Jason Okundaye, 'Black and Gay Back in the Day: A Snapshot of Queer History', *The Face*, 2021, https://tinyurl.com/yc4zsrm3 (last accessed August 2022)

Amaka, 'Sistermatic – An Ode to London's Long-Lost Pioneering Sound System and Collective Run by and for Black Queer Women', 2021, https://tinyurl.com/ycxf2usu (last accessed August 2022)

L'Oréal Blackett, Bustle, 'The Founder of the Black Curriculum Wants Us To Get It Right From The Start', 21 November 2021, bustle.com/rule-breakers/lavinya-stennett-founder-the-black-curriculum (last accessed August 2022)

'These Stunning Photos Celebrate the History of Black Pride through the Ages', *Metro*, 2021, https://tinyurl.com/yj5bysnz (last accessed August 2022)

Calvin Dawkins, 'DJ Biggy C', Spotify Playlist 'It's A Sin – The Black Album', https://tinyurl.com/2p5jch9e (last accessed August 2022)

'In Depth: Is Soho Over', *Attitude Magazine*, 2022 – https://tinyurl.com/mwkwes3j (last accessed August 2022)

London Trans Pride is the 'one day we're not outcasts', BBC, 2019, https://www.bbc.com/news/newsbeat-49447918 (last accessed December 2022)

NYC LGBT Historic Sites Project, 'Paradise Garage', https://tinyurl.com/2ft3w5ep (last accessed August 2022)

Inky Cloak, 'The Thump of the Music, Like Some Powerful Creature Barely Contained', https://tinyurl.com/3uvkjn55 (last accessed August 2022)

2. *EVEN A HOMOSEXUAL CAN BE A REVOLUTIONARY* – BRIXTON

Marcus Garvey, *Message to the People: The Course of African Philosophy*, Majority Press, 1986

'The Week in Audio: Brixton: Flames on the Frontline; The Lazarus Heist; Gangster', *Guardian*, 2021, https://tinyurl.com/mupdxfzk

Revolting Gays, www.revoltinggays.com (last accessed August 2022)

The Institute of Contemporary Arts, 'War Inna Babylon: The Community's Struggle for Truths and Rights', curated by Tottenham Rights, together with independent curators Kamara Scott and Rianna Jade Parker, www.ica.art/exhibitions/war-inna-babylon, 2022 (last accessed August 2022)

Steve Swindells, 'All Human Beings Welcome', https://steveswindells.wordpress.com/tag/steve-swindells/ (last accessed August 2022)

Ishmahil Blagrove Jr, *The Frontline: A Story of Struggle, Resistance and Black Identity in Notting Hill*, Rice N Peas, 2022

BBC, 'Cherry Groce: Memorial Unveiled for Brixton Police Shooting Victim', 2021, www.bbc.com/news/uk-england-london-56873938 (last accessed August 2022)

Library of Congress, 'LGBTQIA+ Studies: A Resource Guide – 1969: The Stonewall Uprising', https://guides.loc.gov/lgbtq-studies/stonewall-era (last accessed August 2022)

Bishopsgate Institute, 'Rebel Dykes Archive', www.bishopsgate.org.uk/collections/rebel-dykes-archive (last accessed August 2022)

Sebastian Buser, 'Women's Anarchist Nuisance Cafe – Various Locations in London Borough of Hackney and Tower Hamlets', 2014, https://site-writing.co.uk/womens-anarchist-nuisance-cafe-a-site-writing-project-2014/ (Accessed 01.06.21)

'Britain: Bloody Saturday, Monday, Apr. 20, 1981', *Time*, https://tinyurl.com/47aesfck (last accessed August 2022)

Black History Studies, 'Educating the Community to Educate Themselves. The New Cross Massacre', https://blackhistorystudies.com/resources/resources/the-new-cross-fire/ (last accessed August 2022)

'Metropolitan Police Chief Apologises over Cherry Groce Shooting', *Guardian*, 2014, https://tinyurl.com/ya9ax5d2 (last accessed August 2022)

'Dorothy "Cherry" Groce Inquest Finds Police Failures Contributed to Her Death', *Guardian*, 2014, https://tinyurl.com/fahrbdfz (last accessed August 2022)

Tate, 'Q&A: Ajamu', 2021, www.tate.org.uk/tate-etc/issue-53-autumn-2021/qa-ajamu (last accessed August 2022)

Outspoken Arts, Ajamu Ikwe-Tyehimba, https://outspokenarts.org/ajamu-ikwe-tyehimba/ (last accessed August 2022)

Urban75, 'The Brixton Fairies and the South London Gay Community Centre, Brixton 1974–6', 14 February 2012, https://tinyurl.com/496ec6d9 (last accessed August 2022)

PRNewswire, 'A Bond across the Pond: A First of its Kind Twinning Joins Two Important Business Improvement Districts (BID) and Forges a Bond Across the Pond in Two Radical Communities of Color', https://tinyurl.com/3kc9xshz, 2021 (last accessed August 2022)

Black History Month, "How Olive Morris Fought for Black Women's Rights in Britain', 29 December 2021, https://tinyurl.com/5dkusb6m (last accessed August 2022)

Rachel Smith and Barbara Vesey, *The Love That Dares: Letters of LGBTQ+ Love Friendship Through History*, Ilex Press, 2022

Lizzie Cocker, 'Olive Morris: Forgotten Activist Hero', https://rememberolivemorris.wordpress.com/category/activism (last accessed August 2022)

Lambeth Archives, 'Olive Morris Collection – Community Leader and Activist', https://tinyurl.com/5dyp2mtd (last accessed August 2022)

Urban75, 'The Brixton Fairies and the South London Gay Community Centre, Brixton 1974–6', 14 February 2012, https://tinyurl.com/496ec6d9 (last accessed August 2022)

London News Online, 'Winifred Atwell Knew the Key to Her Success', 2021, https://tinyurl.com/4zz82rbm (last accessed August 2022)

SOURCES

Oluwatayo Adewole, 'Remembering Pearl Alcock, the Black Bisexual Shebeen Queen of Brixton', 2021, https://tinyurl.com/mr38pakd (last accessed August 2022)

'Policing the Riots: From Bristol and Brixton to Tottenham, via Toxteth, Handsworth, etc', *Crime and Justice*, cjm 87, https://tinyurl.com/mr2ypmtx (last accessed August 2022)

Liberty Human Rights, 'Stop and Search', https://tinyurl.com/y9hrdtvz

Audre Lorde, *The Master's Tools Will Never Dismantle the Master's House*, Penguin, 2018

'Urban75 Remembers One of Brixton's Finest Squatted Community Centres – Brixton: 121 Centre', https://tinyurl.com/avswhvms (last accessed August 2022)

Olive Morris, 'Squatters' Handbook', https://tinyurl.com/ypuabcye (last accessed August 2022)

Urban75, 'The Brixton Fairies and the South London Gay Community Centre, Brixton 1974–6', 14 February 2012, https://tinyurl.com/496ec6d9 (last accessed August 2022)

Grassroots Feminism, '*Shocking Pink* (Magazine, 1981–1982 and 1987–1992)', https://tinyurl.com/24f8rkfe (last accessed August 2022)

LGBT History Festival, 'London Rebel Dykes of the 1980s', https://tinyurl.com/2fsu6m87 (last accessed August 2022)

'Squatting in England: Heritage & Prospects – 2014-05-13', https://tinyurl.com/mwrp4ew5

C. L. R. James, *The Black Jacobins: Toussaint L'Ouverture and the San Domingo Revolution*, Vintage, 1989 (first published 1938)

May Day Rooms, 'Race Today (1973–1988)', https://maydayrooms.org/archive-of-the-month/ (last accessed August 2022)

Huey P. Newton, 'The Women's Liberation and Gay Liberation Movements', 1970, https://tinyurl.com/mxkuy753 (last accessed August 2022)

NSWP Global Network of Sex Work Projects, 'Street Transvestite Action Revolutionaries found STAR House', https://tinyurl.com/j2jx5w66 (last accessed August 2022)

Nadine White, 'Black People's Day of Action: Inside the 1981 New Cross Fire March that Brought Britain to a Standstill', *Huffington Post*, 2021, https://tinyurl.com/bpa6vtpw (last accessed August 2022)

'*Uprising* Review – Steve McQueen's Series on the New Cross Fire is Furious, Devastating TV', *Guardian*, 2021, https://tinyurl.com/2tz7eyrv (last accessed August 2022)

The Menelik Shabazz Film Collection, https://menelikshabazz.co.uk/project/blood-a-go-run (last accessed August 2022)

Terry Fitzpatrick, 'Bengali Housing Action Group', https://tinyurl.com/34yep7m3 (last accessed August 2022)

Stuart Feather, 'A Brief History of the Gay Liberation Front, 1970–73', 21 November 2007, https://tinyurl.com/5fv8dmmp (last accessed August 2022)

Brixton Advice Centre, https://brixtonadvice.org.uk (last accessed August 2022)

Visual AIDS, 'Platforming African-Queerness – Rotimi Fani-Kayode', https://visualaids.org/artists/rotimi-fani-kayode (last accessed August 2022)

Urban75, 'The Brixton Fairies and the South London Gay Community Centre, Brixton 1974–6', 14 February 2012, https://tinyurl.com/496ec6d9 (last accessed August 2022)

Ajamu Studio, www.ajamu-studio.com (last accessed August 2022)

Reni Eddo-Lodge, *Why I'm No Longer Talking to White People About Race*, Bloomsbury Circus, 2017

The New Brixton House, 'Our House', https://brixtonhouse.co.uk/our-house (last accessed August 2022)

Unfinished Histories, 'History of Alternative Theatre', www.unfinishedhistories.com (last accessed August 2022)

Flaminia Giambalvo, 'Sex Workers' Opera – This Opera Gives Sex Workers a Voice', https://tinyurl.com/yckkackx (last accessed August 2022)

3. *THE PANSIES ARE IN BLOOM* – TRAFALGAR SQUARE

Comparitech, 'Surveillance Camera Statistics: Which Cities Have the Most CCTV Cameras?', 2022, https://tinyurl.com/k3jp3fkk (last accessed July 2022)

SOURCES

Guardian, 'Scotland Yard Sets Up Squad to Track Protesters', 07.02.2006, https://tinyurl.com/y9m3t2c7 (last accessed July 2022)

MI5, 'Introduction to Counter-Espionage', www.mi5.gov.uk/counter-espionage (last accessed July 2022)

Graham McKerrow, Guardian, 'Antony Grey Obituary, Campaigner for the Decriminalisation of Homosexuality', 2010, https://tinyurl.com/5ybw5xdt (last accessed July 2022)

Peter Scott-Presland, '1958: Separate Beds, Librettist's Introduction', http://homopromos.org/1958_separate-beds.html (last accessed July 2022)

Interview with Eric Thompson, 30 September 2021

UVA Miller Centre, 'McCarthyism and the Red Scare', https://tinyurl.com/2p8rxjsw (last accessed July 2022)

'You've Probably Heard of the Red Scare, but the Lesser-Known, Anti-Gay "Lavender Scare" Is Rarely Taught in Schools', Time, 2020, https://time.com/5922679/lavender-scare-history/ (last accessed July 2022)

Jess McHugh, '"The Beginning of a Conversation": What It Was Like to Be an LGBTQ Activist Before Stonewall', Time, https://time.com/longform/mattachine-society/ (last accessed July 2022)

Library of Congress, 'LGBTQIA+ Studies: A Resource Guide – The Daughters of Bilitis', https://tinyurl.com/bdhske2c (last accessed July 2022)

Antony Grey, *Quest for Justice: Towards Homosexual Emancipation*, Chatto & Windus, 2011

Interview with Eric Thompson, 30 September 2021

Historic England, 'Experiments in Living', https://tinyurl.com/y5xse8r4 (last accessed July 2022)

National Archives, 'George Ives: Queer Lives and the Family', 2009, https://tinyurl.com/2p8dpuhe (last accessed July 2022)

George Ives – Closet Professor, 'Sacred Band of Thebes – The Order of Chaeronea', https://tinyurl.com/4xawy9xn (last accessed August 2022)

bell hooks, *All About Love: New Visions by bell hooks*, New Visions, 1999

Amy Herzog, 'Sylvester, "You Make Me Feel (Mighty Real)"', *ASAP Journal*, 2020, https://asapjournal.com/sylvester-you-make-me-feel-mighty-real (last accessed July 2022)

Jon Welford, Of Alley, London, 2021, https://tinyurl.com/yckmataa (last accessed December 2022)

'Forty Years of Sheer Heaven at the London Superclub', *Guardian*, 2019, https://tinyurl.com/55yz8kxr (last accessed July 2022)

'Does Homoerotic Beat Poem "Please Master" Belong in AP English Class? Teacher Forced to Resign Over it', *The Washington Post*, 2015, https://tinyurl.com/2p8bvvck (last accessed July 2022)

'Watch Adele Guest-Judge G-A-Y's "Porn Idol" at London's Heaven', *NME*, https://tinyurl.com/bxyavbnv, 2022 (last accessed July 2022)

'Heaven Nightclub Celebrates its 40th Anniversary', *Camden New Journal*, 2020, https://tinyurl.com/3cntypj3 (last accessed July 2022)

Terrence Higgins Trust, 'Learn about Our Namesake Terry Higgins', 2022, https://tinyurl.com/44p3j357 (last accessed July 2022)

BBC, 'Aids – The Unheard Tapes', 2022, www.bbc.co.uk/programmes/m0018t1c (last accessed July 2022)

'AIDS', www.pbs.org/outofthepast/past/p6/1981_1.html (last accessed July 2022)

HIV.gov, 'A Timeline of HIV and AIDS', www.hiv.gov/hiv-basics/overview/history/hiv-and-aids-timeline (last accessed July 2022)

Stewart Who?, 'HIV: Uninvited', 7 November 2021, http://stewartwho.com/opinion/hiv-uninvited/ (last accessed July 2022)

El Hunt, 'Call the Switchboard – The Story behind the UK's Biggest LGBTQ+ Helpline', *Huck Magazine*, 2019, https://tinyurl.com/2p3hsu68 (last accessed July 2022)

'A Policeman's Lot ...', *The Observer*, 2002, www.theguardian.com/the-observer/2002/mar/24/focus.news1 (last accessed July 2022)

'"Like Section 28 and Gay Rights": Fears UK Schools Being Silenced from Discussing Racism', *Guardian*, 2020, https://tinyurl.com/yck35jba (last accessed July 2022)

Peter Tatchell, 'NSW Must Learn from Britain's Disastrous Section 28', *Sydney Sentinel*, 2020, https://tinyurl.com/yc3tejvw (last accessed July 2022)

SOURCES

'Inalienable', www.lawinsider.com/dictionary/inalienable (last accessed July 2022)

'Why "There's No Such Thing as Society" Should Not Be Regarded with Moral Revulsion', *The Conversation*, 2020, https://tinyurl.com/2h5v4eky (last accessed July 2022)

George Severs, '"No Promotion of Homosexuality": Section 28 and the No Outsiders Protests', 2019, https://tinyurl.com/3sscwa4b (last accessed July 2022)

Hannah Kershaw in London School of Tropical Medicine and Hygiene, 'On Remembering the "Don't Die of Ignorance" Campaign', 2018, https://tinyurl.com/4mzpbvwv (last accessed July 2022)

Advocate, 'Larry Kramer's Anger Is Essential in Historic "Plague" Speech', 2020, https://tinyurl.com/56sxn43f (last accessed July 2022)

'40 years ago, the first cases of AIDS were reported in the US', CNN, 2021, https://tinyurl.com/4kd7y5d7 (last accessed December 2022)

'New report reveals rampant discrimination against transgender people by health providers, high HIV rates and widespread lack of access to necessary care', National LGBTQ Task Force, https://tinyurl.com/mrybn2rd (last accessed December 2022)

Interview with Simon Watney, 19 August 2021

History Extra, 'Aids: The Epidemic that Changed Britain', 2021, https://tinyurl.com/mtn5nn6v (last accessed July 2022)

Stonewall, 'History', www.stonewall.org.uk/stonewalls-history (last accessed July 2022)

House of Commons, 'Parental Involvement in Teaching: Equality Act – Wed 26th June 2019', https://tinyurl.com/569wjy8d (last accessed July 2022)

'Margaret Thatcher Statue Egged within Hours of it Being Installed', *Guardian*, 15 May 2022, https://tinyurl.com/2e5x5r3f (last accessed July 2022)

Interesting Literature, 'The True Meaning of "We Are All in the Gutter, but Some of us Are Looking at the Stars"', https://tinyurl.com/ymvv97m5 (last accessed July 2022)

'Protecting Statues – Councils Do What They Can for Historic Monuments', *The Times*, 2007, https://tinyurl.com/2cerw6sk (last accessed July 2022)

Famous Trials, 'The Trials of Oscar Wilde: An Account', https://famous-trials.com/wilde/327-home (last accessed July 2022)

LSE Library, 'Arts and Culture – The Story of Gay Liberation Front in Britain', https://tinyurl.com/54tv5ntu (last accessed July 2022)

Ian Lucas, *OutRage! An Oral History*, Cassell Press, 1998

'A Legacy of Activism: The ACT UP London Archives', Curzon (2018), https://tinyurl.com/48xjhb56 (last accessed July 2022)

'"Gay Men Were Dying of Aids at a Terrifying Rate": Visiting My Friend on the HIV Ward', *Guardian*, 2017, https://tinyurl.com/22jxvd98 (last accessed July 2022)

Edward Siddons, 'In London, Protestors Demand Access to HIV Prevention Drug Prep', *Vice*, 2016, https://tinyurl.com/5nvwsf5j (last accessed July 2022)

'A Catwalk for Power, Resistance and Hope', https://positivelyuk.org/2018/01/10/catwalk-power-resilience-hope/ (last accessed July 2022)

'Saintmaking: The Canonisation of Derek Jarman by Queer "Nuns"', *Guardian*, 2021, https://tinyurl.com/2s4ztdrf (last accessed July 2022)

BBC, 'Hundreds Rally in Downing Street for Full Ban on Conversion Therapy', 10 April 2022, https://tinyurl.com/y8uddxkt (last accessed July 2022)

Peter Tatchell, 'Obituary: Dudley Cave', *The Independent*, 31 May 1999, https://tinyurl.com/2p8637ee (last accessed July 2022)

#AIDSMemoryUK, 'The Official Campaign Lobbying to Create the #TheAIDSMemorial in London', www.instagram.com/aidsmemoryuk/ (last accessed July 2022)

Interview with Eric Thompson, 30 September 2021

Halfway to Heaven, www.halfway2heaven.net/london

4. *THE FAGS HAVE LOST THAT WOUNDED LOOK –*
PICCADILLY

'Lou Reed's "Walk on the Wild Side": What Became of Candy, Little Joe and Co.?', *Guardian*, 2005, https://tinyurl.com/ywzah3z4 (last accessed June 2022)

SOURCES

'Memories of That Night at the Stonewall Inn, From Those Who Were There', *The New York Times*, 2019, https://tinyurl.com/5a9z6cnc (last accessed June 2022)

Matt Houlbrook, *Queer London: Perils and Pleasures in the Sexual Metropolis, 1918–1957*, University of Chicago Press, 2005

Rictor Norton, 'Homosexuality in Eighteenth-Century England – The Gay Subculture in Early Eighteenth-Century London', http://rictornorton.co.uk/eighteen/molly2.htm (last accessed June 2022)

Antony Grey, *Quest for Justice: Towards Homosexual Emancipation*, Chatto & Windus, 2011

British History Online, 'The Shaftesbury Memorial Fountain', 1963, https://tinyurl.com/4ne85m4m (last accessed June 2022)

Zoe Craig, Londonist, '11 Secrets of London's Eros Statue', https://tinyurl.com/mr3yfy49 (last accessed June 2022)

National Association for the Advancement of Colored People, home page at https://naacp.org (last accessed June 2022)

Jacqueline Walker, *Pilgrim State*, Sceptre, 2009

Biography, 'How Harry Hay Became a Pioneer of the Gay Rights Movement', 2021, https://tinyurl.com/2wf4swdz (last accessed June 2022)

NBC News, 'James Baldwin's Sexuality: Complex and Influential', 2017, https://tinyurl.com/4y79kjbk (last accessed June 2022)

Quotes said during a 2014 lecture at Southern Illinois University; further context in Angela Davis, *Freedom Is a Constant Struggle*, Haymarket Books, 2016

LGBT History UK, 'A. E. Dyson (Tony Dyson, 1928–2002) Was a Literary Critic, University Lecturer, Educational Activist and Gay Rights Campaigner', https://tinyurl.com/yeyvkzu5 (last accessed June 2022)

University of Law, 'A Legal Timeline of the Fight for Equality in the LGBTQIA+ Community', https://tinyurl.com/377duam4 (last accessed June 2022)

Peter Tatchell, 'Don't Fall for the Myth that it's 50 Years since We Decriminalised Homosexuality', *Guardian*, 2017, https://tinyurl.com/2ymun7v5 (last accessed June 2022)

Walter Rodney, *How Europe Underdeveloped Africa*, Howard University Press, 1981

'Moments from LGBT History: London Metropolitan Archives', *Guardian*, 2019, https://tinyurl.com/yeyk6nf4 (last accessed June 2022)

Open Learn, 'Lesbianism and the Criminal Law of England and Wales', 2021, https://tinyurl.com/yrx4pk7c (last accessed June 2022)

Radclyffe Hall, *The Well of Loneliness Paperback*, Penguin, 2015

Lily Wakefield, 'Was Queen Anne a Lesbian? The Heartbreaking Truth behind Olivia Colman's Epic *The Favourite*', *Pink News*, 2021, https://tinyurl.com/bdhy2n8p (last accessed June 2022)

Lily Wakefield, 'Buckingham Palace Site May Once Have Been Home to a Gay Brothel', *Pink News*, 2021, https://tinyurl.com/ydn3b7z2 (last accessed June 2022)

Anne Somerset, *Queen Anne, The Politics of Passion*, HarperCollins, 2012

'Lesbian Avengers', https://tinyurl.com/ysx2fncx (last accessed June 2022)

'Florida's Law Limiting LGBTQ Discussion in Schools, Explained', *The Washington Post*, 2022, https://tinyurl.com/yp2z5v62 (last accessed June 2022)

Human Rights Watch, 'Russia's "Gay Propaganda" Law Imperils LGBT Youth', 2018, https://tinyurl.com/mut2bm8x (last accessed June 2022)

Ian Lucas, *OutRage! An Oral History*, Cassell Press, 1998

A Chronology Of OutRage!', Peter Tatchell, https://tinyurl.com/52ntmynj (last accessed December 2022)

ACT UP New York, 'Queers Read This', https://actupny.org/documents/QueersReadThis.pdf (last accessed June 2022)

Jeremy Reed, 'The Dilly: A History of the Piccadilly Rent Boy Scene', Peter Owen Publishers, 2013

Zinn Education Project, 'This Day in History – March 8, 1971: FBI's COINTELPRO Exposed', https://tinyurl.com/5cmymw74 (last accessed June 2022)

Stan Persky, 'Feasting with Oscar: from De Profundis to Post-Queer', 2005, https://tinyurl.com/bdhevudp (last accessed June 2022)

SOURCES

UK Parliament, '1885 Labouchere Amendment', https://tinyurl.com/3xbuj87r (last accessed June 2022)

Podtail, 'We Found Love in the 80s', 2021, https://tinyurl.com/4ptfkrun (last accessed June 2022)

Brian Fairbairn and Karl Eccleston, 'Putting on the Dish', www.brianandkarl.com/PUTTING-ON-THE-DISH, 2015 (last accessed June 2022)

Peter Tatchell, 'Police Failed Dennis Nilsen's Victims. Decades Later, Little Has Changed', *Guardian*, 2022, https://tinyurl.com/jadktse2 (last accessed June 2022)

'23 September 1975: Police to Shut Arcades of Vice', *Guardian*, 23 September 2015, https://tinyurl.com/2fha73p7 (last accessed June 2022)

Bishopsgate Institute, 'Countdown on Spanner Archive 1984–1998', https://tinyurl.com/3mf4zr5c (last accessed June 2022)

Colin Clews in Gay in the 80s, 'From Fighting for Our Rights to Fighting for Our Lives – 1986. Politics: Manchester's Chief Constable James Anderton', https://tinyurl.com/5n8e5c2r (last accessed June 2022)

'Out of the Frying Pan and into the Fire: Part Two of "the Boy on the Meat Rack", the Story of Alan Kerr', *Village*, 2019, https://tinyurl.com/5bu84b2w (last accessed June 2022)

Koshka Duff (ed.), *Abolishing the Police: An Illustrated Introduction*, with images by Cat Sims, is an edited collection on policing abolition, published by Dog Section Press, 2021

Steve Bamlett, 'Reflecting on the Gay Bathhouse', 2021, https://tinyurl.com/mtfhn27r (last accessed June 2022)

The Turkish Baths in Jermyn Street, St James, https://tinyurl.com/mvkuv8vs (last accessed June 2022)

Jason Okundaye, 'Ted Brown: The Man Who Held a Mass Kiss-in and Made History', *Guardian*, 2021, https://tinyurl.com/k7949594 (last accessed June 2022)

Bishopsgate Institute LGBTQ+ Archives, 'Come Together: Gay Liberation Front', https://tinyurl.com/3x8ay3k6 (last accessed June 2022)

LSE, '50 Years on From the Founding of the Gay Liberation Front: Progress Made Since and Applicability Today', 2020, https://tinyurl.com/nze5c3zz (last accessed June 2022)

Arkansas Online, 'Not This Time': In 1969, Patrons of Stonewall Inn Fought Back against Police Harassment, Sparking Movement that Continues Today', 2019, https://tinyurl.com/2bxsdhdt (last accessed June 2022)

'Some People Think Stonewall Was Triggered by Judy Garland's Funeral. Here's Why Many Experts Disagree', *Time*, 2019, https://tinyurl.com/494rzc92 (last accessed June 2022)

'Martin Luther King Jr's Dream Undoubtedly Included LGBT+ People, Say Those Who Knew and Loved Him', *Pink News*, 2022, https://tinyurl.com/y7f6pysv (last accessed June 2022)

Stuart Feather, 'A Brief History of the Gay Liberation Front, 1970–73', 21 November 2007, https://tinyurl.com/5fv8dmmp (last accessed June 2022)

Islington's Pride, 'Collecting and Celebrating Islington's LGBTQ+ Heritage', https://islingtonspride.com/humap/ (last accessed June 2022)

British Library Collections, 'Gay Liberation Front Manifesto', https://tinyurl.com/2whyr6wn (last accessed June 2022)

Stuart Feather, *Blowing the Lid: Gay Liberation, Sexual Revolution and Radical Queens*, Zero Books, 2015

'North, South, East & West: Wherever You Live, Gay is Best', 2021, https://tinyurl.com/mr3d8wxs (last accessed June 2022)

Ryan White, 'This Film Celebrates One of London's Most Beloved (and Debauched) 90s Club Nights', *Vice Magazine*, 2022, https://tinyurl.com/mw73nsfr

Per-spex, 'Taboo, the Legend of Leigh Bowery', 2019, https://tinyurl.com/bp8b7bc8 (last accessed June 2022)

Rupert Smith, 'We Were So Naughty', *Guardian*, 2022, https://tinyurl.com/2n92vzhm (last accessed June 2022)

Queer China UK, 'A Home for the Global Queer Chinese and Allies', https://queerchinauk.com (last accessed June 2022)

Bishopsgate Institute LGBT+ Archives, 'Come Together: Gay Liberation Front', https://tinyurl.com/3x8ay3k6 (last accessed June 2022)

Dan de la Motte, Queer Tours of London – A Mince Through Time – R&D into 1960s gay male experience – Interview with Andrew Lumsden (b.1941)

SOURCES

Lisa Power, An Oral History of the Gay Liberation Front 1970–1973, Cassell, 1995

Jason Okundaye, 'Ted Brown: The Man Who Held a Mass Kiss-in and Made History', *Guardian*, 2021, https://tinyurl.com/k7949594 (last accessed June 2022)

LSE, 'Interview with Ted Brown, Gay Liberation Front Veteran', 2011, https://tinyurl.com/ya4d238s (last accessed June 2022)

Amal Fashanu, 'It's Only a Matter of Time before There Is an Out Gay Premier League Player', *Guardian*, 2022, https://tinyurl.com/3dzj3ns6 (last accessed June 2022)

Sophie K. Rosa, 'Queer Elders Are Going Into Care – and Back into the Closet – Activists Who Started Pride Are Fighting for a Care System that Honours Queer People in Later Life', 2021, https://tinyurl.com/44e5x8u9 (last accessed June 2022)

National Archives, '"London's Greatest Bohemian Rendezvous": the Caravan Club', 2017, https://tinyurl.com/yc3hdzhd (last accessed June 2022)

5. *A CACHE OF DIAMONDS* – WHITECHAPEL

Rictor Norton, 'Homosexuality in Eighteenth-Century England – The Gay Subculture in Early Eighteenth-Century London', http://rictornorton.co.uk/eighteen/molly2.htm (last accessed June 2022)

mudlark121, 'Today in Queer History: Acid-Drag Queen Commune Bethnal Rouge Opens, Bethnal Green, 1973' (01.03.2018), https://tinyurl.com/4vd4sk5x (last accessed May 2022)

David Rosenberg, *Rebel Footprints: A Guide to Uncovering London's Radical History*, Pluto Press, 2019

Stuart Feather, *Blowing the Lid: Gay Liberation, Sexual Revolution and Radical Queens*, Zero Books, 2015

'Drag, Defiance and "No D***heads": How the Glory Became East London's Most Loved LGBTQ+ Pub', *Evening Standard*, 2019, https://tinyurl.com/2d5x2akk (last accessed May 2022)

'For the Last 14 Years, Sink the Pink Has Been the Largest LGBTQ+ Collective and Club Night in the UK', https://sinkthepink.com/ (last accessed May 2022)

'Friends of the Joiners Arms Presents *Lèse Majesté*', https://tinyurl.com/5fm5zs6x (last accessed May 2022)

Lisa Power, *An Oral History of the Gay Liberation Front 1970–1973*, Cassell, 1995

Stuart Feather, *Blowing the Lid: Gay Liberation, Sexual Revolution and Radical Queens*, Zero Book, 2015

Emma Goldman, *Living My Life*, Penguin, 2006

Bethnal Green Working Mens Club – www.workersplaytime.net/

Odbhut Queer Bangla Group UK, 'Dedicated to the Bengali Queer Community in the UK & Globally', https://tinyurl.com/ntybnusn (last accessed May 2022)

'Celebrating 50 Years of Gay Pride in Britain: A Special SOAS Event Celebrating African, Asian and Middle Eastern Contributions to Queer London', 2022, https://tinyurl.com/yva8spat (last accessed July 2022)

Huey P. Newton, 'The Women's Liberation and Gay Liberation Movements', 1970, https://tinyurl.com/mxkuy753 (last accessed August 2022)

Glasshouse London, 'An Exciting New LGBTQIA+ Multidisciplinary Venue Led by Glass House Projects', https://glasshouse.london/ (last accessed May 2022)

Rictor Norton, 'Homosexuality in Eighteenth-Century England – The Gay Subculture in Early Eighteenth-Century London', http://rictornorton.co.uk/eighteen/molly2.htm (last accessed May 2022)

British History Online, 'Bethnal Green: Settlement and Building to 1836–1998', https://tinyurl.com/399t8te3 (last accessed May 2022)

Podtail, 'We Found Love in the 80s', www.wefoundloveinthe80s.com/post/5-ian-ian (last accessed May 2022)

Jeremy Reed, *The Dilly: A History of the Piccadilly Rent Boy Scene*, Peter Owen Publishers, 2013

Amnesty, 'One Year after the Murders of Xulhaz Mannan and Mahbub' Rabbi Tonoy', 25 April 2017, https://tinyurl.com/4xf59tf3 (last accessed May 2022)

Human Dignity Trust, 'Types of Criminalisation', www.humandignitytrust.org/country-profile/bangladesh/ (last accessed May 2022)

SOURCES

Gscene, 'Stand Up to LGBTQ+ Hate Crime Held 3rd London Demonstration', 4 November 2019, https://tinyurl.com/muh6cuns (last accessed May 2022)

Bex Wade, 'Night Pride Is Reclaiming the Streets for LGBTQ People – Demonstrations in London and Bristol Over the Weekend Protested the Shocking Rise in Hate Crimes against the LGBTQ Community', *Vice*, 2021, https://tinyurl.com/yc6hje3b (last accessed May 2022)

News from Unmesh Desai: 57% rise in homophobic hate crime in Tower Hamlets', London assembly, 24 Jan 2022, https://tinyurl.com/7zdyzxp2 (last accessed December 2022)

'EastEnders Fans Call Phil Mitchell a "Gay Icon" after he Punched a Homophobe', *Gay Times*, 2019, https://tinyurl.com/3wnka5ss (last accessed May 2022)

'Hackney History: "Why I Set Up a Self-Defence Class for Gay People in Dalston in the 1980s"', *Hackney Gazette*, 2019, https://tinyurl.com/2szs2x42 (last accessed May 2022)

'Back to the Eighties: Crime, Yucky Subways, and the Guardian Angels!', *The New Yorker*, 2021, https://tinyurl.com/yck872ua (last accessed May 2022)

Pol Allingham, 'Photographing Bender Defenders, a Self-Defence Class for Queer People', *ID Magazine*, 2021, https://tinyurl.com/yckdarcb (last accessed May 2022)

Open Plaques, 'Haroon Shamsher 1965–1999 Founder of Influential Music Collective Joi Lived Here', https://openplaques.org/plaques/42928 (last accessed May 2022)

Alan Gilbey, *East End Backpassages*, Quartet Books, 2012

Peter Ackroyd, *Queer City: Gay London from the Romans to the Present Day*, Vintage, 2018

BBC, 'This Single London Address is Home to Many Cultures', 2017, https://tinyurl.com/yckk6aty (last accessed May 2022)

University College London, 'A Memory Map of the Jewish East End', https://tinyurl.com/59a8va47 (last accessed May 2022)

Ladies Who London, 'Spitalfields – Banglatown, Where London Meets the World', https://tinyurl.com/5adyfwjv (last accessed May 2022)

'The Long History of Criminalising Hijras – The Persecution of Hijras in India Goes Beyond the Infamous Section 377', *Himal South Asian*

Magazine, 2019, https://tinyurl.com/bp52k9dt (last accessed May 2022)

Bethnal Green London, 'The Eternal Message of Brick Lane Jamme Mosque's Sundial Uniting Islam, Judaism and Christianity', 2021, https://tinyurl.com/5n7jk95f (last accessed May 2022)

Ejel Khan, 'My Work as a Gay Muslim', TEDxLambethSalon, 2022, https://tinyurl.com/57nvbuaw (last accessed May 2022)

CNN, '"Watermelon Smiles" and "Piccaninnies": What Boris Johnson Has Said Previously about People in Africa', 2019, https://tinyurl.com/2ycuypcu (last accessed May 2022)

Andrea Meuzelaar, 'The Emergence and Persistence of Racialised Stereotypes on Dutch Television: Tracing the History of Representation of Muslim Immigrants along the Archival Grain', 2021, https://viewjournal.eu/articles/10.18146/view.268/ (last accessed May 2022)

'Edited Extract from Helen Pankhurst's Deeds Not Words: The Story of Women's Rights – Then and Now', 2018, https://tinyurl.com/mwvucast (last accessed May 2022)

Toynbee Hall, 'Resist, Reclaim and Reimagine: Remembering the Battle of Cable Street 85 Years Later', 2021, https://tinyurl.com/c3amsbwe (last accessed May 2022)

Toynbee Hall, 'Our History', www.toynbeehall.org.uk/about-us/our-history/ (last accessed May 2022)

National Archives, 'George Ives: Queer Lives and the Family', 2009, https://tinyurl.com/2p8dpuhe (last accessed May 2022)

National Archives, 'Suffragettes, 1912: "Rather Broken Windows than Broken Promises"', 2018, https://tinyurl.com/4ude6twz (last accessed May 2022)

Rachel Lumsden, '"The Music Between Us": Ethel Smyth, Emmeline Pankhurst, and "Possession"', *Feminist Studies* 41(2), 2015

Gillian Murphy, 'The Women's Library', https://tinyurl.com/ye9m2urp (last accessed May 2022)

Roman Road London, 'Mural on Lord Morpeth in Bow commemorates Sylvia Pankhurst', 2018, https://tinyurl.com/2p9ueewz (last accessed May 2022)

Sacred Cow Saturday, 'Never Mind the Bollocks, Here's the Sex Pistols', https://tinyurl.com/yckty9ch (last accessed May 2022)

SOURCES

Freedom Press, https://freedompress.org.uk/ (last accessed May 2022)

Avispa, 'Emma Goldman: Intersectional Before the Word Existed', 2018 – https://tinyurl.com/ycxpyvyv (last accessed May 2022)

The Gay Left Collective (ed.), *Homosexuality: Power and Politics*, Radical Thinkers series, Verso, 2018

'*Freedom's Founding*: A Journal of Anarchist Communism (1886–1927)', https://freedompress.org.uk/history/

Meagan Day, 'Capitalism Made Gay Identity Possible. Now We Must Destroy Capitalism – An interview with John D'Emilio', *Jacobin Magazine*, 15 August 2020, https://tinyurl.com/skdcsknv (Accessed on 11.11.2021)

'"Staying Alive": The Impact of "Austerity Cuts" on the LGBT Voluntary and Community Sector (VCS) in England and Wales – A TUC Funded Research Report', ResearchGate, June 2014, https://tinyurl.com/mtk9hnr3

East End Women's Museum, 'Miss Muff's Molly House in Whitechapel', 2016, https://tinyurl.com/5m8jxdja (last accessed May 2022)

Dan de la Motte, Queer Tours of London – A Mince Through Time – Molly Houses Tour, with links to 20th Century Gay History, 2nd October 2020, for St Margaret's House

Tim Alderman, 'Gay History: Miss Muff's Molly House in Whitechapel', 2017, https://tinyurl.com/yncjhj2n (last accessed May 2022)

Julie Begum, 'How a Racist Murder of Altab Ali Changed the Way the Bengalis Saw Themselves in Britain', https://tinyurl.com/4pzbhnyj (last accessed May 2022)

Liberty Human Rights, 'Stop and Search', https://tinyurl.com/y9hrdtvz (last accessed May 2022)

Totally London, 'The Altab Ali Park in Whitechapel', 2021, https://tinyurl.com/bdd48eyd (last accessed May 2022)

History Extra, 'Desired, Stolen, Cursed: The History of the Koh-i-Noor Diamond', 2020, https://tinyurl.com/mr4dzzkf (last accessed May 2022)

The East London Mosque – https://tinyurl.com/yc352nnc

Independent, 'Finsbury Park Attacker Turned Violent by Far-Right Posts from Tommy Robinson and Britain First', Police Say, 2018, https://tinyurl.com/4rv26tue (last accessed May 2022)

Rainbow Coalition Against Racism, https://tinyurl.com/bdz66dt2 (last accessed May 2022)

LGBT+ Against Islamophobia, www.facebook.com/LGBTAI/ (last accessed May 2022)

Rainbow Hamlets, https://rainbowhamlets.wordpress.com/ (last accessed May 2022)

Mumia Abu-Jamal, 'Frantz Fanon and His Influence on the Black Panther Party and the Black Revolution', in *Frantz Fanon and Emancipatory Social Theory: A View from the Wretched*, Brill, 2019

'The London Squatters Who Resisted Evictions in the '70s – "Housing for all!"', *Huck Magazine*, 2022, https://tinyurl.com/5fatx3cp (last accessed May 2022)

May Day Rooms, 'Archive of the Month: Race Today (1973–1988)', 2021, https://maydayrooms.org/archive-of-the-month/ (last accessed May 2022)

Muslim LGBT Network, https://muslimlgbtnetwork.wordpress.com (last accessed May 2022)

'The History of the Blind Beggar', www.theblindbeggar.com/history.html (last accessed May 2022)

Friends of the Joiners Arms, www.instagram.com/friendsjoinersarms/ (last accessed May 2022)

Dan Glass, *United Queerdom: From the Legends of the Gay Liberation Front (GLF) to the Queers of Tomorrow*, Bloomsbury Publishing, 2020

6. *YOU THINK THE DEAD WE LOVED EVER TRULY LEAVE US?* – KING'S CROSS

'Harry Potter's Platform 9¾', https://tinyurl.com/2dwzuukj (last accessed April 2022)

Chi Luu, 'The Unspeakable Linguistics of Camp', 2018, https://tinyurl.com/3ns2smht (last accessed April 2022)

Mike Jackson, 'Lesbians and Gays Support the Miners', https://tinyurl.com/2p9emc23 (last accessed April 2022)

Andrew Whitehead, 'Red Flag over St Pancras', 2015, https://tinyurl.com/2vcz7nua (last accessed April 2022)

SOURCES

Irish Emigration Museum, 'Remembering Mark Ashton: A Proud Advocate of Socialism and Gay Rights', https://tinyurl.com/22wsrxdm (last accessed April 2022)

Mark Kermode, 'Pride Review – Power in an Unlikely Union', *Guardian*, 2014, https://tinyurl.com/bdd9hwbm (last accessed April 2022)

Federation of International Employers, 'The History of European Working Time Laws 1784–2015', https://tinyurl.com/yjhh3hwv (last accessed April 2022)

mudlark121, 'Today in London Housing History, 1946: Mass Squat of Duchess of Bedford House', Kensington, 2020, https://tinyurl.com/yck5sbxy (last accessed April 2022)

Interview with Mike Jackson, 15 March 2022

Andrew Whitehead, *Curious King's Cross*, Five Leaves Publications, 2018

'Framed Youth – The Revenge of the Teenage Perverts', 1983, https://vimeo.com/22654557 (last accessed August 2022)

Colin Clews, 'Pub: The Bell, Kings Cross, London, Guest Blogger Rob Pateman Remembers a Legendary 80s London Pub', 2017, https://tinyurl.com/yu4a3j9j (last accessed April 2022)

'Spotify – Movement at the Bell 09/12/1984', https://tinyurl.com/5h67fyb4 (last accessed August 2022)

'"We Specialised in the Freakish": The Glory Days of the Scala Cinema', *Guardian*, 2018, https://tinyurl.com/bdfrm7v3 (last accessed April 2022)

Attitude, 'A Brief History of Trade, London's First Gay After-Hours Club', 2015, https://tinyurl.com/43y9c9sv (last accessed August 2022)

Rose Collis, 'Events and Activism – Highlights', https://tinyurl.com/3c8d2z7n (last accessed August 2022)

Jimmy Somerville, 'Jesus Christ! Alan Shearer – What a Little Sex Bomb!', *Guardian*, 2014, https://tinyurl.com/5cnk2nb5 (last accessed April 2022)

'Rebel Dykes Review – the Unstoppable Rise of the Raddest of the Radical Lesbians', *Guardian*, 2021, https://tinyurl.com/4b4evnv2 (last accessed April 2022)

Royal Commission on the Ancient and Historical Monuments of Wales, 'LGBT History Month: Lesbians and Gays Support the Miners, 1984–85', https://tinyurl.com/25ewmnxz (last accessed April 2022)

Camden New Journal, 'Bronski Beat Performance Went Down in History', 2022, https://tinyurl.com/4awws9jj (last accessed April 2022)

J. K. Rowling, *Harry Potter and the Deathly Hallows*, Bloomsbury, 2007

British History Online, 'Battle Bridge Estate – Survey of London: Volume 24, the Parish of St Pancras Part 4: King's Cross Neighbourhood, 1952', https://tinyurl.com/2dwhw7ur (last accessed April 2022)

Matt Brown, Is Boudicca buried beneath Platform 10 at King's Cross?, Gasholder, 2021, https://tinyurl.com/5b24dvj6 (last accessed December 2022)

Scott Wood, 'Is Boudica Buried in London?', 2016, https://tinyurl.com/ycy76usk (last accessed April 2022)

'Bohemian Rhapsody Was Freddie Mercury's Coming Out Song', *The Wire*, 2017, https://tinyurl.com/yrjeumwt (last accessed April 2022)

Museum of Youth Culture, 'Arts and Culture – Never Going Underground – Queer Party and Protest in Manchester', https://tinyurl.com/yc5myuth (last accessed April 2022)

Gal-dem, 'Trans Inclusivity in Sexual Violence Services Is Perfectly Achievable – These Organisations Are Leading by Example', 2021, https://tinyurl.com/4eakfyth (last accessed April 2022)

J. K. Rowling, *Harry Potter and the Deathly Hallows*, Bloomsbury, 2007

'Rebel Dykes Review – the Unstoppable Rise of the Raddest of the Radical Lesbians', *Guardian*, 2021, https://tinyurl.com/4b4evnv2 (last accessed April 2022)

Chris Godfrey, 'Section 28 Protestors 30 Years on: 'We Were Arrested and Put in a Cell up by Big Ben', *Guardian*, 7 March 2018, https://tinyurl.com/yvyak7dk (last accessed April 2022)

'Manchester Stop Clause 28 / Never Going Underground / Gay Rights Rally', 20 February 1988, https://tinyurl.com/2c29zrjw (last accessed April 2022)

John Tierney, 'The Big City; In 80s, Fear Spread Faster Than AIDS', 2001, https://tinyurl.com/w5zb8479 (last accessed April 2022)

SOURCES

'Facing the Past – We Mustn't Forget the Tabloids' Sins against the Gays', *Huck Magazine*, 2021, https://tinyurl.com/bdjduhpa (last accessed April 2022)

'A Policeman's Lot ...', *The Observer*, 2002, https://tinyurl.com/4cs3yzmp (last accessed August 2022)

'Garden Named after Mark Ashton', *Morning Star*, https://tinyurl.com/yc45cv53 (last accessed April 2022)

Ryan Gilbey, 'Kink, Drink and Liberty: A Queer History of King's Cross in the 80s', *Guardian*, 2017, https://tinyurl.com/5c6cupbd (last accessed April 2022)

J. K. Rowling, *Harry Potter and the Goblet of Fire*, Bloomsbury, 2000

BLKOUT, 'Dennis Carney on the Front Line', 2018, https://blkoutuk.com/archives/6224 (last accessed April 2022)

Glasgow Womens Library, 'Camden Lesbian Centre and Black Lesbian Group: The Fight for a Home', https://tinyurl.com/43f298zu (last accessed April 2022)

'Camden Lesbian Centre', https://tinyurl.com/5ccp7yk9 (last accessed April 2022)

Audre Lorde, *Zami: A New Spelling of My Name: A Biomythography*, Crossing Press, 1982

Lesbians Talk, *Making Black Waves*, Scarlet Press, 1993

'Crossroads Women Runs the Crossroads Women's Centre in Kentish Town', http://crossroadswomen.net/ (last accessed April 2022)

Queer Britain, https://queerbritain.org.uk (last accessed April 2022)

Gas Holder, 'See Abandoned Bagley's Nightclub Morph into Coal Drops Yard', 2019, https://tinyurl.com/2p8k6nvc (last accessed April 2022)

Jessica Furseth, 'Raves and Resistance: The Hidden History of Kings Cross – The Disappearing City', *Huck Magazine*, https://tinyurl.com/yrdkfk5a (last accessed April 2022)

Genius, 'Baby D – "Let Me Be Your Fantasy" Lyrics', https://tinyurl.com/4tusby8a (last accessed April 2022)

Dave Swindells, 'From Bagley's to Spiritland', https://tinyurl.com/3w66w2my (last accessed April 2022)

My London, 'Remembering Bagleys – the lost King's Cross rave venue that was so grimy your clothes would go black if you touched the walls', https://tinyurl.com/pw5mxhhy (last accessed August 2022)

'The Last Bar Standing? For Some, Coming Here Changed Their Lives', *Islington Tribune*, 2022, https://tinyurl.com/yrdjfvhb (last accessed April 2022)

Murray Healey, *Gay Skins: Class, Masculinity and Queer Appropriation (Sexual Politics)*, UNKNO, 1996

Islington Pride Humap, 'Colin Devereaux aka Dockyard Doris', https://tinyurl.com/2e8vy4sj (last accessed April 2022)

My London, 'Bid to Save Islington LGBTQ+ Bar 'More Than Just a Pub but a Community' for 30 years', 2021, https://tinyurl.com/2e8ssfs7 (last accessed April 2022)

Interview with Mike Jackson, 15 March 2022

'Have You Got Lesbian Fighting Song? The Pride Anthems that Time Forgot', *Guardian*, 2022, https://tinyurl.com/32t5t3ce (last accessed August 2022)

London Friend, https://londonfriend.org.uk/ (last accessed April 2022)

'Yvonne Sinclair (1934–2013) sailor, changeback, activist, actor,' Zagria Blogspot, 2013, https://tinyurl.com/4yp3ktzh (last accessed December 2022)

El Hunt, 'Call the Switchboard – The story behind the UK's biggest LGBTQ+ helpline', *Huck Magazine*, 2019, https://tinyurl.com/2p3hsu68 (last accessed April 2022)

Galop, https://galop.org.uk/388

'London Gay Teenage Group', https://tinyurl.com/yc6tszu7 (last accessed April 2022)

Curzon, 'A Legacy of Activism: The ACT UP London Archives', 2018, https://tinyurl.com/48xjhb56 (last accessed April 2022)

mudlark121, 'Today in Queer History: Acid-Drag Queen Commune Bethnal Rouge Opens, Bethnal Green, 1973' (01.03.2018), https://tinyurl.com/4vd4sk5x (last accessed August 2022)

Peter Scott-Presland, 'Amiable Warriors: A History of the Campaign for Homosexual Equality and Its Times', Paradise Press, 2015

Andrew Lumsden, 'Rainbow Planet', 2019, www.andrewlumsden.co.uk/publications.html (last accessed April 2022)

'How 1967 Changed Gay Life in Britain: "I Think for My Generation, We're Still a Little Bit Uneasy", *Guardian*, 2017, https://tinyurl.com/4ders5y5 (last accessed April 2022)

'How a Radical Kings Cross Bookshop Was HQ to McLibel and Spawned Pride Marches', *Islington Gazette*, 2021, https://tinyurl.com/4hvd53ye (last accessed April 2022)

Islington New, '"Gay Is Good": Heartfelt Messages Found in the Basement of Radical King's Cross Bookshop', 2020, https://tinyurl.com/bdddayzn (last accessed April 2022)

Mark Ashton Red Ribbon Fund, https://mark-ashton.muchloved.com/Home (last accessed April 2022)

UK AIDS Memorial Quilt, www.aidsquiltuk.org/ (last accessed April 2022)

The Food Chain, www.foodchain.org.uk (last accessed April 2022)

Institute of Race Relations, https://irr.org.uk/ (last accessed April 2022)

Helios Centre, https://helioscentre.org.uk (last accessed April 2022)

Gay's the Word, www.gaystheword.co.uk/ (last accessed April 2022)

'Garden Named after Mark Ashton', *Morning Star*, https://tinyurl.com/yc45cv53 (last accessed April 2022)

7. *ALL POWER TO THE PEOPLE!* – LADBROKE GROVE

My London, 'The Notting Hill Caribbean Cafe that Became Centre of UK's Black Panther Movement – This Modest Restaurant Made History', 2022, https://tinyurl.com/2urm9dv9 (last accessed August 2022)

'Marxist, Feminist, Revolutionary: Remembering Notting Hill Carnival Founder Claudia Jones', *Vogue*, 2020, https://tinyurl.com/4uszj4m7 (last accessed May 2022)

UOM History, 'The West Indian Gazette: A Symbiotic Dialogue between the Local and the Global', 2019, https://tinyurl.com/3w79669u (last accessed May 2022)

Institute of Contemporary Arts, 'War Inna Babylon: The Community's Struggle for Truths and Rights', curated by Tottenham Rights, together with independent curators Kamara Scott and Rianna Jade Parker, 2022, www.ica.art/exhibitions/war-inna-babylon (last accessed August 2022)

Micha Frazer-Carroll in Runnymede Trust, 'Black History Legacies: Claudia Jones', 2020, https://tinyurl.com/3662ft6s (last accessed May 2022)

Our Migration Story, 'Murder in Notting Hill', https://tinyurl.com/4kamp6dw (last accessed May 2022)

Notting Hill Carnival, 'Arts and Culture – The History of Mas – Exploring the Origins of Mas and its Significance to Notting Hill Carnival', https://tinyurl.com/mr45en2b (last accessed May 2022)

'Portobello Carnival Film Festival', 2009, https://tinyurl.com/38fpte7a (last accessed May 2022)

Margaret Busby, 'The Notting Hill Carnival Has an Unsung Hero, Rhaune Laslett', *Guardian*, 2014, https://tinyurl.com/24e84kxb (last accessed May 2022)

Notting Hill, 'The Life of a Simple Bookshop Owner Changes When He Meets the Most Famous Film Star in the World', 1999, www.imdb.com/title/tt0125439/ (last accessed May 2022)

'The Film that Speaks to Britain's Youth in Words They Understand', *Guardian*, 2006, https://tinyurl.com/ya8zb3e9 (last accessed May 2022)

Octavia Foundation, 'Grove Roots', 2013, https://tinyurl.com/45hnhcv8 (last accessed May 2022)

Close Up Film Centre, 'How the West Was Won', https://tinyurl.com/3r36wskt (last accessed May 2022)

Stuart Feather, *Blowing the Lid: Gay Liberation, Sexual Revolution and Radical Queens*, Zero Books, 2015

'One Love: The Rastafarian Origin Story', 2011, https://tinyurl.com/dft79j7n (last accessed May 2022)

The Music, 'Jamaica's Reggae Musos Are Fighting Back Against Homophobia', 2017, https://tinyurl.com/4k25ekt7 (last accessed May 2022)

Ishmahil Blagrove, Jr, *The Frontline: A story of Struggle, Resistance and Black Identity in Notting Hill*, Rice N Peas, 2022

James Greig Omar Shweiki, 'Coming Out Against Imperialism', *Tribune Magazine*, 2021, https://tinyurl.com/yx25bunn (last accessed May 2022)

SOURCES

Institute of Contemporary Arts, 'War Inna Babylon: The Community's Struggle for Truths and Rights', curated by Tottenham Rights, together with independent curators Kamara Scott and Rianna Jade Parker, 2022, www.ica.art/exhibitions/war-inna-babylon (last accessed August 2022)

Them, 'Queer Caribbeans Speak Out About One of Dancehall's Most Homophobic Songs', 2020, https://tinyurl.com/3xz52t9v (last accessed May 2022)

ABC News, 'One Love, One Hate, One Hope: Tackling Homophobia in Jamaica', 2017, https://tinyurl.com/2p89d64c (last accessed May 2022)

Caribbean Entertainment Hub, 'Reggae Super Star Lila Ike Make Waves With Her Tweet "I am Into Women"', 2015, https://tinyurl.com/5n8zc6yv (last accessed May 2022)

18 Karat Reggae, 'How Koffee's "Toast" is Becoming a Lesbian Anthem', https://tinyurl.com/2p858dpv (last accessed August 2022)

ABC News, 'From the Start, Black Lives Matter Has Been about LGBTQ Lives – Two of Three Black Lives Matter Founders Identify as Queer', 2020, https://tinyurl.com/52ec4x9m (last accessed May 2022)

Faggamuffin Bloc Party, www.faggamuffinblocparty.com/ (last accessed August 2022)

Reuters, 'Barbados Removes Nelson Statue in Break with Colonial Past', 2020, https://tinyurl.com/4asw899h (last accessed May 2022)

UNAIDS, UNAIDS congratulates Barbados on its decision to repeal colonial-era laws that criminalised same sex sexual relations, 2022, https://tinyurl.com/79b7drnm (last accessed December 2022)

Human Rights Campaign, 'How HIV Impacts LGBTQ People', 2017, https://tinyurl.com/2bx2p37v (last accessed May 2022)

Caribbean Collective Mag, 'Jason Jones: The LGBTQ+ Activist Breaking Ground in Trinidad and the United Kingdom', https://tinyurl.com/4pbyvk9a (last accessed May 2022)

Kaleidoscope Trust, 'Meet Our Team', www.kaleidoscopetrust.com/team.php (last accessed May 2022)

'Perfect storm': Royals Misjudged Caribbean Tour, Say Critics', *Guardian*, 2022, https://tinyurl.com/raajzfx6 (last accessed August 2022)

BBC, '1989: Diana opens Landmark Aids Centre', https://tinyurl.com/y8e9e9sn (last accessed May 2022)

LSE Library, 'Arts and Culture – OutRage! – Telling the Story of LGBT Campaigning in the UK', https://tinyurl.com/3zun8erd (last accessed May 2022)

'Grenfell Shows Us There's No North/South Divide. The Gap is between Rich and Poor', *Guardian*, 2017, https://tinyurl.com/y8tc6r52 (last accessed May 2022)

'Theresa May Calls Her Response to Grenfell Fire "Not Good Enough"', *Guardian*, 2018, https://tinyurl.com/2uwhpeft (last accessed May 2022)

Architects Journal, 'Government "Collusion" Led to Combustibles Loophole, Grenfell Inquiry Hears', 2021, https://tinyurl.com/mtzf4vbm (last accessed August 2022)

Irish News, 'London Fire: We Warned of "Catastrophic Event", says Grenfell Tower Action Group', 2017, https://tinyurl.com/ycks85a9 (last accessed May 2022)

Singleton Argus, 'Silent Vigil at Grenfell Fire Anniversary', 2018, https://tinyurl.com/ysjru6a9 (last accessed May 2022)

George Padmore Institute, 'New Cross Massacre Campaign', https://tinyurl.com/425sdryc (last accessed May 2022)

'How the New Cross Fire Became a Rallying Cry for Political Action', *Guardian*, 2021, https://tinyurl.com/3fvjjepf (last accessed May 2022)

'Group that Led Grenfell Refurbishment Sees Profits Jump 50%', *Financial Times*, 2018, https://tinyurl.com/2p9azt6f (last accessed May 2022)

UK Cladding Action Group, '£15 Billion in Profit since Grenfell for Firms that Built Dangerous Homes', 2021, https://tinyurl.com/yc4tkm8t (last accessed May 2022)

Stuart Feather, *Blowing the Lid: Gay Liberation, Sexual Revolution and Radical Queens*, Zero Books, 2015

Ian Lucas, *OutRage! An Oral History*, Cassell Press, 1998

'Saintmaking: The Canonisation of Derek Jarman by Queer "Nuns"', *Guardian*, 2021, https://tinyurl.com/2s4ztdrf (last accessed May 2022)

SOURCES

Penguin, 'Remembering Derek Jarman: AIDS Activist, Diarist, Writer', 2019, https://tinyurl.com/3amncdv9 (last accessed May 2022)

SOAS, 'Nubian Jak Community Trust Blue Plaques', 2020, https://tinyurl.com/yakeu47w (last accessed May 2022)

UOM History, 'The West Indian Gazette: A Symbiotic Dialogue between the Local and the Global', 2019, https://tinyurl.com/3w79669u (last accessed May 2022)

British Newspaper Archive, 'Exploring the Notting Hill Race Riots of 1958–2022', https://tinyurl.com/yc7y4pxn (last accessed May 2022)

Adam Elliott-Cooper, *Black Resistance to British Policing*, Manchester University Press, 2021

Hilary A. Moore, *Beyond Policing: A Handbook for Community-Led Solutions to the Violence of Policing in Western Europe*, Rosa Luxemburg Stiftung, 2021

'From the Archive, 2013, Kristallnacht', *Guardian*, https://tinyurl.com/5t4tp4cp (last accessed May 2022)

Portobello Film Festival, 2008, https://tinyurl.com/mwu2fz4z (last accessed December 2022)

'"The Late 50s Were Turbulent Times": The Scene of the Murder of Kelso Cochrane', *Guardian*, 2017, https://tinyurl.com/2s5trtyv (last accessed May 2022)

My London, 'The Horrific Notting Hill Murder of Kelso Cochrane and Why Carnival Can Never Be Cancelled', 2022, https://tinyurl.com/2dhhtemf (last accessed August 2022)

mudlark121, 'Today in London's History: White Crowds Launch Notting Hill Race Riots, 1958–2016', https://tinyurl.com/2p92cwv7 (last accessed May 2022)

BBC, 'Windrush Generation: Who Are They and Why Are They Facing Problems?', 2021 www.bbc.com/news/uk-43782241 (last accessed May 2022)

'British Nationality Law Reform Aims to Remove Windrush Anomalies', *Guardian*, 2021, https://tinyurl.com/3hnunab7 (last accessed May 2022)

Rainbow Railroad, www.rainbowrailroad.org (last accessed May 2022)

Ishmahil Blagrove Jr, *The Frontline: A Story of Struggle, Resistance and Black Identity in Notting Hill*, Rice N Peas, 2022

London is the Place for Me, 'Black Britons, Citizenship and the Politics of Race Kennetta Hammond Perry', Pages 249–284, Published: December 2015, https://doi.org/10.1093/acprof:oso/978019024 0202.002.0008 (last accessed May 2022)

Malcolm X, *The Autobiography of Malcolm X: With a New Foreword by Attallah Shabazz*, Ballantine Books, 1987

Black Past, 'Organisation of Afro-American Unity', 2009, https://tinyurl.com/yu39z7vw (last accessed May 2022)

Black Cultural Archives, 'Arts and Culture – Black Cultural Archives – The Black Power Movement', https://tinyurl.com/nkknn8zu (last accessed August 2022)

Tiemo Talk of the Town, 'Bob Marley and The Wailers Honoured with Blue Plaque at Legendary SARM Studios', 2019, https://tinyurl.com/y8t6bztp (last accessed May 2022)

Sound on Sound, 'Recording George Michael's "Older"', https://tinyurl.com/nhc2kx57 (last accessed May 2022)

'How George Michael Used His Single "Outside" to Tell People He Would Not Be Shamed for His Sexuality – It Was a Direct Response to His Arrest and the Public Reaction in 1998', *The Independent*, 2016, https://tinyurl.com/45us4td7 (last accessed May 2022)

'There Was So Much Death', *Guardian*, 2005, https://tinyurl.com/5n6 juf8b (last accessed May 2022)

Hornet, 'This Christmas, Let's Remember George Michael Was a Communist Who Fought for Coal Miners' Rights', 2020, https://tinyurl.com/yys8ynhf (last accessed May 2022)

'George Michael On Parkinson 1998, Part 1', https://tinyurl.com/bdd68n52 (last accessed May 2022)

'Nina Simone: "Are You Ready to Burn Buildings?"', *Guardian*, 2015, https://tinyurl.com/yksj99av (last accessed May 2022)

Repeating Islands, 'It Was like a Family: Remember the Mangrove, Notting Hill's Caribbean Haven', 2018, https://tinyurl.com/yaswz3s5 (last accessed May 2022)

Ishmahil Blagrove Jr, *The Frontline: A Story of Struggle, Resistance and Black Identity in Notting Hill*, Rice N Peas, 2022

SOURCES

Ruth Feldstein, '"I Don't Trust You Anymore": Nina Simone, Culture, and Black Activism in the 1960s', *Journal of American History* 91(4), March 2005, www.jstor.org/stable/3660176 (last accessed May 2022)

Nina Simone & Lauryn Hill, 'The Miseducation of Eunice Waymon (Full Album)', Amerigo Gazaway, 2018, https://tinyurl.com/yvcbf8r3 (last accessed August 2022)

PBS, 'The Story behind Nina Simone's Protest Song, "Mississippi Goddam"', 14 January 2021, https://tinyurl.com/yy2uarra (last accessed May 2022)

Variety, 'Steve McQueen on "Uprising", His Docuseries Companion to "Small Axe", and the Power of Music', 2021, https://tinyurl.com/4p47e5h3 (last accessed May 2022)

Black History Month, 'The Mangrove Nine – We Remember the Protest 50 Years Ago in Notting Hill Gate', 2021, https://tinyurl.com/bdfk3dwt (last accessed May 2022)

Interview with Ted Brown, 1 August 2022

GCN, '10 Out and Proud Bisexual Celebrities', 2015, https://tinyurl.com/873kdm65 (last accessed May 2022)

'Watch Nina Simone Define the Role of an Artist', *Far Out Magazine*, 2022, https://tinyurl.com/2zjdxpdu (last accessed August 2022)

Dick Hebdige, *Cut 'n' Mix: Culture, Identity and Caribbean Music*, Routledge, 1987

'Portobello Carnival Film Festival', 2009, https://tinyurl.com/38fpte7a (last accessed May 2022)

Stuart Feather, *Blowing the Lid: Gay Liberation, Sexual Revolution and Radical Queens*, Zero Books, 2015

Interview with Nettie Pollard, 7 August 2022

'Faraday Road (Notas)', https://tinyurl.com/3du7tva9 (last accessed May 2022)

Lisa Power, *An Oral History of the Gay Liberation Front 1970–1973*, Cassell, 1995

'LGBTQ+ Rights – In the Pink', *Guardian*, 2002, https://tinyurl.com/49u757n3 (last accessed May 2022)

The GLF Transvestite, Transsexual and Drag Queen group, 1972, Zagria Blogspot, 2012, https://tinyurl.com/3a2v94fr (last accessed December 2022)

East End Women's Museum, 'May Hobbs and the Night Cleaners Campaign', 2020, https://tinyurl.com/288d7uz3 (last accessed May 2022)

Andy Beckett, *When the Lights Went Out: Britain in the Seventies*, Faber & Faber, 2010

Stuart Feather, *Blowing the Lid: Gay Liberation, Sexual Revolution and Radical Queens*, Zero Books, 2015

'Firebrands in Frocks: The Radical Drag Queens of The Gay Liberation Front', *QX Magazine*, 2016, https://tinyurl.com/358p8m8t (last accessed May 2022)

'The End of Homophobic Discrimination', *The Independent*, 2010, https://tinyurl.com/5yjf697y (last accessed May 2022)

Pictures of London's School Strike of 1972, 'The Pupil Power Demonstration Protested against Caning, Detention, Uniforms and 'Headmaster Dictatorships', 2013, https://tinyurl.com/mr2etnp9 (last accessed May 2022)

Interview with Nettie Pollard, 7 August 2022

'The Fabulous Life of Bette Bourne', *Guardian*, 2009, https://tinyurl.com/2p8pje5f (last accessed May 2022)

'A Hidden Treasure in Portobello', www.thetabernaclew11.com/ (last accessed May 2022)

Lysistrata – Aristophanes | Summary, Characters & Analysis | Classical Literature, https://tinyurl.com/3rry3et6 (last accessed December 2022)

'What Is "Radical Drag" and Who Were Bloolips?', *Gay Star News*, 2019, https://tinyurl.com/yc74mxkp (last accessed May 2022)

'Mark Ravenhill Helps Bette Bourne Look Back in A Life in Three Acts', *The Village Voice*, 2010, https://tinyurl.com/4jw6t3db (last accessed May 2022)

Close Up Film Theatre, 'How the West Was Won', https://tinyurl.com/3r36wskt (last accessed May 2022)

Ishmahil Blagrove Jr, *The Frontline: A Story of Struggle, Resistance and Black Identity in Notting Hill*, Rice N Peas, 2022

'The Angry Brigade's John Barker, 40 Years on: 'I Feel Angrier than I Ever Felt Then', *Guardian*, 2014, https://tinyurl.com/4cnusnb8 (last accessed May 2022)

SOURCES

'Tom Daley on His LGBTQ+ Awakening: 'I Had My Head in My Hands. I Felt So Dark about Being British', *Guardian*, 2022, https://tinyurl.com/4ckd3p37 (last accessed May 2022)

'*My Beautiful Laundrette*: A Queer Fairytale', *Out Write News Mag*, 2022, https://tinyurl.com/4vhv8sah (last accessed May 2022)

Frankie Green, 'Various Writings on Experiences of Women's Liberation, Gay Liberation and Other Political Activism – The Gay Liberation Front ... and Subsequent Related Stuff, Letters etc', https://tinyurl.com/2x9kafje (last accessed May 2022)

Glasgow Women's Library, '"You Are Looking at a Roaring Dyke" – Remembering Jackie Forster', July 2018, https://tinyurl.com/3mp33pp6 (last accessed May 2022)

British Library, 'Jackie Forster Remembers the Founding of Sappho', 1990, https://tinyurl.com/23nzsxze (last accessed August 2022)

Stuart Feather, 'A Brief History of the Gay Liberation Front, 1970–73', 2007, https://tinyurl.com/5fv8dmmp (last accessed August 2022)

'Gay Liberation Front: Looking Back at the Revolutionary LGBTQ Group 50 Years on', *Attitude Magazine*, 2022, https://tinyurl.com/buetzm72 (last accessed August 2022)

Stuart Feather, *Blowing the Lid: Gay Liberation, Sexual Revolution and Radical Queens*, Zero Books, 2015

'*Bette Bourne: It Goes with the Shoes* – Review', *Guardian*, 2014, https://tinyurl.com/5fz7dwhr (last accessed August 2022)

8. *SHORT QUEER POWER STOPS*

Islington's Pride, 'Collecting and Celebrating Islington's LGBTQ+ Heritage', https://islingtonspride.com/humap (last accessed March 2022)

Sam Stroud, '50 Years of Gay Liberation', 2020, www.redpepper.org.uk/50-years-gay-liberation/ (last accessed March 2022)

Islington Pride Map, 'Paradise Club & The Block', https://tinyurl.com/d2v54nda (last accessed March 2022)

'World's Biggest LGBT Community Celebrating our East to West Diversity with Unity & Pride since 1995', 2013, https://clubkali.com/dj-ritu/ (last accessed March 2022)

Harringay Online, 'Amy Winehouse Back to Black Video Filmed in Abney Park, Stoke Newington', 2018, https://tinyurl.com/2j46z2mp (last accessed March 2022)

'Abney Park – Nellie Power', https://tinyurl.com/33tdbbnx (last accessed March 2022)

'Champagne, Charlie and the Rest', *Guardian*, 2006, https://tinyurl.com/v2742rwt (last accessed March 2022)

The History Project, 'Hanky Panky: An Abridged History of the Hanky Code', 2019, https://tinyurl.com/y5x8mrcp (last accessed March 2022)

Time Out, 'There's a Pride March in Peckham on Saturday to Support Migrants in London', 2017, https://tinyurl.com/msz85bjc (last accessed March 2022)

Red Pepper, 'Ida-Sofie Picard introduces Lesbians and Gays Support the Migrants', 2016, https://tinyurl.com/294we7zp (last accessed March 2022)

'The RVT Gets Asset of Community Value Status', 2014, https://tinyurl.com/2t3fzk65 (last accessed March 2022)

'Cheerio, Duckie: Regulars Look Back at the LGBTQ+ Club that Broke the Mould', *Guardian*, 2022, https://tinyurl.com/478s2w8u (last accessed March 2022)

Wotever World, https://woteverworld.com/ (last accessed March 2022)

Duckie, Purveyors of Progressive Working Class Entertainment, https://duckie.co.uk (last accessed March 2022)

'David Hoyle: "Drag Is Accessible to Everybody Irrespective of Gender"', *Another Mag*, 2021, https://tinyurl.com/mr3an4da (last accessed August 2022)

'Paul O'Grady Relives Horrifying, Homophobic Police Raid on Lily Savage Show at London's Legendary Royal Vauxhall Tavern', *Pink News*, 2021, https://tinyurl.com/wwts3n47 (last accessed August 2022)

SOURCES

Apple Podcasts, 'Busy Being Black – Lady Phyll and a Busload of Black Lesbians', 2022, https://tinyurl.com/bdexcz8f (last accessed August 2022)

The Kaleidoscope Trust, https://tinyurl.com/5bjz2ens (last accessed August 2022)

'Lady Phyll Reflects on the Powerful Moment She Rejected Her MBE: "It's Based on the Toxic Legacy of Empire"', *Pink News*, 2020, https://tinyurl.com/22bcrmxc (last accessed August 2022)

Zoya Raza-Sheikh, '10 Black British LGBTQ+ Icons You Should Know About', *Gay Times*, 2021, https://tinyurl.com/rt3zhczm (last accessed August 2022)

'HIV Campaigners Mark World Aids Day by Dumping Manure at UKIP Office in Station Road, South Norwood', *Croydon Guardian*, 2014, https://tinyurl.com/2espss7c (last accessed August 2022)

Inside Croydon, 'McKenzie's UKIP Branch Forced Out after Manure Stunt', 2014, https://tinyurl.com/5bc4zcyt (last accessed August 2022)

Bishopsgate Institute, www.bishopsgate.org.uk/ (last accessed August 2022)

Bex Wade, 'Night Pride Is Reclaiming the Streets for LGBTQ People', *Vice*, 2021, https://tinyurl.com/yc6hje3b (last accessed August 2022)

'Britain's Longest-Serving Trans Prisoner Is Now Helping Trans People Locked up in the Wrong Prisons', *Pink News*, 2020, https://tinyurl.com/yshrsnnp (last accessed August 2022)

'How Pride Changed Everything for a Growing Group of Brave LGBTQ+ Travellers', *Cambridge News*, 2020, https://tinyurl.com/4m97xtvu (last accessed August 2022)

Pride of Arabia, https://prideofarabia.com/ (last accessed August 2022)

SWANA Alliance, www.swanaalliance.com

mudlark121, 'Today in London's Parklife: 1000s Destroy Enclosure Fences, Hackney Downs, 1875', 11 December 2017, https://tinyurl.com/ba2m232n (last accessed August 2022)

Eve Hartley, 'Sisters Uncut Celebrates "Win" Over Hackney Social Housing With Town Hall Stunt', *Huffington Post*, 2016, https://tinyurl.com/2p8vpukw (last accessed August 2022)

'RIP Shoreditch: Why the Closure of The White Horse Is the End of an Era – Activist Strippers Are Throwing a Funeral Rave in the East End, in an Unlikely Protest at the Closure of a Shoreditch Strip Pub', *Time Out*, 2016, https://tinyurl.com/55vj3ucu (last accessed August 2022)

Stacey Clare, *The Ethical Stripper: Sex, Work and Labour Rights in the Night-time Economy*, Unbound, 2022

Soho House, 'Harpies: Sexual Fantasies from IRL to Online and Back Again', https://tinyurl.com/ywsk7y7c (last accessed August 2022)

Human Rights Watch, 'Russia: New Anti-Gay Crackdown in Chechnya – Police Detain, Torture Men in Grozny', 2019, https://tinyurl.com/3ajp8az6 (last accessed August 2022)

Jason Ritchie, 'Pinkwashing, Homonationalism, and Israel–Palestine: The Conceits of Queer Theory and the Politics of the Ordinary', 2014, https://tinyurl.com/6x8m5stb (last accessed August 2022)

London Palestine Action, 'A Network of People in London Taking Creative Action against Israeli Apartheid, London Queers Say NO to Israel's Pinkwashing, YES to BDS!', https://tinyurl.com/3mwkf87b (last accessed August 2022)

Established in 2011, Kaleidoscope Trust is a UK-based charity focused on fighting for the human rights of LGBT+ people across the Commonwealth, www.kaleidoscopetrust.com/ (last accessed August 2022)

All Out, https://allout.org/en (last accessed August 2022)

'Remembering the Coleherne and the Earl's Court Gay Scene', https://tinyurl.com/2w35jnvc (last accessed August 2022)

Absolute Crime, 'The Gay Slayer: The Life of Colin Ireland Serial Killer', https://tinyurl.com/27jzw7m5 (last accessed August 2022)

British Social Attitudes, 'Homosexuality', https://tinyurl.com/mrxd2rcp (last accessed August 2022)

'Section 28 Backer Brian Souter: I'm Not Homophobic and I Have Gay Friends', *Pink News*, 2014, https://tinyurl.com/y98v8bdt (last accessed August 2022)

London School of Economics, 'Sociology and the Gay Liberation Front – Bob Mellors at LSE', 2017, https://tinyurl.com/bdh9vpb2 (last accessed August 2022)

SOURCES

Roodepoort Record, 'Today in History: WHO Removed Homosexuality from its List of Mental Illnesses', 17 May 2018, https://tinyurl.com/35mwxaez (last accessed August 2022)

Peter Tatchell, 'The 1972 Protest against Prof. Hans Eysenck's Advocacy of Aversion Therapy as a "Cure" for Homosexuality', 2016, https://tinyurl.com/4ktu7mb3 (last accessed August 2022)

Historic England, 'Le Duce', https://tinyurl.com/bdzxx3ct (last accessed August 2022)

Hannah Hoch and Til Brugman, 'Lesbianism, and Weimar Sexual Sub-culture', 2013, https://tinyurl.com/2p8tb7dv (last accessed August 2022)

National Archives, 'LGBTQ+ history: Maud Allan and "Unnatural Practices among Women"', 2019, https://tinyurl.com/yck6ty75 (last accessed August 2022)

Peter Ackroyd, QUEER CITY: Gay London from the Romans to the Present Day, Abrams, 2018

When Fanny met Stella, QX Magazine, 2015, https://tinyurl.com/2v2cmefh (last accessed December 2022)

London Life with Liz, 'Fanny and Stella: The Young Men Who Shocked Victorian England', 2020, https://tinyurl.com/23acus8t (last accessed August 2022)

Matt Houlbrook, *Queer London: Perils and Pleasures in the Sexual Metropolis, 1918–1957*, University of Chicago Press, 2005)

Cellar Door, www.cellardoor.biz/ (last accessed August 2022)

Islington Humap, 'Reach Out and Touch – Hyde Park, W2 2UH Vernal Scott', https://tinyurl.com/ykhvf4vr (last accessed August 2022)

Guardian, Chris Godfrey, 'Section 28 Protestors 30 Years on: "We Were Arrested and Put in a Cell up by Big Ben"', 2018, https://tinyurl.com/yvyak7dk (last accessed May 2022)

mudlark121, 'Today in London Religious History, 1971: the Gay Liberation Front Mash Up Reactionary Christian Festival of Light', 2019, https://tinyurl.com/38fcx2ku (last accessed June 2022)

Stuart Feather, *Blowing the Lid: Gay Liberation, Sexual Revolution and Radical Queens*, Zero Books, 2015

Index

INDEX